# Tools to Stop Overthinking

A Teen Guide to Relief From Anxiety and
Stress in an Age of Overwhelm

**Jennifer Costanza, MA, LMFT**

# Table of Contents

# Introduction

Picture a grand theater, bathed in the soft glow of twinkling lights. The crimson velvet curtains rise and reveal a stage. The performance of a lifetime is about to begin. This isn't just any performance. This one's yours. This theater, this stage, this spotlight is a metaphor for life. You're both the star performer and the director, armed with the power to script your destiny. But amidst all the applause and excitement, there's also something else—the buzz of thoughts, constant and relentless, playing in the background like an orchestral symphony.

Now imagine the songs in this symphony. Sometimes, they are in sync, each note harmoniously complementing the other, uplifting your spirit. But there are times when the harmony breaks. A single thought starts to dominate, repeating itself like a song stuck in a loop. And before you know it, it isn't just one song but many, all blaring at once, muddling the harmony, overshadowing the performance. This is overthinking.

We all experience it—especially during our teenage years when every day feels like a new act in life's grand play, filled with endless possibilities and an array of challenges. It's a whirlwind, and amidst this whirlwind, our thoughts become an unending broadcast, a ceaseless radio station playing in our minds. But what if you could control the broadcast? What if there was a way to change the channel, adjust the volume, and curate the playlist? What if you could turn the chaos of overthinking into a beautiful symphony, a harmony that empowers and uplifts rather than overwhelms? Sounds interesting, right? Well, you're in for a treat!

As a teen, your mind can sometimes feel like a jam-packed highway during rush hour—horns blaring, people shouting, and ideas moving at a hundred miles an hour, all leading to gridlock. It's a world where text messages, social media updates, homework assignments, extracurriculars, friendships, and personal goals all compete for the driver's seat in your thoughts. Throw in the normal confusion and anxieties of growing up, and it's no wonder you might often find yourself stuck in a cycle of overthinking. But what if there was a roadmap that could guide you through the chaos, helping you navigate this frenzied highway with ease and grace? This book is designed to be that roadmap.

This journey begins with acknowledging a simple yet overlooked fact: overthinking isn't your enemy. It's a natural part of your brilliant mind. It's a result of your brain's incredible capacity to process information, solve problems, and create solutions. But like any superpower, it can be overwhelming if you don't know how to control it.

Overthinking, when unchecked, can lead to mental and emotional fatigue, hampering your ability to perform and engage effectively with the world around you. But don't worry, you're not alone in this. Countless teens across the globe grapple with overthinking on a daily basis. Imagine, for a moment, that you're at a party. You make a comment, and it doesn't land as you'd hoped. Perhaps there were a few awkward laughs or, even worse, silence. Suddenly, you're spiraling into a loop of second-guessing and embarrassment that seems inescapable.

Does this scenario sound familiar? If it does, you're an over-thinker. But here's the good news: overthinking isn't a life sentence of stress and confusion. Managed correctly, it can become a powerful tool for creativity and problem-solving.

Over the next few chapters, you'll gain insight into the impact of overthinking on various aspects of your life, from productivity to emotional health. You'll learn how to recognize and deal with overthinking fatigue, a common yet often overlooked condition. We'll explore a range of self-care practices to help you restore balance and energy. In addition, we'll dive deep into the intricacies of maintaining a healthy balance between work and rest, highlighting how vital this balance is for productivity and overall well-being.

We're all guilty of procrastination, aren't we? This book will empower you with strategies to overcome it. We'll break down tasks into manageable pieces and discover the beauty of setting priorities. We'll venture into the realm of time management, a skill that's invaluable in today's fast-paced world.

Perhaps most importantly, this book will help you build your own support network, equipping you with tools to communicate effectively and seek help when needed. It's about helping you understand that it's okay to ask for help, that reaching out isn't a sign of weakness, rather strength. We'll guide you in creating your own self-care, work-rest, and support plans, and provide you with practical exercises to solidify these concepts. Every teen's journey is unique, so these plans will be tailored to your specific needs and circumstances.

This book is not a quick fix or a magic formula, but a guide. Think of it as a compass, pointing you in the direction of healthier thought habits and patterns. It's a path that requires a willingness to reflect, learn, and grow. But don't worry, you won't be walking this path alone. You'll be joining a community of fellow travelers who, like you, are committed to making the most of their brilliant minds.

Every chapter in this book is a step towards understanding your mind better, towards harnessing the power of your thoughts and transforming overthinking from a burden into a superpower. So, are you ready to explore new perspectives and practical tools that will help you manage overthinking? If you are, then let's get started on this exciting journey. Remember, the world needs your ideas, your creativity, and your energy. By learning to manage overthinking, you're not only improving your own life but also empowering yourself to make a positive impact on the world around you. And who knows? By the end of this journey, you might just find that overthinking has become your greatest ally.

So, here you are, standing at the backstage of life's grand performance. The audience is in anticipation, the spotlight awaits, and your greatest act is about to begin. This isn't just an introduction to a book; it's an invitation to embark on an exciting, transformative path—the journey of mastering the art of overthinking. Are you ready to step into the limelight, take control of the stage, and orchestrate your mind's symphony? Let's raise the curtain together. Let the performance of a lifetime begin!

# Chapter 1:

# Understanding Overthinking

Picture this: you're sitting in front of your computer, a blank document staring back at you. It's the English essay that's due tomorrow and all you can think of is the dreadful *what if*. "What if it's not good enough?" "What if the teacher hates it?" "What if, what if, what if..." and before you know it, the night has slithered away, leaving behind an untouched essay and a whirlpool of exhausting thoughts.

Sound familiar? If you're nodding your head, you've just experienced overthinking, a silent invader who takes control of your mind, breeding chaos and uncertainty. Welcome to the reality of millions of teenagers around the world, including you.

This chapter is your first step in reclaiming your peace of mind, by truly understanding the maze of overthinking. We start by peeling back the layers to reveal what overthinking really is—a constant, repetitive contemplation that leaves little room for clear thought or action. We'll dive into its characteristics and discover how it's closely entwined with feelings of anxiety, stress, and indecisiveness.

Next, we'll bring you face-to-face with the startling prevalence of overthinking in teens. Picture an auditorium filled with your peers. A recent study indicates that nearly half of them are wrestling with the same thoughts that keep you up at night. We'll probe into why adolescents, more than any other age group, grapple with overthinking. From the pressure to fit in to the burden of academic excellence and the hormonal roller coaster, we'll touch all bases.

Then, we'll explore the age-old nature versus nurture debate as it applies to overthinking. Is there a genetic lottery that predisposes certain individuals to overthinking, or is it a learned behavior, sculpted by our environments and experiences? Regardless of where it originates, the power to manage and redirect overthinking lies with you. Finally, we'll engage in a practical exercise of introspection. Picture yourself as a detective, investigating your own experiences with overthinking. You'll scrutinize specific instances, identify patterns and triggers, and evaluate the emotional impact it's had on you.

So, let's set off on this enlightening journey. With each page you turn, you'll become more adept at navigating the complex web of overthinking, taking you closer to the peace of mind you seek. After all, understanding the problem is the first step to solving it. Buckle up, because it's going to be an eye-opening ride.

# Definition and Characteristics of Overthinking

For all you young thinkers out there...

Overthinking might feel like your brain is running a marathon that never ends. It's when you're trapped in your own thoughts, going over the same ideas and worries again and again. Picture your mind like a hamster running on a wheel, it's constantly moving but not getting anywhere. That's overthinking.

While it's perfectly normal to think things through, overthinking is like thinking on steroids—excessive, repetitive, and often unhelpful. It can feel like your thoughts are a pack of wild horses, and you're struggling to reign them in. This is especially tricky during the teen years, when your brain is dealing with all sorts of changes and challenges.

So, what does overthinking look like? Let's discuss some key characteristics.

## Rumination

This is when your mind is like a rewind button, constantly replaying events, conversations, and feelings from the past. You might find yourself asking the same questions over and over: "Why did I say that?" "What did they mean by that?" "What could I have done differently?" While reflecting on past experiences can be helpful for learning and growth, rumination often involves a fixation on negative experiences or emotions. Experiencing emotions like guilt, regret, and self-blame may arise as a consequence. The key to managing rumination is to recognize when it's happening and redirect your focus to more constructive thoughts or actions.

## Obsessiveness

This is when a single thought, concern, or idea seems to dominate your mind. Imagine a song stuck on repeat—that's your brain with obsessive thoughts. You might try to push these thoughts away, but they often bounce back even stronger. Obsessiveness is frequently driven by fear or uncertainty. By recognizing the fear at the root of obsessive thoughts and challenging the validity of these fears, you can begin to break free from their grip.

## Difficulty Letting Go of Thoughts

Picture your thoughts as birds fluttering around your mind. Most of them will eventually fly away, but sometimes, certain thoughts can be more stubborn, sticking around and pecking at your peace of mind. When you're overthinking, these thoughts can keep you up at night, distract you during the day, and make it hard for you to focus on the here and now. Developing skills like mindfulness and self-compassion can help you gently let go of these lingering thoughts.

# Connection Between Overthinking, Anxiety, Stress, and Indecisiveness

Delving into the world of overthinking, we soon discover an intricate web linking it with anxiety, stress, and indecisiveness. This dance of the mind, while tricky to navigate, is essential to understand, especially for a young adult grappling with life's uncertainties.

Imagine your thoughts as cars driving on a highway, each one heading to a destination, serving a purpose. Now picture a traffic jam, cars bumper-to-bumper, honking, and drivers feeling frustrated and helpless. Overthinking is like this traffic jam, where the normal flow of thoughts gets congested, causing distress signals in the form of anxiety, stress, and indecisiveness.

## Anxiety and Overthinking

Anxiety and overthinking often exist as a tag team in the wrestling match of our minds. Anxiety, characterized by a sense of worry or fear, can instigate overthinking as we attempt to gain control over an uncertain situation or predict outcomes. Conversely, overthinking can fuel anxiety by turning hypothetical problems into seemingly imminent catastrophes. It's like tossing a ball back and forth, each throw escalating the game's intensity.

Remember, while it's natural to worry about the future or replay past events in your mind, when these thoughts start looping incessantly, causing distress or interfering with your daily life, it's the signal that normal anxiety has tipped into the realm of overthinking.

## Stress and Overthinking

Stress, the body's reaction to any change requiring an adjustment or response, also has a strong connection with overthinking. When faced with a challenging situation, such as a big exam or a disagreement with a friend, it's common to mull over the details, trying to find solutions or make sense of things. But when this thinking turns obsessive, it amplifies stress, creating a vicious cycle.

It's like being stuck in a hamster wheel: the more you think, the more stressed you become, and the more stressed you become, the more you think. Breaking this cycle involves recognizing when you're stuck in this loop and consciously practicing stress-relieving techniques like deep breathing, mindfulness, and/or physical exercise.

### *Indecisiveness and Overthinking*

Overthinking and indecisiveness are two sides of the same coin. When you're caught in an overthinking spiral, making decisions can feel like trying to find your way out of a maze with infinite paths. You might get stuck, analyzing every potential outcome, dwelling on every possible risk, or questioning your every preference. This *analysis paralysis* can make even simple decisions feel overwhelming.

But remember, it's perfectly okay not to have all the answers, and making mistakes is part of being human. Sometimes, the best decision is just to make a decision, to take one step forward, even if you're not entirely sure it's the right step.

# Overthinking in Teens

As we traverse the often-tumultuous seascape of teenage years, a consistent companion is the pervasive habit of overthinking. When examined closely, this is not just a global phenomenon but also an issue of growing concern, garnering increased attention in recent years.

### *The Prevalence*

First, let's dive into some hard numbers. Globally, one in seven, or approximately 14% of 10 to 19-year-olds, experience mental health conditions, a significant proportion of which can be attributed to overthinking-related disorders such as anxiety, depression, and behavioral disorders. Anxiety disorders involving excessive worry (a direct result of overthinking) are especially prevalent, affecting 3.6% of 10 to 14-year-olds and 4.6% of 15- to 19-year-olds. Depression, another manifestation of overthinking, affects 1.1% and 2.8% of these respective age groups (World Health Organization, 2021).

What is more, the impact of overthinking isn't merely transient. Neglecting to address mental health conditions during adolescence can have long-term ramifications, affecting both physical and mental well-being in adulthood and limiting the ability to live fulfilling lives. Overthinking and its repercussions thus have the power to shape the trajectory of an individual's life, reinforcing the critical need to address this issue.

## The Contributors to Overthinking

Adolescence is a critical period filled with significant physical, emotional, and social changes. This is the stage when young minds are trying to understand themselves and the world around them. This exploration, coupled with academic pressures, social expectations, hormonal changes, and an onslaught of digital media, often sets the stage for overthinking.

The teenage years can bring about a lot of stress due to the pressure to fit in with friends and figuring out who you really are. Sometimes, teenagers tend to overthink because they notice differences between what they're actually going through and what they imagine or hope for their future, which can be influenced by media and societal expectations based on gender. Teens who go through tough situations, face discrimination, exclusion, stigma, or have limited access to the right support and services, are more prone to experiencing mental health challenges due to these additional stress factors.

## You are not Alone

Teens, it's essential to understand that you are not alone in your struggles with overthinking. Almost every teenager grapples with these concerns at some point. The teen years are often marked by an intense inner life in which worry, self-doubt, and rumination can play a significant role.

Take the story of Mia, for example, a bright and active high school student. She found herself tangled in her thoughts, constantly replaying her interactions with friends, dissecting her performance in school, and incessantly worrying about her future. Over time, she realized that her overthinking was not a solitary battle but a shared experience with many of her peers. When Mia began opening up about her thoughts, she discovered similar narratives among her friends. They were all grappling with their versions of overthinking. This shared realization was a significant first step towards dealing with their collective issue.

# The Innate and Learned Aspects of Overthinking

Overthinking is an intricate phenomenon born of a complex interplay between our genetic makeup, brain chemistry, upbringing, environmental factors, and learned behaviors. To understand this maze better, let's delve into the innate and learned aspects of overthinking.

## *The Innate Aspects of Overthinking*

Just like our hair color, height, or predisposition to certain physical conditions, our tendencies to overthink can also be an inheritance from our genetic lineage. Certain individuals might possess unique brain chemistry or genetic factors that predispose them to overthink. In essence, they might be hardwired to ruminate and reflect more than others.

For instance, a significant volume of research points towards the role of genetics in mental health conditions like anxiety disorders, where overthinking is a salient feature. Variations in certain genes might affect the balance of neurotransmitters in the brain, making an individual more susceptible to anxiety and, consequently, overthinking (Arnold et al., 2004).

However, it's important to remember that genetic predisposition does not equate to inevitability. Genetics only set the stage, they do not write the script. While some individuals may be more predisposed to overthinking due to their unique brain chemistry or genetics, it does not mean they are destined to become chronic overthinkers.

## *The Learned Aspects of Overthinking*

Equally significant are the learned aspects of overthinking that develop over time due to environmental factors, upbringing, and learned behaviors. We learn to overthink through our experiences and interactions with the world around us.

For example, if a child grows up in an environment where worry and fear are the norm, they might learn to overthink as a coping strategy. Similarly, constant exposure to academic pressures, social expectations, and peer comparisons might ingrain overthinking patterns in a teenager's mind.

Our brains are remarkably plastic, constantly changing and adapting in response to our experiences. Hence, overthinking, as a learned pattern, can become a default neural pathway, particularly when it's repeatedly reinforced.

# Managing and Overcoming Overthinking

Whether overthinking is an innate tendency or a learned habit, the empowering news is that it can be managed and overcome. Even if your genetic code nudges you towards overthinking or your life experiences have drilled this pattern into you, you are not a passive recipient of this fate.

Harness the power of neuroplasticity—the brain's ability to rewire and create new pathways. You can develop strategies to break the cycle of overthinking, cultivating healthier patterns of thought. Cognitive behavioral techniques, mindfulness practices, and professional therapy are some tools that have shown efficacy in managing overthinking.

The human brain is a work-in-progress, continually evolving and adapting. Therefore, despite our genetic predispositions or learned behaviors, each one of us has the capacity to sculpt our brains, choosing the thought patterns that serve us best. Remember, our genetic or environmental inheritance may influence our starting point, but they don't determine our journey's trajectory.

Whether you were born an overthinker or have become one due to life's circumstances, remember that you possess the power to change your thought patterns. You have the capability to grow, adapt, and evolve, redirecting the course of your life one thought at a time. Remember, you are not alone in this journey, and there is help and support available to guide you along the way.

# Practical Exercise: Reflecting on Personal Experiences of Overthinking

Let's embark on a journey of self-exploration, shining a light on the shadows of overthinking that we may unknowingly nurture within ourselves. This exercise is designed to help you reflect on your personal experiences with overthinking, recognize its patterns, triggers, and emotional impact. Grab a journal or open a new digital note—you're about to have a heart-to-heart with your mind.

### *Identifying Instances of Overthinking*

Start by reflecting on times when you've found yourself caught in a whirlpool of thoughts. These could be moments when you've spent hours mulling over something said or done, replaying a scenario repeatedly, or worrying excessively about a future event.

- What was the situation that led you to overthink?

- How much time did you spend ruminating over this situation?

- Did it prevent you from doing other important things?

Remember, there's no right or wrong answer here. This is about understanding your mind's tendencies, not passing judgment on them.

## Exploring the Triggers

Triggers are specific events, thoughts, or feelings that initiate a cycle of overthinking. Think about the instances you identified above.

- Were there any common triggers?

- Were these related to specific events, people, or personal insecurities?

- Did certain environments or situations induce overthinking more than others?

By understanding what triggers your overthinking, you can better anticipate these episodes and gradually learn to handle them more effectively.

## Recognizing Patterns

Overthinking, like any other habit, often follows a pattern. Understanding this pattern can help you intercept it before it spirals.

- Are there certain times of the day when you're more prone to overthink?

- Do you tend to overthink more when you're alone, stressed, or tired?

- Are there recurring themes in your overthinking episodes, such as fear of failure, social acceptance, perfectionism?

## Evaluating the Emotional Impact

Overthinking can take a toll on your emotional well-being, leading to anxiety, stress, or feelings of inadequacy. Reflect on how overthinking impacts your emotions.

- How do you feel during and after an episode of overthinking?

- Does overthinking drain your energy or make you feel anxious or stressed?

- Does it affect your confidence or self-esteem?

## Looking at Coping Mechanisms

Finally, think about how you generally deal with episodes of overthinking.

- Do you have any strategies or coping mechanisms that you use?

- How effective have these been in helping you break the cycle of overthinking?

Remember, this exercise is not about blaming or criticizing yourself. It's about understanding your mind better and gaining insight into its patterns and habits. Overthinking is a common human experience, something we all grapple with from time to time. The key is to learn from these experiences, equip ourselves with effective strategies, and work towards a healthier mental landscape.

# Conclusion

Overthinking, a mental pathway where thoughts whirl and twirl, is a prevalent experience among teenagers. It's a complex interplay between the innate fabric of our minds and the experiences we gather as we grow. It thrives in the crevices of uncertainty, self-doubt, and worry, often fueled by societal pressures, academic stress, and emotional turbulence that mark adolescent years. Understanding this reality, we dived into global statistics to establish the magnitude of this issue. We explored the innate and learned aspects of overthinking, illuminating the interplay between our unique brain chemistry, genetic predispositions, and environmental influences. We also guided you through a practical exercise to facilitate personal reflection on your experiences with overthinking, aiding you in recognizing patterns, triggers, and emotional impact.

This chapter has been an exploration into the intricacies of overthinking, a journey of understanding and self-awareness. However, amidst all of this, the most important takeaway is that overthinking, whether innate or learned, is not an insurmountable monster. It's a mental habit that can be understood, managed, and ultimately, transformed. Understanding is the first step. The next steps involve learning coping mechanisms, developing emotional resilience, and fostering a mindset of acceptance and mindfulness. It's a journey, often challenging but entirely achievable. After all, our minds are capable of extraordinary things when we direct them with purpose and kindness.

As we conclude this chapter, remember you are not alone in this journey. Every teen has their unique struggles with overthinking, and it's through understanding and mutual support that we can navigate these challenging years. There's a whole world of discovery ahead, and this is just the beginning of your journey toward a healthier, happier mind.

# Chapter 2:

# The Inner Workings of Your

# Unique Brain

A secret, mysterious web lies within each of us: the human brain. Like a unique fingerprint, every brain is different, a complex blend of genetics, environment, and experiences, making each one of us who we are. Now, imagine if you had the power to navigate this complex web, to truly understand its inner workings. This is precisely the voyage we are about to embark on in this chapter.

You might find yourself often lost in a whirlwind of thoughts, falling into the rabbit hole of overthinking. However, the twists and turns of your thoughts are not your enemy, but rather a reflection of the unique mind you possess. Overthinking is not a defect; it is a characteristic feature of your brain's dynamic landscape. In this chapter, we will venture deeper into the fascinating depths of your unique brain, particularly focusing on overthinking, exploring its sources and understanding its implications.

Here, we will dissect the individual differences in overthinking tendencies, unraveling the thread of influence extending from your genes to your daily environment and personal experiences. You'll come to understand that the source of your overthinking is not a monolithic, unchangeable flaw but a multifaceted attribute of your unique mind.

This chapter will emphasize the transformative powers of self-acceptance and self-compassion. You'll see how these essential components can become your compass, guiding you toward freedom from unproductive overthinking patterns and toward a more understanding, compassionate relationship with your mind. Finally, we will delve into a practical exercise that will help you identify your personal strengths and qualities. This exercise will illuminate how these unique attributes of your own can be powerful allies in managing overthinking. With self-reflection and understanding, you'll see how what might seem like a weakness can indeed become a strength.

So, gear up! As we prepare to embark on this exploration of the unique landscapes of your mind, remember that you are not merely an observer but the adventurer charting a path through this mysterious and incredible terrain that is your brain. There's much to discover, understand, and embrace. This journey towards self-understanding and self-acceptance starts now.

# Understanding Individual Differences in Overthinking Tendencies

## *The Concept of Neurodiversity*

Before we delve into the intricacies of overthinking tendencies, it's essential to understand the concept of neurodiversity. This term, popular in the realms of psychology and neuroscience, is a viewpoint that sees people with differences in how their brains work and behave as simply part of the natural variation found in the human population. In simpler terms, neurodiversity celebrates the idea that we all have unique brains that work in their individual ways. Just as we all have diverse appearances, talents, and preferences, our brains too, are varied, each possessing its unique strengths and challenges.

## *Overthinking and Neurodiversity*

One such difference that can occur in our brain function is the tendency to overthink. Some of us have brains that like to ponder, analyze, and, occasionally, overanalyze. You might find yourself thinking about a conversation you had yesterday, questioning the tone you used or contemplating the implications of a casual remark made by a friend. Sometimes, this overthinking can cause anxiety or stress, but at other times, it can lead to more profound insights and better problem-solving.

In the lens of neurodiversity, overthinking isn't viewed as a flaw or a problem to be solved. Instead, it's seen as part of your unique brain function. It's essential to note that this doesn't mean overthinking can't cause distress or that you can't develop strategies to manage it when it becomes overwhelming. But it does mean that overthinking, like every other neurodivergent trait, has its strengths.

For instance, overthinkers often have excellent attention to detail, noticing things others may overlook. They're often good at seeing different angles of a situation, which can make them excellent problem solvers. They can be highly creative, coming up with novel solutions or ideas that others may not consider. Their tendency to reflect deeply on experiences can lead to personal growth and self-understanding.

## Embracing Your Overthinking Tendencies

So, if you identify as an overthinker, here's a reassurance: it's okay. Overthinking is not a flaw; it's a part of who you are. It's part of your unique neural makeup, and while it can sometimes feel challenging, it also comes with its own set of superpowers.

Embrace your individuality. Understand that your overthinking brain is capable of incredible depth, insight, and creativity. Don't pressure yourself to think or act like everyone else—your unique perspective is valuable and needed.

That said, it's also important to equip yourself with strategies to manage overthinking when it becomes distressing or counterproductive. This can include mindfulness techniques, physical activity, expressive writing, or talking things out with a trusted friend or mentor. Remember, you're not trying to stop overthinking, you're learning to channel it in ways that work best for you.

Understanding our individual differences, including overthinking tendencies, through the lens of neurodiversity can empower us to embrace our unique minds. It's not about labeling our thought patterns as good or bad but rather acknowledging, accepting, and harnessing our unique cognitive styles. And most importantly, it's about knowing that however your brain works, it's a remarkable part of who you are. Your unique brain, with all its quirks and idiosyncrasies, is your superpower.

# Genetics, Environment, and Experiences in Shaping Overthinking Patterns

### The Genetic Blueprint

In the human genome, our personal biological roadmap, lie intricate details about our potential cognitive patterns, including overthinking. Science has shown us that our predisposition towards certain mental and behavioral traits can be partially encoded in our DNA, passed down from our parents and ancestors. That's not to say there's an overthinking gene, but rather clusters of genes that might influence traits like anxiety or heightened awareness, which could contribute to overthinking tendencies.

Just like the color of our eyes or our natural aptitude for music or sports, our propensity for overthinking could be tied to our genetic makeup. It's important to note that having these genetic tendencies doesn't necessarily mean you'll become an overthinker. Much like a blueprint, genetics outlines possibilities, not certainties.

### The Environment

While our genes may lay the groundwork, our environment plays a significant role in shaping these genetic tendencies. The term *environment* covers a broad spectrum, including our upbringing, family dynamics, societal influences, culture, and education, all of which can mold our overthinking tendencies.

For instance, growing up in a family where overthinking and anxiety are common might normalize this behavior for you. Conversely, a family that encourages open communication and problem-solving could provide tools to manage overthinking. Societal influences, such as the pressure to succeed or conform, can also fuel overthinking tendencies. Learning to navigate these environmental factors is a crucial step towards understanding and managing our overthinking patterns.

## Personal Experiences

Our life is a mosaic of experiences, each piece shaping us in unique ways. Personal experiences, including trauma or significant life events, can intensify or trigger overthinking patterns.

Imagine a significant life event, like a big move or a change in family dynamics. Your brain might respond to this change by going into overdrive, analyzing all possible outcomes and implications. Traumatic experiences, too, often lead to overthinking as the brain tries to make sense of what happened or to prevent it from happening again.

It's important to recognize these experiences and their impact on our thinking patterns. By doing so, we can begin to understand why we might overthink certain situations and work on effective strategies to manage these tendencies.

## Interplay of Genetics, Environment, and Experiences

In understanding our overthinking tendencies, it's crucial to recognize the interplay between genetics, environment, and experiences. None of these factors act in isolation. Your genetic predispositions interact with your environment and experiences, creating a unique cognitive pattern—that's you.

So, while you might have a genetic inclination towards overthinking, your environment and experiences can shape how this tendency manifests and how you manage it. It's a complex, dynamic interaction, and understanding it can be empowering. It shows us that while we may not choose our genes or control every aspect of our environment or experiences, we can choose how we respond, cope, and grow.

In the end, each of us is a unique blend of nature and nurture, genes and environment, experiences and resilience. Understanding this blend can help us embrace our overthinking tendencies, not as flaws, but as a part of our unique, multifaceted selves.

# A Path Towards Self: Acceptance and Compassion

Understanding the complexities of your mind and the overthinking tendencies that come with it is only half the battle. The other half? Embracing self-acceptance and fostering self-compassion.

## *Self-Acceptance: Embrace Your Overthinking*

Overthinking can feel like a mental whirlwind that leaves you feeling exhausted and overwhelmed. But remember, it's not a flaw; it's a part of who you are. Embracing your overthinking tendencies is the first step towards self-acceptance. This doesn't mean resigning yourself to a lifetime of overthinking. Rather, it's about acknowledging it without judgment or self-blame. It's recognizing that you have a unique mind that might delve deeper and think harder.

Let's say you have a propensity for playing out every scenario in your head before a major event. That's okay. It's not a character defect; it's just how your brain processes information. The key lies in harnessing this trait positively and knowing when to pause. As you grow and learn more about yourself, you'll start to see your overthinking not as a hurdle, but as a part of your complex, unique self.

## Self-Compassion: The Healing Balm for Overthinking

Navigating through the whirlpool of overthinking can be daunting, and that's where self-compassion becomes indispensable. Think of it as a soothing balm for your bustling mind, a gentle reminder that it's okay to be imperfect, to make mistakes, and to have difficult days.

Just as you would show kindness and understanding to a friend, extend the same to yourself. Did you overanalyze a conversation with a friend and worry about it all night? Instead of berating yourself for overthinking, offer yourself some kindness. Acknowledge that your mind was trying to protect you from potential conflict or misunderstanding.

## Cultivating Self-Compassion

How does one foster self-compassion, especially in the face of overthinking? Here are a few strategies.

### Practice Self-Care

Self-care isn't just about pampering yourself; it's about attending to your physical, emotional, and mental needs. That might mean getting regular exercise, prioritizing sleep, or taking time each day to relax and do something you enjoy. By taking care of your physical well-being, you create a stronger foundation for emotional resilience.

### Use Positive Self-Talk

Our thoughts shape our reality. When you catch yourself falling into a pattern of negative self-talk, consciously replace it with kindness and understanding. Instead of saying, "I shouldn't overthink everything," try, "It's okay that I overthink sometimes. I'm learning how to manage it better each day."

Remember, you don't have to navigate this journey alone. Reach out to friends, family, or a trusted counselor. Share your feelings and experiences. Sometimes, just the act of verbalizing your thoughts can provide new perspectives and make you feel less alone.

At the end of the day, the journey to self-acceptance and self-compassion isn't a destination but an ongoing process. It's about continuously learning, growing, and showing up for yourself, just as you are, overthinking tendencies and all. And remember, you are not alone on this journey.

# Practical Exercise: Unearthing Your Personal Strengths and Qualities

Embracing your unique strengths and qualities is not just a journey of self-discovery, but also a crucial step towards personal growth. It's like conducting an exciting archaeological dig within yourself, unearthing your hidden talents and skills that make you special. And yes, this includes your tendency to overthink, which can actually be harnessed as a strength when channeled appropriately. Let's delve into a practical exercise designed to help you identify and celebrate these unique traits.

## *Step 1: Self-Reflection*

Begin by finding a quiet, comfortable place where you can sit undisturbed. You'll need a notebook and a pen. Now, jot down your thoughts in response to these prompts:

- What are some things you do really well? Think about skills or tasks you excel at, whether it's related to school, hobbies, sports, or interpersonal skills.

- What are some qualities you like about yourself? It could be your curiosity, kindness, determination, creativity, or any other personal trait you value.

- What do others often compliment you for? This could provide insight into strengths you might not have recognized.

## Step 2: Harnessing Overthinking as a Strength

Next, consider your overthinking tendencies. While overthinking can often seem like a burden, it can also be viewed as a sign of a creative and analytical mind. Ask yourself:

- Have there been times when your overthinking helped you understand a situation better or come up with a unique solution?

- How can you channel your overthinking into proactive problem-solving or creative thinking?

- What strategies can you use to keep your overthinking in check, like setting aside specific thinking time, practicing mindfulness, or jotting down your thoughts in a journal?

## Step 3: Celebrating Your Strengths

Take a moment to review your list of strengths, talents, and qualities. Consider each one and acknowledge how it contributes to who you are. Remember, no strength is too small or insignificant to celebrate.

Next, think about how you can apply these strengths to overcome the challenges posed by overthinking. Perhaps your creativity can help you devise new coping strategies. Or maybe your analytical skills can be used to dissect and understand your thought patterns better. Finally, keep this list somewhere you can easily see it—on your desk, by your bedside, or even as a note on your phone. Refer to it often, especially in times of self-doubt or when overthinking feels overwhelming. This list is a tangible reminder of your unique strengths and abilities, a testament to your potential.

Remember, you are not defined by your overthinking tendencies but by the myriad of strengths and qualities that make you unique. Understanding and embracing these strengths is a significant step towards mastering your overthinking and fostering self-acceptance.

## Conclusion

Understanding your emotions and embracing your individual differences, especially in overthinking tendencies, is an essential part of personal growth and emotional well-being. It's crucial to acknowledge the intricate interplay of genetics, environment, and personal experiences in shaping these tendencies. Remember, self-acceptance and self-compassion are vital tools in navigating these complex emotional landscapes. Being comfortable with the ebb and flow of your emotions, and accepting the things you can and cannot control, can lead to greater emotional stability. Also, identifying your personal strengths and qualities can provide a constructive perspective on overthinking, turning it from a perceived weakness into a strength. At the end of the day, remember that you are unique, and your overthinking tendencies are a part of your unique makeup, not a flaw to be eradicated. You have the power to channel this trait in positive ways and use it as a tool for personal growth and success.

# Chapter 3:

# Unraveling the Underlying Causes

Ever found yourself caught in an incessant loop of overthinking, drowning in a storm of thoughts, making mountains out of molehills? It's like your mind is a television with a remote that's stuck on the channel surf button, constantly flipping through a variety of channels, unable to rest on one. If this sounds familiar, welcome to the chapter that is the map to the maze of your mind, illuminating the shadowy corners where the seeds of overthinking are planted and nurtured.

In this chapter, we're going on a journey that will delve into the common causes of overthinking. We'll pick apart limiting beliefs, expose the crippling weight of perfectionism, and scrutinize the iron grip of control. Are these influences whispering in the background, quietly orchestrating your thoughts? We're about to find out.

We'll also venture into the less explored territories of trauma and anxiety, looking at how these often-overlooked factors contribute to the relentless cycle of overthinking. It's a difficult expedition, but remember, the first step towards changing something is understanding it. Moreover, this chapter won't just lay bare the root causes of your overthinking; it will equip you with tools to deal with them. You'll engage in a practical exercise, challenging your limiting beliefs through self-reflection. We'll guide you as you unravel your intricate thought patterns and help you reconstruct them into a supportive mental framework.

Our sources for this journey are diverse and solid, ranging from scientific publications to introspective guides. They provide a strong basis for our exploration, backing up the personal with the empirical and the subjective with the objective.

This chapter is a treasure trove of understanding, acceptance, and transformation. The key takeaway? Overthinking is not a personal failure but a complex interplay of various internal and external factors. But the power to change it is within you. So, let's take that first step into the labyrinth and discover the amazing mind that is uniquely yours. Let's begin the unraveling.

# Overthinking: Understanding the Causes and Ways to Break Free

Overthinking is a common phenomenon, but when it becomes a constant, it can wreak havoc on your mental well-being and hinder productivity. It's akin to being stuck in a loop where you endlessly analyze your thoughts and behaviors, second-guess decisions, and worry about potential future scenarios. Overthinking often arises from certain underlying causes like perfectionism, fear of failure, or a need for control, and can be intensified by past traumas or unresolved issues. However, with self-awareness and effective strategies, it's possible to break free from this cycle. This guide aims to provide insights into the common underlying causes of overthinking and the methods to break free.

## Understanding Common Underlying Causes of Overthinking

### Perfectionism

The constant pursuit of flawlessness and the highest standards can contribute to overthinking. Perfectionism often stems from a fear of making mistakes and the belief that anything less than perfect is unacceptable. The perfectionist mindset often leads to excessive self-criticism, prolonged decision-making processes, and the habit of focusing more on flaws than achievements. For instance, Stacy Caprio, a successful entrepreneur and founder of Her.CEO, an online platform for female entrepreneurs, experienced this firsthand. Despite her success, she found herself hesitant to start new tasks out of fear of not executing them perfectly. This fear and hesitation led her to avoid tasks, causing her to overthink situations more often than not. It's a real-life example of how even successful individuals can fall into the trap of perfectionism.

### *Fear of Failure*

Fear of failure often keeps us stuck in a cycle of constant worrying and rumination. Overthinking can be fueled by the fear of making a mistake, disappointing others, or not living up to expectations. This fear might prevent us from taking risks or trying new things, hindering personal growth and progress.

### *Need for Control*

Overthinking can also be a result of the desire to control every aspect of our lives. The thought of not being able to control outcomes can cause anxiety and lead to overthinking. Trying to anticipate every possible outcome or scenario can be exhausting and unproductive.

# Impact of Past Traumas, Negative Experiences, or Unresolved Issues

Overthinking can also be the result of past traumas, negative experiences, or unresolved issues. These past experiences can shape our thoughts and beliefs about ourselves and the world around us. For instance, someone who has experienced failure in the past might overthink out of fear of repeating the same mistakes or, someone who has experienced rejection or criticism might overthink out of fear of experiencing these feelings again. Unresolved issues or experiences can lead us to ruminate, keeping us stuck in a cycle of overthinking.

## Addressing Underlying Causes

Addressing the underlying causes of overthinking is crucial for breaking free from its grip. It starts with self-awareness—recognizing and understanding our thought patterns and what triggers overthinking. Once we identify these triggers, we can begin to challenge and change our thoughts and behaviors.

For instance, for those who overthink due to perfectionism, learning to see the bigger picture and adjusting their standards can be beneficial. Accepting that there's a point of diminishing returns in aiming for perfection can help in shifting their mindset. For those who fear failure, reframing failure as a learning opportunity and embracing the idea that making mistakes is a part of growth can help reduce overthinking. For those with a need for control, understanding that not everything can be controlled and learning to accept uncertainty can alleviate overthinking.

## Key Measures to Break Free From Overthinking

### Reframe Your Mindset

Recognize the negatives of overthinking and see the bigger picture. You might realize that spending hours worrying about a minor detail isn't worth the stress and doesn't significantly enhance the outcome.

### Adjust Your Standards

It's essential to remember that not everything needs to be perfect. Show your work to others for feedback and adjust your standards based on the feedback received.

## Break the Cycle of Rumination

Identify your triggers for rumination and develop strategies to disrupt the cycle. This could involve distracting yourself with a task or seeking support from a trusted friend or mentor.

## Develop a Checklist

Creating a checklist for tasks can help direct your focus towards achievable, discrete goals rather than an elusive idea of perfection.

## Seek Support and Get Perspective

It's okay to ask for help. Friends, family, mentors, and professionals can provide support, encouragement, and a fresh perspective.

## Reflect and Monitor Progress

Regularly review your progress. Ask yourself whether there were instances where you overcame overthinking, what strategies worked best, and where there is room for improvement. Recognizing progress, however small, can boost your confidence and encourage you to continue on your journey.

## Practice Mindfulness and Relaxation Techniques

Trying out mindfulness techniques such as meditation, deep breathing, and yoga can be helpful in reducing overthinking. These practices can bring you back to the present moment and help you feel more grounded. These techniques can also help manage stress and anxiety, which often fuel overthinking.

### Engage in Physical Activity

Regular physical activity, such as walking, running, or playing a sport, can be a great outlet for reducing stress and clearing your mind. Getting regular exercise can boost the production of endorphins, which are natural mood boosters in our bodies. This can be a great way to break the cycle of overthinking and improve your overall mood.

### Limit Time Spent Overthinking

Set aside a specific time to process your thoughts, and once that time is up, move on to a different task. This can help prevent you from getting stuck in a cycle of overthinking.

### Seek Professional Help

If overthinking is significantly impacting your quality of life, it may be helpful to seek professional support. Therapists and psychologists are trained to help you navigate your thoughts and learn healthy ways to cope with overthinking, such as developing effective strategies and addressing any underlying issues that might be causing it. By doing so, you can gain better control over your thoughts and find ways to manage them more effectively.

Remember, overcoming overthinking is a process that takes time, patience, and practice. It's not about completely eliminating all negative or worrying thoughts but rather learning to manage them better and not let them take over your life. You are more than your thoughts and have the power to change your thinking patterns and behaviors.

# Limiting Beliefs, Perfectionism, and Control

As we navigate through adolescence, we are often influenced by an array of beliefs, some of which can be limiting and act as fuel to our overthinking tendencies. These are deep-seated convictions that can constrain us, creating an invisible barrier between us and our goals. "I'm not good enough," "I have to be perfect," or "I can't handle failure" are common examples of limiting beliefs that might ring a bell in your mind.

When these limiting beliefs take root in our psyche, they act like tiny stones in our shoes, making each step toward our dreams more painful than it needs to be. Over time, they can become so ingrained that they form the backdrop of our thought process, causing us to overanalyze situations, doubt our abilities, and worry excessively about the future.

## *Limiting Beliefs*

These are deep-seated convictions that can constrain us. Examples include thoughts such as "I'm not good enough," "I have to be perfect," or "I can't handle failure." When these limiting beliefs become ingrained in our psyche, they lead us to overanalyze situations, doubt our abilities, and worry excessively about the future.

## *Perfectionism*

Perfectionism is a relentless mindset demanding excellence in everything we undertake. It sets a high and often unattainable standard leading to constant self-evaluation and criticism. We tend to magnify even minor flaws, which contributes to the cycle of overthinking.

## *Control*

As teenagers, we often desire control over our lives and our futures. The fear of uncertainty and the desire for certainty can provoke overthinking. We may overanalyze past actions and worry about future possibilities, which fuels our overthinking tendencies.

Recognizing the impact of limiting beliefs, perfectionism, and the need for control is the first step toward managing them. Accepting that uncertainty is a part of life and that it's okay not to have control over everything helps reduce overthinking. Overcoming limiting beliefs, shedding the weight of perfectionism, and embracing life's unpredictability are key elements in personal growth. It's important to remember that we are braver than our fears, stronger than our doubts, and more capable than we think.

# Addressing Trauma, Anxiety, and Other Factors Contributing to Overthinking

Our experiences, emotions, and environment play a significant role in shaping our thought patterns. Overthinking, a habit that can undermine our happiness and productivity, often stems from deeper issues such as trauma, anxiety, and other psychological factors. It's essential to unpack these root causes to understand better and address the habit of overthinking.

## *Trauma and Overthinking*

Past traumas or negative experiences have a profound impact on our thoughts. Traumatic experiences often cause people to relive moments of distress, leading to intrusive thoughts that continuously play in their minds. These intrusive thoughts can become habitual, sparking a cycle of overthinking as we constantly replay and analyze the traumatic events and our responses to them. It's important to recognize this pattern and seek professional help, if necessary, to heal from these experiences.

## *Anxiety's Role*

Anxiety often magnifies overthinking tendencies. The intrinsic worry that accompanies anxiety leads to a perpetuation of rumination and nervous introspection. This can manifest as concern about the future, constantly trying to predict outcomes, or replaying past events to try to identify where things went wrong. Learning to manage anxiety, perhaps through techniques such as mindfulness or Cognitive Behavioral Therapy (CBT), can help to reduce the intensity and frequency of overthinking.

### Other Contributing Factors

Other factors like chronic stress, low self-esteem, and feelings of inadequacy also contribute to overthinking. When we are continually stressed, our minds may default to overthinking as a coping mechanism. Similarly, when we harbor feelings of low self-worth, we may overanalyze our actions and decisions, constantly second-guessing ourselves. Addressing these issues directly, perhaps through therapy, self-care practices, or supportive relationships, can interrupt the cycle of overthinking.

Overcoming overthinking is not a quick fix; it's a journey that involves addressing underlying issues, practicing self-compassion, and developing healthier thought habits. Remember, it's completely okay to seek help along the way. After all, understanding is the first step towards improvement.

# Practical Exercise: Challenging Limiting Beliefs Through Self-Reflection

Tackling overthinking often begins by addressing the limiting beliefs that fuel it. This exercise aims to help you identify, challenge, and replace these self-limiting beliefs with more empowering perspectives, fostering a healthier mental environment. Let's dive into the process.

### Step 1: Identifying Your Limiting Beliefs

Find a quiet, comfortable space where you can think clearly. Equip yourself with a pen and a notebook for this reflective journey. Start by writing down any recurring thoughts or beliefs that seem to trigger your overthinking. Some prompts to get you started might include:

- What are some negative beliefs I often hold about myself?

- When do these beliefs typically arise? Are there specific situations that seem to trigger them?

## Step 2: Questioning Your Limiting Beliefs

After jotting down your limiting beliefs, it's time to question their validity. For each belief, ask yourself:

- Is this belief objectively true? Can I find solid evidence that supports it?

- Is this belief always true, or are there instances where it isn't valid?

- Is this belief helping me, or is it holding me back?

## Step 3: Replacing Your Limiting Beliefs

Now that you've identified and questioned your limiting beliefs, it's time to replace them with more empowering and realistic perspectives. For each limiting belief, consider a more positive, balanced belief you could adopt. Write these next to your limiting beliefs. Some questions to guide this process might include:

- What's a more accurate, balanced belief that could replace the limiting one?

- How does this new belief make me feel about myself and my abilities?

- How can I reinforce this new belief in my daily life?

## *Step 4: Cultivating Self-Compassion and Self-Acceptance*

The last step is all about treating yourself with kindness and compassion. Changing deeply ingrained beliefs takes time, and there will be moments of backsliding. It's important to be patient with yourself and celebrate each small victory. Consider these prompts:

- How can I show myself compassion if I catch myself reverting to a limiting belief?

- How can I celebrate my progress in adopting new, healthier beliefs?

Review your answers regularly, updating them as your beliefs and feelings evolve. This exercise is not a one-time event but an ongoing process. Be patient with yourself, and remember that each step you take, however small, is a step towards overcoming overthinking.

# Conclusion

Overthinking, especially in teenagers, is a multifaceted issue influenced by a range of factors, including limiting beliefs, perfectionism, the need for control, past trauma, anxiety, and more. However, it's important to remember that overthinking can be managed and even harnessed as a strength with the right mindset and tools. By understanding and confronting the roots of overthinking, challenging limiting beliefs, and fostering self-compassion, teenagers can transform their overthinking tendencies into a catalyst for personal growth and resilience. Just as each individual is unique, so too is their journey through overthinking, with the journey itself often proving to be a valuable source of self-discovery and empowerment.

# Chapter 4:

# The Pros and Cons of

# Overthinking

Do you find yourself caught in the spiraling vortex of your thoughts, as though you're on an unstoppable merry-go-round? Are you wrestling with questions, second-guessing your decisions, and playing *what if* scenarios until your mind feels like a crowded room of chattering voices? Welcome, my friend, to the fascinating realm of overthinking. It's a world that can be as enticingly intriguing as it can be frustratingly exhausting.

In this chapter, we will delve into the compelling landscape of overthinking, laying bare its intricate layers and complex characteristics. This journey is not intended to label or stigmatize the act of overthinking but rather to empower you with a more comprehensive understanding of this cognitive phenomenon. The essence of this chapter resides in the understanding that, like many things in life, overthinking carries with it a dual nature—it has its beneficial potential and its detrimental consequences. Once we discern between the two, we can consciously navigate this network of thoughts more effectively.

Our exploration will start with a surprising revelation: overthinking is not entirely your enemy. You might scoff at the thought, but bear with me. We will discuss how, under specific circumstances, overthinking can be a valuable tool that facilitates comprehensive decision-making and effective planning. Overthinking, when channeled correctly, can even lead to heightened self-awareness. However, a coin, as you know, always has two sides. Overthinking, when it mutates from a constructive thinking process into an endless spiral of rumination, can become a destructive force. It can instigate a cascade of unwanted consequences, including heightened anxiety, strained relationships, and hindered productivity. We'll delve into these negative impacts to understand how overthinking might be silently sabotaging our mental peace and happiness.

Just as Goldilocks sought the perfect porridge that was neither too hot nor too cold, the key to harnessing the power of overthinking lies in finding a balance. Too much of it can drown us in a sea of doubts, while too little might leave us unprepared for life's myriad challenges. This chapter will explore the delicate equilibrium between productive and unproductive overthinking, offering guidance on how to strike the right balance.

To make this knowledge practical and tangible, we will introduce an exercise. You'll be creating a list of pros and cons of your personal overthinking tendencies. This exercise aims to promote self-reflection and provide you with a blueprint for understanding when overthinking is a helpful ally and when it morphs into an unwelcome intruder.

So, buckle up! We're about to embark on a thrilling exploration of our complex minds, wrestling with the intricate dance of overthinking, and learning how to choreograph it to our own tune. Your adventure into understanding and managing overthinking starts here.

# Recognizing the Potential Benefits of Overthinking

Overthinking is often viewed as an obstacle, something that keeps us stuck in our heads while life carries on around us. But what if we viewed it differently? What if overthinking was, in fact, a tool that could be honed and used to our advantage? Let's explore how.

## Overthinking as a Decision-Making Tool

Overthinking can serve as a deep-dive into the waters of decision making. Rather than making rash or impulsive choices, overthinkers take the time to consider every angle, every outcome, and every consequence. This thorough analysis can lead to more informed and calculated decisions. For instance, if you're deciding on a college major, a dash of overthinking allows you to visualize different scenarios related to each option.

## Effective Planning and Goal-Setting

Overthinking can also contribute to effective planning and goal-setting. Consider it like this: our goals and plans are like journeys on a map, and overthinking can be the process of identifying all the routes, rest stops, potential roadblocks, and alternative paths. If you're setting a goal to improve your grades, for example, overthinking may help you plan out study schedules, identify areas where you need extra help, and prepare you for potential challenges.

## Increased Self-Awareness

Overthinking can serve as a spotlight that we shine on our innermost thoughts and emotions. When we overthink, we delve deep into our motivations, our fears, our desires, and our values. We question not just what we think, but why we think that way. This process can lead to greater self-awareness and personal growth. For instance, if you're feeling anxious about a friendship, overthinking could help you identify the root cause of your worries and understand your emotional needs better.

However, like all tools, overthinking needs to be used wisely and with care. If left unchecked, it can lead to stress, anxiety, and a sense of feeling stuck. Balancing the act of thinking deeply with the act of moving forward is crucial.

Here are some pro tips to help you use overthinking to your advantage.

## Observe Rather Than Chastise

Instead of beating yourself up for overthinking, simply acknowledge it. Treat your thoughts as something external that you can observe and learn from.

## Recognize Thought Traps

Be mindful of getting stuck in unhelpful thought patterns, like imagining worst-case scenarios. Learn to identify these traps and use techniques to neutralize them.

## Set a Deadline

Give your overthinking a time limit. It's like giving your mind a secure space to explore freely, but with boundaries to ensure it doesn't spiral out of control.

## Practice Mindfulness

Practicing mindfulness assists in maintaining a sense of presence and minimizes the inclination to become entangled in the whirlwind of one's thoughts.

## Exercise Regularly

Exercise can help clear your mind and reduce the stress that comes with overthinking. It's a healthy way to give your mind a break.

## Challenge Negative Thoughts

Instead of letting your thoughts control you, challenge them. Question their validity, confront them head-on, and over time, their power over you will diminish.

Remember, it's perfectly normal to overthink sometimes. The trick is to recognize when you're doing it, understand why, and then use it as a tool for personal growth and informed decision-making. So, next time you find yourself diving headfirst into the whirlpool of your thoughts, take a deep breath and remember that you're not alone. With a bit of practice and patience, you can turn your tendency to overthink into a superpower.

# Negative Consequences and Pitfalls of Excessive Overthinking

While overthinking can sometimes be used as a tool for more comprehensive decision-making and self-awareness, there's a fine line between thoughtful introspection and excessive rumination. Crossing this line can lead to some significant negative consequences.

### *Impacts on Mental and Emotional Well-Being*

Overthinking can often amplify our worries and fears, leading to heightened anxiety and increased stress levels. Like a snowball rolling down a hill, a simple worry can quickly grow into an avalanche of concern. For instance, a small worry about a test result can spiral into concerns about overall academic performance, future college prospects, and even potential career paths. This constant state of worry can leave you feeling emotionally exhausted, taking a toll on your overall well-being.

### *Effects on Relationships*

Overthinking can also impact our relationships negatively. Constant rumination can create a barrier of doubt and insecurity that hinders open and honest communication. Overanalyzing a friend's offhand comment or misreading a text message can lead to misunderstandings and, over time, result in withdrawal and distrust. These misinterpretations can strain friendships and cause unnecessary conflict.

### Impediments to Productivity and Progress

Overthinking often creates a mental gridlock, halting our ability to make decisions and move forward. It's like being stuck at a crossroads, forever weighing the pros and cons without ever taking a step. This excessive analysis and doubt can result in missed opportunities and hinder progress. For instance, you might spend so much time pondering over a summer job application that by the time you decide to apply, the deadline has already passed.

It's natural to think deeply about certain aspects of life. But when thinking turns into overthinking, it's essential to recognize the signs and take steps to manage it. Overthinking is a maze, but with the right strategies, you can navigate it effectively and come out stronger on the other side.

# The Balance Between Productive and Unproductive Overthinking

Overthinking isn't necessarily a negative process. In fact, it can become a valuable tool when utilized correctly. The secret to harnessing overthinking lies in striking a delicate balance between productive and unproductive rumination. This balance, when mastered, can transform overthinking from a burdensome hurdle into a powerful catalyst for personal growth and achievement.

### The Balancing Act

Let's take a look at the difference between productive and unproductive overthinking. Productive overthinking, or deep thinking, can lead to self-awareness, careful decision-making, and better problem-solving abilities. It involves considering different perspectives, anticipating outcomes, and strategizing effectively. On the other hand, unproductive overthinking often involves dwelling on past mistakes, fearing the future, and getting stuck in a loop of negative thoughts. Recognizing this distinction is the first step towards finding the balance.

## The Role of Self-Awareness

Self-awareness plays a pivotal role in identifying when overthinking starts to become a hindrance rather than a help. The ability to catch yourself in the act of unproductive overthinking is a powerful tool. It allows you to consciously choose to divert your mental energy towards more constructive thought processes. To develop this self-awareness, you might try practicing mindfulness or meditation, both of which can help you become more attuned to your thoughts and patterns of thinking.

## Setting Boundaries and Redirecting Overthinking Energy

Setting mental boundaries can be an effective strategy to curb unproductive overthinking. These boundaries could involve designating specific times during the day for deep thinking and decision-making, thereby preventing your thoughts from occupying your entire day. Furthermore, when you find yourself overthinking, try to redirect that energy toward more productive endeavors. For instance, if you find yourself fretting about a future project, channel that energy into researching, planning, or starting the project instead of simply worrying about it.

Creating a healthy mental environment is essential to manage overthinking effectively. One of the best ways to achieve this is by setting boundaries and directing your thoughts and energies toward more productive endeavors. Here's how you can do that.

## Create a Thinking Time

Establish a specific period in your daily routine for deep thought or rumination. This can help to contain overthinking to a designated time, preventing it from consuming your entire day. This *thinking time* can be used to productively analyze situations, solve problems, or plan future actions.

## Mindful Activities

Mindfulness entails actively and attentively participating in the present moment, being fully engaged and aware. Activities such as meditation, yoga, or even a simple walk in nature can help bring your attention back to the present, reducing the tendency to overthink past events or worry about the future.

## Journaling

Writing your thoughts down can be a therapeutic way to clear your mind. It can help you visualize your thought patterns, identify triggers for overthinking, and find solutions to your problems. Plus, it's a constructive use of the energy you might otherwise spend on overthinking.

## Physical Activity

Regular exercise is known to reduce stress and anxiety levels, which can, in turn, alleviate overthinking. Whether it's a team sport, a solo run, or a dance class, physical activity can help clear your mind and redirect your energy in a positive direction.

## Positive Affirmations

Practicing positive affirmations can help combat negative thought patterns associated with overthinking. Repeating phrases like "I am capable" or "I can handle this" can foster a more optimistic mindset and can be an effective way to channel your overthinking energy.

## Problem-Solving Approach

When you find yourself overthinking a situation, try shifting your mindset to a problem-solving approach. Instead of dwelling on the issue, focus on identifying potential solutions. This strategy redirects overthinking toward a more productive outcome. Remember, these strategies are tools to help manage overthinking, but it is perfectly acceptable if one does not immediately achieve perfection in their mindfulness practice. It takes time and practice to develop these skills, so be patient with yourself. The goal isn't to eliminate overthinking entirely but rather to control it and use it as a tool for growth and self-improvement. Your thoughts are powerful—channel them in the right direction, and they can lead you to great heights.

Overthinking is not inherently detrimental. In fact, it can be a powerful tool for self-reflection and critical analysis. The challenge lies in distinguishing between productive and unproductive overthinking, and then consciously guiding your thought processes towards more constructive paths. This balance, once mastered, can become an invaluable asset in navigating the complexities of the teenage years and beyond.

The journey toward mastering this balance is not an overnight task, it's a continuous learning process. But with patience, practice, and persistence, you can transform overthinking from an obstacle into an opportunity for personal growth and development.

# Practical Exercise: Creating a Pros and Cons List of Overthinking Patterns

The act of overthinking can have a dual effect, encompassing both positive and negative aspects. On the positive side, it enables thorough analysis of situations, nurtures creative ideas, and contributes to thoughtful decision-making. On the other hand, it can also lead to stress, anxiety, and indecision when left unchecked. An excellent way to understand and manage your overthinking patterns is to create a personal pros and cons list. Here's how you can do that.

## Step 1: Identify Your Overthinking Patterns

Take some quiet time to reflect on how and when you tend to overthink. Maybe it's when you're facing a tough decision, anticipating a significant event, or rehashing a conversation you had earlier in the day. Write down these patterns and situations.

## Step 2: Create a List of Pros and Cons

Take a sheet of paper and draw a line down its center. Label one side as Pros and the other side as Cons. This simple division allows for a clear separation and organization of the positive and negative aspects you wish to list. Now, think about the effects of your overthinking.

Under Pros, list the positive outcomes of your overthinking. These might include things like a better understanding of a complex problem, coming up with a creative solution, or preventing potential mistakes by thinking through all possible scenarios.

Under Cons, write down the negative outcomes of your overthinking. This could be things like increased anxiety, wasted time, missed opportunities, or trouble sleeping.

### Step 3: Reflect on Your List

After finalizing your list, allocate a moment for introspection and contemplation regarding the contents you have penned down. Are there more pros or cons? Are there certain situations where the benefits of overthinking outweigh the negatives, and vice versa? Can you identify any patterns or triggers for when overthinking becomes problematic?

### Step 4: Apply Your Insights

Use the insights gained from this exercise to guide your actions moving forward. Perhaps you've discovered that overthinking before a big test helps you perform better, but overthinking social interactions causes you unnecessary stress.

With this understanding, you can try to channel your overthinking productively while setting boundaries to prevent it from causing harm. For example, you could designate a specific study time for in-depth analysis while consciously practicing mindfulness during social situations to keep your thoughts from spiraling. Remember, this exercise isn't about labeling overthinking as *good* or *bad* but about understanding how it affects you personally. Each individual possesses unique characteristics, and methods that prove effective for one person may not necessarily yield the same results for another. The goal is to find a balance that allows you to harness the power of your thoughts without letting them control you.

# Conclusion

Overthinking, a common aspect of the adolescent experience, is not inherently detrimental. It is a powerful tool when wielded with discernment, enabling nuanced understanding, creative problem-solving, and conscientious decision-making. However, unchecked overthinking can also spiral into a vortex of anxiety, stress, and indecisiveness, undermining mental well-being, straining relationships, and hindering productivity. By developing self-awareness, setting boundaries, and redirecting thought energy productively, it's possible to strike a balance that maximizes the benefits of this cognitive tendency while mitigating its drawbacks. Exercises like creating a personal list of pros and cons of overthinking patterns can be invaluable in this journey of self-discovery and personal growth, empowering teens to navigate their tumultuous years with wisdom, resilience, and equanimity.

# Chapter 5:

# Shifting Perspectives on

# Overthinking

In the loud, cacophonous world of our thoughts, it's easy to become lost, and this is especially true when we fall into the vortex of overthinking. We've all been there, our thoughts spiraling into an unending loop of *what ifs* and *could haves*. But what if there was a way to not only escape this mental quagmire but also harness its potential? That's exactly what we will discover in this chapter.

As you read through the pages of this chapter, you'll learn how to challenge and overcome the negative beliefs associated with overthinking. We'll uncover the common misconceptions and peel back the layers of societal narratives that vilify this attribute, reframing it instead as a useful tool, rather than a burden. With examples from successful individuals who've spun their overthinking tendencies into gold, you'll see the hidden potential that's been residing within you.

This chapter will also guide you on a journey towards mindfulness and present-moment awareness, which are powerful antidotes to overthinking. You'll learn about mindfulness as a practice that embraces your thoughts and emotions without judgment, allowing you to observe your overthinking patterns without getting entangled in them. Through simple and practical techniques like deep breathing and body scan exercises and practice, you can develop the ability to concentrate on the present moment, fostering a sense of tranquility and mastery over your thoughts. From there, we'll transition into the uplifting realm of gratitude and positive thinking, which play a crucial role in balancing your mental scales. We'll explore how a mindset of appreciation can shift your focus from overthinking to relishing the present moment. By introducing techniques like affirmations and visualization, you'll learn to replace negative thought patterns with positive ones, creating a brighter internal narrative.

Last but not least, we'll get hands-on with a practical exercise that'll challenge you to reframe your overthinking scenarios. You'll dive into real-life situations where overthinking took the reins, but this time, you'll find ways to view them in a new light. We'll work together to uncover the hidden benefits or lessons in these instances, fostering a perspective that empowers you and encourages personal growth.

Get ready to revolutionize the way you perceive overthinking, turning what is often seen as a liability into an asset. Brace yourself for an enlightening journey towards a more grounded and present mindset, equipped with a new-found understanding of the power that resides within your thoughts.

# Rethinking Overthinking: From Liability to Asset

Overthinking often gets a bad reputation, especially in our fast-paced, results-driven society. We often hear phrases like *analysis paralysis* or *it's all in your head*, emphasizing the negative connotations surrounding overthinking. But what if I told you that we could reshape these negative beliefs about overthinking and make them work in our favor?

Contrary to the prevailing narrative, overthinking isn't necessarily a bad thing. Yes, it can be a source of anxiety and stress when we let our thoughts spiral into endless loops of worry and self-doubt. However, overthinking also implies that we have an active and engaged mind, capable of deep reflection and critical thinking. Now, wouldn't it be marvelous if we could channel that energy more positively?

# Challenging Negative Beliefs About Overthinking

To start, let's challenge some common misconceptions about overthinking. One prevalent belief is that overthinking always leads to negative outcomes. It's important to understand that while it can lead to indecision and unnecessary stress, it doesn't always have to. The key is learning to control and guide our overthinking tendencies rather than letting them control us.

Another common misconception is that overthinkers are inherently pessimistic. This is not necessarily true. Overthinking is not a reflection of one's attitude towards life; rather, it is a cognitive process of diving deeper into thoughts and scenarios. Overthinkers can be just as capable of optimism and positivity as anyone else!

## Reframing Overthinking

Instead of viewing overthinking as a problem, let's try a different perspective. Overthinking means we're able to scrutinize every detail, consider multiple viewpoints, and generate a variety of potential solutions. These skills are invaluable in many aspects of life, from academics and careers to interpersonal relationships.

Think about it: who would make a great detective, journalist, scientist, or writer? Someone who observes, thinks deeply, asks probing questions, and isn't afraid to challenge the status quo—sounds a lot like an overthinker, right? Remember, the goal here isn't to stop overthinking entirely (which is nearly impossible). Instead, we aim to cultivate mindfulness and learn to harness our overthinking tendencies constructively. It's about channeling your natural inclination to think deeply into productive outlets like problem-solving, creativity, and personal growth.

## Embracing Overthinking: Successful Overthinkers

Still not convinced? Let's look at some successful individuals who have turned their overthinking into a superpower.

Take, for instance, the famed scientist Albert Einstein. He was known for his deep and often convoluted thought processes, which led him to revolutionize physics with his theory of relativity. Or consider renowned author J.K. Rowling, whose intricate plotlines and character developments in the Harry Potter series bear testimony to her detailed thought processes.

In each of these cases, these individuals leveraged their tendencies to think deeply and consider every possible outcome, proving that overthinking can indeed lead to exceptional results.

Overthinking doesn't have to be a liability; it can be one of your greatest assets. It all boils down to how you perceive it and, more importantly, how you control and direct it. So, the next time you find yourself deep in thought, remember—you're not just overthinking; you're exercising your ability to engage with the world in a unique and deeply thoughtful way. Embrace it and watch as your overthinking tendencies transform from your Achilles heel to your superpower.

# Mindfulness and You

In our pursuit to master overthinking, there is an incredible tool we have at our disposal: mindfulness. If overthinking had a superhero sidekick, mindfulness would be it. It's like a gentle spotlight, illuminating the patterns of our thoughts and emotions without getting swept away by them.

## What is Mindfulness?

Mindfulness is the practice of being fully present and engaged in the here and now, without judgment. Picture this: you're sitting on the bank of a gently flowing river. The river represents your stream of consciousness, filled with thoughts, emotions, and sensations. When you're mindful, you're merely observing this river from the bank, not jumping in and getting carried away by the current.

With mindfulness, we cultivate an attitude of curiosity and kindness towards ourselves and our experiences. This non-judgmental observation helps us notice our thought patterns, including the ones leading to overthinking, without letting them overwhelm us.

## How can Mindfulness Help Overthinkers?

Now you may ask, "But how can sitting and observing my thoughts help me with my overthinking?" Great question! And here's the answer.

Mindfulness helps us see our overthinking tendencies as they truly are: just thoughts. By observing them without judgment, we learn to detach ourselves from these thoughts, to see them as separate from who we are. This understanding frees us from the chains of overthinking, allowing us to notice a thought or emotion, acknowledge its presence, and then let it pass without getting entangled in it.

## Embracing Mindfulness: Practical Techniques

Now that we understand what mindfulness is and how it can help us, let's explore some simple yet powerful practices that you can start incorporating into your daily routine. These techniques are designed to cultivate present-moment awareness and help you regain control of your overthinking tendencies.

## Deep Breathing

One of the easiest ways to bring your attention back to the present moment is through deep breathing. This practice is as simple as it sounds but has profound effects on our minds and body. Here's a quick exercise you can try.

Sit comfortably and close your eyes. Take a deep breath in, filling your lungs completely, and then slowly exhale, emptying your lungs entirely. While you breathe, redirect your focus to the sensation of the breath as it enters and exits your body. Concentrate your attention on the rhythmic flow of inhalation and exhalation. In the event that your mind drifts away (as it often does), gently redirect your attention to your breath. Dedicate a few minutes each day to this practice, gradually extending the duration as you become more at ease.

### *Body Scan*

Another powerful mindfulness technique is the body scan. This practice involves slowly shifting your attention through different parts of your body, observing any sensations you feel along the way. Start from the tips of your toes and gradually move up to the top of your head. Notice the sensations—warmth, coolness, tension, relaxation—without trying to change or judge them.

The beauty of these mindfulness practices is that they can be done anywhere, anytime. Whether you're waiting for the bus, studying for a test, or lying in bed before sleep, you can always take a moment to ground yourself in the present moment. Remember, mindfulness is not about emptying your mind or stopping your thoughts. It's about becoming an observer of your thoughts, not a participant. So, embrace mindfulness, and witness as it opens up a new avenue to understanding and navigating your overthinking tendencies better. After all, the journey to mastering overthinking starts with a single mindful breath.

# The Power of Positivity: Cultivating Gratitude and Positive Thinking

Life is like a kaleidoscope of experiences, filled with ups, downs, twists, and turns. We have our share of triumphs and trials, joys and sorrows, fears and dreams. However, our outlook on life and how we perceive these experiences play a significant role in how we feel and think. Enter the art of cultivating gratitude and the practice of positive thinking.

## Gratitude: A Shift in Focus

Think of gratitude as a lens through which we view our life experiences. It's a simple yet profound practice that shifts our focus from what's wrong or missing in our lives to appreciating what we have. It can be an antidote to overthinking, helping us center our thoughts on the present moment's blessings instead of ruminating on past regrets or future anxieties.

Scientific research indicates that individuals who consistently engage in gratitude practices often experience a range of benefits, including an enhanced immune system, reduced blood pressure, and improved sleep patterns. Moreover, they experience more joy, optimism, and happiness, feel less lonely and isolated, and even have more compassion and kindness toward others (Ackerman, 2017).

So, how can you cultivate a gratitude practice in your life? Initiate a gratitude journaling habit. Each day, take a moment to record three things you are grateful for, regardless of their size. It could be as simple as relishing a delightful breakfast or immersing yourself in a captivating book, a chat with a friend, or the warmth of the sun on your face. What matters is that you genuinely appreciate these things and allow yourself to feel gratitude.

## Positive Thinking

While gratitude can help shift our focus from the negatives to the positives, cultivating positive thinking equips us with the mental tools to counteract negative thought patterns. Positive thinking involves using techniques such as affirmations and visualization to instill an optimistic outlook and resilience in the face of adversity.

## Affirmations

Affirmations are positive statements that you repeatedly tell yourself, reinforcing a constructive mindset and counteracting negative self-talk. For instance, if you find yourself overthinking about a test, you might use affirmations like, "I am prepared and will do my best," or "I am capable and intelligent."

Write down a few affirmations that resonate with you and repeat them to yourself throughout the day. Over time, these positive statements can help you build a mindset that empowers rather than discourages you.

## *Visualization*

Visualization is another powerful tool for positive thinking. It involves mentally picturing a desired outcome or goal, creating a vivid, sensory-rich image in your mind. You might visualize acing that math test, delivering a killer presentation, or even just having a peaceful, stress-free day. By regularly visualizing these positive scenarios, you can foster a sense of confidence and preparedness, further combating overthinking.

Cultivating gratitude and positive thinking is like nurturing a garden. It takes time, patience, and consistent effort, but the results—a mind blooming with optimism, resilience, and appreciation—are well worth it. Remember, you have the power to shape your thought patterns and, by extension, your experiences. And that power starts with a single grateful thought and a positive affirmation.

# Reframing Overthinking

In the dance of life, overthinking often steps on our toes. But what if we could change the rhythm and learn to move gracefully with it? Reframing overthinking scenarios is a practical way to do just that. It's about viewing these scenarios from a different perspective, one that highlights benefits and encourages personal growth. This chapter will guide you through a hands-on exercise to do just that.

## Understanding Reframing

Before we delve into the exercise, let's clarify what reframing means. Reframing is a technique used in cognitive psychology to help change the way we view situations, experiences, ideas, or emotions that might seem negative or unhelpful. It's about shifting our perspective to see things in a new light, ideally one that brings positivity, resilience, and empowerment.

# Exercise: The Art of Reframing Overthinking

Now, let's get practical. This exercise will help you reframe real-life overthinking scenarios and harness them for personal growth. It will require you to be open, honest, and reflective, but remember, this is a judgment-free zone. So, grab a pen and some paper, or open up a new note on your phone or computer, and let's begin.

## Step 1: Identify the Scenario

First, think about a recent situation where you found yourself overthinking. It could be anything—a test you took, a conversation you had, a decision you had to make. Write it down in a few sentences, focusing on why it caused you to overthink.

## Step 2: Uncover Negative Beliefs

Identify the negative beliefs or fears that fueled your overthinking. Were you worried about failure? Did you fear judgment from others? Jot these down as well. Recognizing these negative beliefs is the first step in reframing them.

### *Step 3: Seek the Silver Lining*

Now, consider the potential benefits or lessons from this overthinking scenario. Did it make you more prepared for a challenge? Did it make you realize something important about yourself? Write down any positives you can think of, no matter how small they seem.

### *Step 4: Reframe With Empowerment*

Finally, look at the scenario again, but this time, from an alternative, empowering perspective. Could this experience be an opportunity for growth? Could it be a stepping stone toward resilience? Rewrite the scenario, emphasizing these empowering aspects. By the end of this exercise, you'll have reframed your overthinking scenario, uncovering the positive aspects hidden beneath the surface. This process is about acknowledging that overthinking isn't merely a stumbling block but potentially a stepping stone towards personal growth.

Remember, it's normal to find this exercise challenging at first—after all, you're reshaping habitual thought patterns. But with consistent practice, you'll find it easier to reframe overthinking scenarios and foster a mindset that empowers, rather than hinders, you.

Practicing the art of reframing is like learning a new language—the language of positive perspective. And just like any other language, the more you practice, the more fluent you become. So, whenever you find yourself caught in the whirlwind of overthinking, take a step back, grab your metaphorical pen and paper, and start reframing.

# Conclusion

In the dynamic landscape of teenage years, overthinking can often feel like a relentless storm. However, through understanding and navigating these mental torrents, we can transform them into powerful tools for self-awareness and growth. It's all about challenging negative beliefs, embracing mindfulness, cultivating gratitude, and employing practical techniques to reframe scenarios. As you walk this path, remember overthinking isn't a flaw, it's a feature of the deeply analytical and reflective mind, one that, when guided correctly, can lead to profound insights and breakthroughs. So take the reins of your overthinking tendencies, steer them towards positivity and empowerment, and witness the flourishing of your true potential.

# Chapter 6:

# What Happens When Overthinking is not Helpful

Overthinking, like an insistent echo, reverberates through the hallways of the mind. It takes hold of ordinary contemplations and transmutes them into an overgrown web, a constant game of mental hide-and-seek that enthralls us into exhaustive circles. As teenagers, your minds are radiant, teeming with curiosity and brimming with questions that seek answers. However, what happens when this inherent curiosity skews into a spiral of overthinking? What occurs when the thirst for answers is so overpowering that it leads to mental and emotional fatigue, affecting not only your relationships but also your productivity and decision-making abilities?

In this chapter, we will delve into the profound and often intricate world of overthinking. Through a combination of scientific insights, shared experiences, and expert advice, we will explore the potential pitfalls that come from overindulging in our thoughts. We will paint a comprehensive picture of the consequences of excessive rumination, from the psychological distress it can instigate, to the profound impact it can have on our relationships and overall effectiveness in daily tasks.

But our journey doesn't stop there. With a thorough understanding of the potential detriments, we will arm ourselves with the tools needed to combat these undesirable effects. As we navigate this complex web, we'll discover self-care strategies and exercises that can help you break free from the cycle of overthinking. By the end of this chapter, you'll not only have a deep understanding of how overthinking can obstruct your path to emotional well-being but also the means to divert and reframe these thought patterns into a healthier perspective.

So prepare to delve deep, unravel the threads of overthinking, and emerge with the strength to transform your mental habits. Together, we'll explore, learn, and strive to cultivate a more positive mindset— step by step, thought by thought.

# The Impact of Overthinking on Mental and Emotional Well-Being

We've all been there, obsessively replaying a conversation in our heads or tirelessly pondering over a decision until we're spiraling down a rabbit hole of unending thoughts. This act of overthinking is a common experience, but when it escalates, it can have profound impacts on our mental and emotional well-being. In this comprehensive guide, we delve into the impact of overthinking on our lives, offering insights from mental health experts, practical strategies for combating it, and illuminating ways to better understand this habitual pattern.

## The Enigma of Overthinking

Overthinking, according to clinical psychologist Julie Pike, is inherent to our human nature (WtopNews, 2021). However, when these thoughts spin out of control, we often find ourselves stuck in a loop of catastrophizing scenarios. This pattern, as psychologist Sophie Lazarus points out, may provide a sense of control in the short term, but it could lead to serious repercussions for our well-being and our overall engagement with life in the long term (Berjot & Gillet, 2011).

## Understanding Anxiety: The Fuel to Overthinking

Jeri Coast, a licensed clinical social worker, explains that worrying and overthinking is part of our natural response to stress and potential danger. Anxiety, therefore, serves as the fuel to overthinking. The challenge lies in striking a balance between healthy, problem-solving thinking and debilitating overthinking (USNews, 2023).

## Impact of Overthinking on Mood and Sleep

Overthinking can negatively impact mood, leading to heightened levels of depression and irritability. Furthermore, the constant barrage of thoughts can interfere with sleep, leading to fatigue and contributing to a cycle of exhaustion.

## Practical Strategies to Combat Overthinking

In order to stop overthinking, one must first recognize when they're doing it. There are 17 expert-approved tactics to break free from the cycle of overthinking. These include catching oneself, looking for thought patterns, setting worry deadlines, practicing mindfulness, and turning to activities such as listening to music or exercising.

### Harnessing Anxiety as a Learning Tool

Anxiety isn't always detrimental. In fact, it can be harnessed as a tool for improvement. Morra Aarons-Mele, host of the *The Anxious Achiever* podcast, suggests leveraging your anxiety to enhance your performance and leadership skills.

### The Power of Mindfulness and Exercise

Practicing mindfulness and engaging in regular physical activity are effective strategies for managing anxiety and reducing overthinking. Mindfulness exercises allow for a break from the problem, leading to more efficient problem-solving, while exercise helps clear the mind and settles racing thoughts.

Overthinking can have a significant impact on one's mental and emotional well-being. Recognizing this pattern and employing effective strategies can help mitigate these effects and improve overall health.

The understanding that overthinking is a common experience that can be controlled is the first step toward a healthier mind.

# Overthinking in Relationships: The Hidden Strain

Overthinking is not a phenomenon that exists in isolation. Its impact extends far beyond one's individual mental and emotional well-being, often seeping into interpersonal relationships. When we overthink, we put relationships under the microscope, dissecting every interaction, and attempting to decipher hidden meanings in words, actions, or even silences.

## *Miscommunication and Misunderstandings*

A major drawback of overthinking is the breeding ground it creates for miscommunication. For an overthinker, a conversation isn't just an exchange of words, it's a riddle embedded with hidden meanings. This tendency to magnify simple interactions can distort the real intent behind them, leading to unfounded misunderstandings and unnecessary conflict. It's not just the words either. Overthinkers might overanalyze non-verbal cues or perceived slights, turning innocent oversights into imagined insults.

These misunderstandings can lead to feelings of hurt, confusion, and resentment. Over time, they can drive a wedge in relationships, creating a distance that might seem insurmountable. Overthinkers might find themselves constantly on the defense, preparing for perceived attacks that are purely figments of their imagination. In this never-ending network of miscommunication, it becomes difficult for them to engage in healthy, open dialogues, thus straining their relationships.

## *Overanalyzing Interactions and Making Assumptions*

The tendency to overanalyze interactions is another trait common in overthinkers. They might scrutinize every word, every action, every silence for hidden implications. Such an intense focus on decoding behaviors can lead to them making erroneous assumptions about others' thoughts and intentions. This habit of *mind-reading* is more akin to conjuring illusions, leading to misguided conclusions and unwarranted anxiety.

This habit can also result in feelings of constant pressure. Overthinkers might worry excessively about how they are perceived by others, fueling their anxiety. They might spend hours rehashing past conversations or actions, looking for clues about others' perceptions of them. This obsessive analysis not only stresses them but also strains their relationships, creating tension and fostering miscommunication.

# Impact on Trust, Vulnerability, and Intimacy

Overthinking can have profound effects on the bedrock of any relationship—trust, vulnerability, and intimacy.

When we overthink, we question every word, every action, scrutinizing them for hidden meanings. This habit can make it difficult to trust others, leading to a constant state of doubt and suspicion. This lack of trust can erect barriers in a relationship, hampering open and honest communication. It can also lead to a fear of betrayal, causing overthinkers to hold back their feelings and thoughts. This guardedness can prevent real intimacy from taking root in a relationship.

Vulnerability—showing our authentic selves to others—is crucial for deep connections. However, overthinking can make vulnerability seem like a daunting prospect. It paints a picture of potential rejection or ridicule, inhibiting us from showing our true selves. This fear of vulnerability can hinder deeper emotional connections, depriving relationships of the honesty and authenticity they need to thrive.

In essence, overthinking doesn't merely affect us as individuals; it has far-reaching implications for our relationships as well. However, recognizing its impact is the first step towards mitigating its harmful effects. With understanding and effort, we can steer away from the traps of overthinking and work towards healthier, more fulfilling relationships.

## Indecisiveness and Missed Opportunities

One notable fallout of overthinking is its deleterious impact on decision-making abilities. Indecisiveness often tags along with overthinking, turning even trivial choices into mental tugs-of-war. The constant second-guessing, the endless weighing of pros and cons, can trap an overthinker in a state of analysis paralysis. It's like standing at a crossroads where each path seems to lead to an equally foreboding uncertainty.

This indecisiveness can also lead to missed opportunities. While the overthinker is tangled in the web of *what ifs*, life does not pause. The world keeps moving, and opportunities that require prompt action may slip by unnoticed. Overthinking, therefore, can become a roadblock to seizing new possibilities, stunting personal growth and progress.

## Decreased Productivity and Efficiency

Overthinkers often have an unintentional knack for taking simple tasks and transforming them into complex challenges. A simple homework assignment, a minor group project, or a basic household chore could turn into an exhausting ordeal due to overthinking. The overthinker's mind tends to dissect each task into minute fragments, overanalyze each fragment, and thus increase the overall perceived difficulty.

This tendency to overcomplicate tasks invariably leads to decreased productivity. It not only consumes a significant amount of time but also drains mental energy, leading to exhaustion and burnout. Tasks that could have been completed efficiently now seem overwhelming, leaving little time and energy for other activities. Overthinking, in this way, becomes a productivity killer, inhibiting efficiency and promoting procrastination.

## Inaction and Stagnation: The Overthinking Trap

Overthinking can create a vicious cycle of inaction and stagnation. The constant analysis and re-analysis can make any decision, any action, seem fraught with potential danger and error. This fear of making a wrong move can paralyze overthinkers into a state of inaction. They may find themselves stuck in their comfort zones, unable to make the leap toward change or progress.

This cycle of inaction can lead to stagnation. Personal growth requires action, experimentation, and occasional failure. However, overthinking can instill a fear of failure, making it difficult to take the necessary risks for growth. Over time, this inaction can lead to feelings of dissatisfaction and unfulfillment, reinforcing the cycle of overthinking.

Overthinking, while seeming like a harmless mental exercise, can have serious ramifications on productivity, decision-making, and personal growth. However, recognizing these impacts is the first step towards breaking free from the shackles of overthinking. Having a deep understanding of these challenges enables us to skillfully maneuver past them and make progress towards cultivating a more positive state of mind.

# Exercise: Crafting Your Personalized Self-Care Plan

Overthinking can often seem like a complex maze with no apparent exit. However, an effective self-care plan can serve as a roadmap guiding you out of this maze. This exercise will guide you in creating your own personalized self-care plan, designed to help manage and mitigate the effects of overthinking. Remember, this is your plan tailored by and for you. Grab a notepad and a pen, or open a new note on your phone or computer, and let's begin.

## Step 1: Self-Care Inventory

The first step is to identify self-care activities that you already engage in or enjoy. These can range from physical activities like yoga or a sport, to creative ones like painting or playing an instrument, to simple activities like reading, listening to music, or taking a warm bath. Write down these activities as they will form the base of your self-care plan.

## Step 2: Stress Triggers and Coping Mechanisms

Next, take a moment to reflect on the situations that typically trigger your overthinking. This could be certain people, environments, topics, or even times of the day. Note these down. Alongside each trigger, list out one or two coping mechanisms or activities from your self-care inventory that you can engage in when faced with these triggers.

## Step 3: Daily Dose of Self-Care

Now, it's time to weave these self-care activities into your everyday routine. Plan out your typical day and identify slots where you can incorporate these self-care activities. It's essential to set realistic expectations. Remember, even a few minutes of self-care can have significant benefits.

## Step 4: Emergency Self-Care Kit

Sometimes, overthinking can hit us unexpectedly. For such occasions, create an emergency self-care kit. This can include quick stress relief activities such as deep breathing exercises, short meditations, or even uplifting songs or videos that always manage to put a smile on your face.

## Step 5: Review and Refine

Lastly, remember that your self-care plan is not set in stone. As you grow and evolve, so should your plan. Regularly review and refine it to best suit your current needs and circumstances.

By the end of this exercise, you will have created a personalized self-care plan, a powerful tool in combating overthinking. With regular practice, these self-care activities will become a natural part of your routine, helping you manage stress, promote emotional well-being, and reduce the negative impact of overthinking. After all, it's not just about surviving, but thriving in the face of overthinking.

# Conclusion

As we reach the conclusion of our exploration, it's crucial to remember that overthinking is not an insurmountable barrier but rather a challenge that can be navigated with understanding, practice, and patience. The repercussions of overthinking—whether it's on relationships, productivity, or decision-making—can certainly be daunting. Yet, equipped with awareness, practical strategies, and a personalized self-care plan, we can transform this hurdle into an opportunity for growth. Overthinking, like any aspect of our psyche, forms a part of who we are. It's not about eliminating it entirely but about understanding its dynamics and learning how to manage it effectively. As you progress on this journey, remember it's okay to stumble, to pause, and to take a moment for yourself. After all, dealing with overthinking isn't a race—it's a journey, one that leads to a more self-aware, resilient, and empowered version of you.

# Chapter 7:

# Channeling Overthinking in Useful

# Ways

Picture this: you've been tasked with building a boat. The boat must be able to withstand violent storms, navigate treacherous waters, and sail across vast, uncharted oceans. The thought alone overwhelms you, doesn't it? You begin to doubt your abilities. A boat? That's too massive a task! You know nothing about boat construction, let alone handling storms or treacherous waters. Fear sets in. Overthinking begins to stir, like a gusty wind, swirling around in your mind.

We've all been there, standing on the brink of an intimidating task, teetering on the precipice of crippling overthinking. But here's the thing: You don't need to construct an entire boat at once. Instead, focus on one plank of wood, one nail at a time. You see, the key lies in breaking down tasks and setting achievable goals, small enough to hold in your hand and clear enough to navigate your thoughts. This chapter is your compass, guiding you in transforming that intimidating image of a boat into a step-by-step blueprint, which allows you to tackle the project in manageable stages.

In this chapter, we'll embark on a journey of embracing self-acceptance and self-compassion, acknowledging our propensity to overthink and learning to navigate it with kindness and understanding. This is our first step: reframing self-talk and embracing our imperfections. It's okay to overthink. It's okay to be imperfect. In fact, it's more than okay—it's human.

As we move forward, we'll delve into the art of breaking tasks down into manageable goals, the kind that can be held in the palm of your hand, carefully examined and effectively accomplished. This, my friends, is our lifeboat in the stormy sea of overthinking. A single plank does not make a ship, but align them, nail by nail, and soon you'll be looking at your very own vessel.

Further, we'll explore the intricacies of finding a balance in life and setting boundaries. Yes, it's important to dedicate time to deep thinking, to challenge our minds and engage our intellect, but it's equally important to offset this with activities that instill relaxation, joy, and connection. You'll learn to designate *thinking time* and *non-thinking time*, ensuring your mind doesn't always sail on the turbulent sea but finds safe harbor in serene waters too. And finally, as we set our compasses toward the horizon, we'll step into a practical exercise: identifying your personal goals and charting a course of action. We'll dissect each goal, plank by plank until you're not staring at a daunting vessel but instead at a tangible, achievable action plan.

In this chapter, we'll not only build our boats, but we'll learn to navigate our thoughts, one wave at a time. We'll explore. We'll conquer. We'll set our sails and brave the vast ocean of overthinking. So, strap on your life vests, adventurers, because we're about to embark on a journey of self-discovery, resilience, and growth. Let the journey begin!

# Embracing Self-Acceptance and Self-Compassion

We are all like works of art in progress. As we grow, we shape and define our own personalities, crafting ourselves with experiences, choices, and emotions. Just like how an artist values each stroke of their brush, each thought we have is a vital part of who we are, even the ones that tend to overthink. Understanding and accepting this inherent nature is an integral part of embracing self-acceptance and self-compassion.

Life is like a constantly unfolding story with us at the center of it all. Being a teenager is a lot like being the protagonist in the most intense part of the story. It's a roller coaster of feelings, experiences, and choices that shape us into who we will become. During this time, it's quite normal to get caught in the whirlwind of thoughts that race through our minds. Yes, we all tend to overthink sometimes, and that's okay! Overthinking can be a sign of a mind that's creative, analytical, and sensitive. It's an indication that your brain is engaging with problems and trying to solve them.

## *Reframing Self-Talk and Embracing Imperfections*

What's important is how we deal with overthinking. The first step is accepting it as a part of who we are. Instead of getting frustrated when you find yourself stuck in a loop of thoughts, acknowledge it. You can say to yourself, "Right now, I'm overthinking, and that's okay." This simple act of self-acceptance is the cornerstone of building self-compassion.

Self-compassion is like a warm blanket we wrap around ourselves when the world feels cold. It's the act of treating ourselves with kindness and understanding, just as we would with a dear friend. When we practice self-compassion, we acknowledge our imperfections without judgment. After all, we are all perfectly imperfect, and these imperfections are what make us unique.

Imagine your mind as a garden. The way we talk to ourselves determines the kind of seeds we plant in this garden. Each thought and each word is a seed that will eventually grow. If we constantly criticize and judge ourselves, we plant seeds of negativity, which can sprout into self-doubt and anxiety. On the other hand, when we practice self-compassion and positive self-talk, we plant seeds of self-love and acceptance, nurturing a garden that blooms with confidence and resilience.

One of the best ways to cultivate this inner garden is by reframing our self-talk. When we catch ourselves being harsh or negative, we can gently guide our thoughts toward a more compassionate dialogue. For instance, instead of saying, "I'm terrible at this," we can say, "I'm still learning, and it's okay to make mistakes." This slight shift in perspective can make a significant difference.

## *Embracing Imperfections*

Embracing imperfections is another important part of this journey. Remember, it's our quirks, our unique perspectives, and even our mistakes that make us who we are. They add depth to our character and give us the chance to grow. Every time we stumble and fall, we get back up stronger and wiser. And that's beautiful!

Self-compassion plays a significant role in reducing self-judgment and creating a more nurturing inner dialogue. When we are compassionate towards ourselves, we establish healthy boundaries, both emotional and mental. We acknowledge our needs, our feelings, and our limitations without feeling guilty or selfish. This ability to express our needs assertively is a crucial part of self-care.

So, remember, being a teenager can be overwhelming, but it's also an exciting journey of self-discovery. As you navigate through this vibrant maze of life, don't forget to carry with you the keys of self-acceptance and self-compassion. They will help unlock doors to a more understanding, patient, and loving relationship with yourself.

You are a masterpiece in the making, an extraordinary blend of thoughts, emotions, and experiences. So, treat yourself with kindness, embrace your imperfections, and let your unique light shine!

# Task Management and Goal Setting

The journey to self-improvement often requires us to take on tasks and set goals, both big and small. However, the idea of facing enormous tasks or setting ambitious goals can feel overwhelming, especially when your mind is already brimming with thoughts. It's like staring at a towering mountain you're expected to climb—the height alone can make you want to retreat. However, by breaking down tasks and setting achievable goals, we can conquer these mountains one step at a time.

## The Dilemma of Overthinking and Overwhelm

Overthinking often has a knack for turning molehills into mountains. When you're confronted with a large task or a complex problem, your mind might start creating a web of *what ifs* and *buts*, leading to feelings of stress and being overwhelmed. It's as if you're trying to climb the entire mountain in a single leap. This sense of overwhelm can freeze your progress, and the task at hand may appear more daunting than it truly is.

## Taming the Task

What if we told you that you don't need to conquer the mountain in one stride? Every large task can be broken down into smaller, more manageable steps, which can drastically reduce the sense of overwhelm. This is similar to how a long journey is comprised of numerous steps or how a large puzzle is made up of many small pieces. The idea is to focus on one piece or one step at a time, making the process much less intimidating.

Start by dividing the task into smaller, bite-sized portions. For instance, if you have a large project for school, break it down into parts like research, outlining, drafting, and editing. Each of these parts can be further divided if needed. This way, you're focusing on one piece of the puzzle at a time, which is far more manageable and less overwhelming.

## Setting Achievable Goals

Just like breaking down tasks, setting achievable goals can also reduce overthinking and provide a sense of direction and accomplishment. Goals are like the milestones you set on your journey up a mountain. They help track your progress, motivate you, and make the journey seem feasible.

When setting goals, ensure they are SMART: Specific, Measurable, Achievable, Relevant, and Time-bound (Mind Tools, 2022). This means your goals should be clear and well-defined, have a way to measure success, be attainable, align with your larger objectives, and have a set timeline. Remember, your goals should challenge you but not overwhelm you.

Let's say you aspire to read more books. Instead of setting a vague goal like "I want to read more," make it SMART: "I will read one book per month for the next six months." This goal is specific, measurable (you can track the number of books read), achievable (one book per month is realistic), relevant (if you aim to enhance your knowledge or vocabulary), and time-bound (six months) (Mind Tools, 2022).

### Reaping the Rewards

By breaking tasks into manageable parts and setting achievable goals, you can create a sense of accomplishment. Every small task you complete or goal you achieve is a victory. Celebrating these victories, no matter how small, can boost your confidence, motivate you further, and alleviate tendencies to overthink.

In the end, remember, your journey is your own. Your mountain to climb is unique to you. It's okay to take one step at a time and set your own pace. Embrace the power of breaking down tasks and setting achievable goals, and you'll find that no mountain is too high to climb.

# Crafting Balance in Life and Setting Boundaries

Life is like a dance, a delicate waltz of activities and emotions. To maintain our equilibrium amidst this dance, we need to achieve a balance—a harmony between deep thinking and activities that spark joy, relaxation, and connection. We must also set boundaries to protect our peace and ensure our mental energy isn't entirely consumed by overthinking.

## The Importance of Life Balance

In the vast sea of our thoughts, it's easy to lose sight of the shore. Spending too much time in the depths of overthinking can pull us away from the experiences that breathe color into our lives. It's important to balance time spent on introspective thinking with activities that light up our souls. Not only does this bring us joy, but it also allows us to remain connected with ourselves and others, fostering a healthier outlook on life.

## Strategies for Establishing Healthy Boundaries

As with all things in life, it's beneficial to set limits to the time you spend overthinking. Consider allocating specific *thinking time* during your day for deep introspection and problem-solving. This could be a quiet moment in the morning with a cup of coffee or an evening stroll in your favorite park.

Similarly, dedicate *non-thinking time* for activities that allow you to unwind and shift your focus from your thoughts. This could be reading a captivating book, painting, or even meditating. By setting these boundaries, you're allowing your mind to have a balanced diet of introspection and distraction, thus preventing overthinking from monopolizing your time and energy.

### Hobbies, Social Activities, and Self-Care

Hobbies and social activities are incredibly effective in adding vibrancy to your life and diverting your attention away from excessive overthinking. They are not merely distractions but are avenues for self-expression, creativity, and connection. From playing a musical instrument to gardening or joining a sports team, the options are endless. These activities offer a sense of accomplishment and fulfillment that can buoy your spirits and help maintain mental balance.

Meanwhile, self-care practices are vital in nourishing both your physical and mental well-being. This could involve taking a relaxing bath, practicing yoga, journaling your thoughts and feelings, or simply enjoying a quiet moment with a cup of tea. Undertaking self-nurturing behaviors can offer a stabilizing influence, an essential break amidst the constant whirl of existence. In addition, allocating meaningful moments with those close to us or engaging in communal activities can generate a feeling of unity. This assists in fostering a sensation of being grounded and diminishes the likelihood of feeling adrift in one's own contemplations.

### *Finding Fulfillment in Balance and Boundaries*

Crafting a balanced life and setting healthy boundaries is like composing a symphony, where different notes and rhythms harmonize to create a beautiful melody. It's not about negating overthinking but rather orchestrating a lifestyle that accommodates introspective thinking without allowing it to drown out other essential aspects of life.

Remember, life is more than an arena for problem-solving and deep thinking. It's a colorful canvas that welcomes a spectrum of experiences and emotions. Your life balance and the boundaries you set are the palette and brushstrokes that define your unique masterpiece. Embrace them, and you'll be well on your way to a fulfilling, harmonious life.

# Drawing Your Map: Identifying Goals and Creating an Action Plan

Overthinking can often feel like being lost in a dense forest of thoughts with no clear path. This exercise will guide you in drawing your own map to navigate this forest, using goal setting and action planning to redirect your overthinking energy. This is your map, designed by you and for you. So, grab a notepad and a pen, or open a new note on your phone or computer, and let's get started.

## Step 1: Discovering Your Destinations

Your first step is to identify areas of your life where you'd like to channel your overthinking energy. Reflect on your interests, aspirations, or areas you wish to improve. These are your destinations. Write them down—these will be the places you aim to reach in your journey.

## Step 2: Setting Your Goals

Now, take your identified areas and refine them into specific, achievable goals. Think of these as the landmarks you want to visit at each destination. Make sure these landmarks are realistic and align with your abilities and interests.

## Step 3: Crafting Your Route

Next, you'll craft your route to each landmark—your action plan. Break each goal down into manageable steps and create a timeline for each. Keep your steps realistic, as setting too steep a path can increase overthinking.

## Step 4: Packing Your Progress Tracker

Just as you might take a GPS or map on a hiking trip, you'll need a progress tracker for your journey. This tool will help you monitor your progress towards each goal, see how far you've come, and identify what adjustments might be needed.

## Step 5: Stocking Up on Celebration Supplies

Finally, don't forget to pack some celebration supplies! Every step you complete towards your goals deserves recognition. Whether it's a small treat, a moment of relaxation, or a pat on the back, celebrating your achievements will fuel your journey.

## Step 6: Review and Replot

Keep in mind that your map isn't set in stone. Just as explorers might find new paths or obstacles, you'll likely need to replot your map as you progress. Regularly review and adjust your plan to best suit your current circumstances and needs.

# Conclusion

Navigating the world of teenage years can be an intense journey, particularly when overthinking enters the fray. Yet, as we've discovered, it's not an insurmountable challenge. By embracing self-acceptance and self-compassion, breaking down tasks into manageable steps, finding a balance in life, setting boundaries, and channeling overthinking energy into achieving personal goals, teens can transform overthinking from a stumbling block into a stepping stone. These strategies provide a road map to not only cope with overthinking, but also to harness it as a tool for self-reflection and personal growth. Ultimately, it's about learning to steer the ship of our minds, even when sailing through the stormy seas of overthinking.

# Chapter 8:

# Practical Tools for Managing

# Overthinking

It's a common teen drama: lying in bed at night, staring at the ceiling, and your mind is buzzing like a bee hive. You're reliving that awkward moment from the school lunchroom or obsessing over that text message you sent two hours ago and still have no reply to. Like a relentless cinema reel, your mind plays every scenario that could possibly go wrong at your first part-time job interview or how that algebra test tomorrow will be an absolute disaster. This, my friends, is the notorious beast known as 'Overthinking' that often holds us hostage in its unending maze. In this chapter, we'll arm ourselves with the right tools to tame this beast and navigate through minds with greater ease and confidence.

You're probably no stranger to the phrase, "you're overthinking this." But what exactly is *overthinking*, and more importantly, how do we stop this relentless mental chatter from driving us up the wall? Let's unpack this.

As we embark on our exploration of managing overthinking, we'll start by understanding the crucial role of self-awareness. Imagine being a detective in your own mind, tracking down patterns of overthinking and their triggers. Techniques like mindfulness, journaling, and reflective exercises will be our flashlights, helping us navigate the complex web of our thoughts. Just like Sherlock Holmes, we'll become adept at recognizing and decoding our thought patterns and emotional states.

Next, we will learn about cognitive restructuring, a powerful tool that enables us to challenge and reframe the limiting beliefs that often fuel our overthinking. It's like being in a debate with your own thoughts and winning, every time! This technique helps us counteract negative thoughts and develop a more constructive and positive mindset. You'll discover strategies like identifying evidence for and against limiting beliefs, creating alternative perspectives, and practicing affirmations. But, we can't always silence the negative thoughts or uncomfortable feelings. And that's okay. We'll explore how to acknowledge and accept these feelings through emotional regulation. We'll learn to ride the waves of our emotions with techniques such as deep breathing, grounding exercises, and expressive writing. Think of it as your personal emotional first-aid kit, always ready to provide relief and prevent your feelings from spiraling into overthinking.

Finally, we'll roll up our sleeves and dive into a practical exercise of thought stopping and thought replacement. This is like learning martial arts for your mind. Every time overthinking attempts to strike, you'll be ready to block and counter with more positive and constructive thoughts. It's a practical skill that you can use anytime and anywhere overthinking starts creeping in.

So let's begin, shall we? It's time to reclaim our mental space and escape the clutches of overthinking. Get ready to be the master of your mind, not its prisoner. Because we're not just surviving the teenage years, we're thriving through them!

# Understanding the Role of Self-Awareness in Managing Overthinking

Self-awareness is integral to managing overthinking. It's like having a compass that guides you through your mental landscape, allowing you to recognize patterns of overthinking and their triggers. One of the first steps towards developing self-awareness is understanding that certain coping skills, while they may seem effective in the short term, can be detrimental in the long run.

For example, substances like alcohol and drugs may numb your pain temporarily but introduce new problems like health, legal, financial, and social issues. Similarly, overeating, oversleeping, and excessive venting may feel like temporary escapes, but they don't solve the problem and can lead to harmful cycles. Avoiding problems, even with *healthy* activities, can still be an unhealthy coping skill if it keeps you from addressing and resolving the issues at hand.

## Techniques to Cultivate Self-Awareness

That's where self-awareness comes into play. Being self-aware means recognizing your emotions, behaviors, and thoughts—the very factors that lead to overthinking. So, how can you foster self-awareness?

Mindfulness, journaling, and reflection exercises are some effective ways. Mindfulness involves being present in the moment and consciously acknowledging your feelings and thoughts without judgment. This practice not only cultivates self-awareness but also aids in emotion regulation. Mindfulness-based interventions have been observed to induce alterations in brain regions associated with attention systems, emotion regulation, and self-referential processing, as evidenced by neuroimaging studies.

Journaling, on the other hand, offers a tangible way to track your thoughts and emotions. By putting your feelings and thoughts on paper, you can spot patterns, triggers, and even potential solutions. The act of writing also helps to declutter the mind, reducing overthinking.

Reflection exercises are another powerful way to enhance self-awareness. They require you to look back on your experiences, behaviors, and feelings to understand them better. Through reflection, you can discover your triggers, recognize your patterns of overthinking, and explore healthier coping mechanisms.

Part of self-awareness is being proactive in developing coping skills that manage future obstacles effectively. This might involve planning ahead for challenges or setting realistic goals. For instance, if you're feeling stressed about an upcoming event, proactive coping might involve identifying potential stressors and devising a plan to manage them.

While cultivating self-awareness and proactive coping skills, remember that what works for others may not work for you. You might need to try different strategies before finding what suits you best, be it walking in nature, engaging in a hobby, or watching a funny video. The goal is to build your own toolkit of coping strategies tailored to your unique needs and circumstances.

In essence, self-awareness is your compass in navigating your mental landscape, helping you manage overthinking. By understanding your triggers, acknowledging your feelings, and proactively developing effective coping strategies, you can lead a more balanced and emotionally healthy life. This process, like any journey, takes time and practice. So be patient with yourself and remember, every step towards self-awareness is a step towards a healthier you.

# Unraveling Cognitive Restructuring

Cognitive restructuring stands as a pillar of strength when dealing with the complex maze of overthinking and limiting beliefs. This potent technique, hailing from the realm of CBT, fundamentally revolves around identifying, challenging, and reshaping thoughts that are unhelpful or detract from our overall sense of well-being and achievement.

It's like reprogramming your mind, shifting away from entrenched negative thought patterns or limiting beliefs, and moving towards perspectives that are more balanced, empowering, and constructive. Essentially, cognitive restructuring aims at transforming the lens through which you view your thoughts, fostering a positive shift in your mindset.

Imagine your mind as a garden and each thought as a seed. Negative thoughts, like weeds, can take root and spread if left unchecked, impacting the growth of healthy, positive thoughts. Cognitive restructuring is akin to being a mindful gardener, spotting these weeds, understanding why they grow, and replacing them with healthier alternatives.

This process is not about denying challenges or difficulties but rather acknowledging them and choosing to nurture thoughts that lead to resilience, personal growth, and overall wellness. When applied consistently, cognitive restructuring can become an empowering tool, helping you to navigate the turbulent waters of adolescence and beyond with greater ease and confidence.

## Challenging Limiting Beliefs: The First Step

Before we can change our thoughts, we first need to identify them. Limiting beliefs are thoughts or ideas that hold us back, hinder our progress, and cultivate a negative mindset. These might be beliefs like "I'm not good at math" or "I can never be a good public speaker." The key here is to become aware of these thoughts, to catch them in their tracks. This is where the skills of self-awareness and mindfulness come into play.

## Gathering Evidence: For and Against

Once you've identified your limiting beliefs, the next step is to challenge them. You can do this by gathering evidence both for and against these beliefs. For instance, if your limiting belief is that you're not good at math, think about times when you've done well in math or successfully solved math problems. This is evidence against the belief. Conversely, consider the instances that make you feel inadequate in math. Is it because of a few poor test scores, or is it based on one negative comment someone made? By objectively examining evidence from both sides, you can create a more accurate picture that isn't dictated solely by your negative thoughts.

## Creating Alternative Perspectives

After gathering evidence, the next step in cognitive restructuring is to create alternative perspectives. Let's stick with the math example. An alternative perspective could be, "While I've struggled with a few math concepts, I've also successfully solved several problems. With practice and perseverance, I can improve my math skills." This reframing process takes your limiting belief and turns it into something more balanced, constructive, and grounded in reality.

## Practicing Affirmations

Affirmations are positive, empowering statements that you can use to counteract further limiting beliefs. They are particularly effective when they're specific, personal, and realistic. For instance, instead of the vague statement, "I'm good at math," a more effective affirmation might be, "I am capable of understanding and mastering math concepts with practice and dedication."

## Applying Cognitive Restructuring

Cognitive restructuring can be applied to any area of your life where you find yourself overthinking or where limiting beliefs arise. It's particularly effective in areas where your negative thoughts are persistent and have a significant impact on your behavior or emotional state.

For example, let's say you're constantly anxious about making friends because you believe that you're not interesting enough. You can apply cognitive restructuring by first identifying this belief, then challenging it by finding evidence for and against it, creating an alternative perspective, and reinforcing it with affirmations like, "I have unique experiences and interests that others may find intriguing."

Remember, the process of cognitive restructuring requires practice and patience. Overcoming limiting beliefs and changing thought patterns doesn't happen overnight. However, with consistent practice, this powerful technique can help you shift your mindset and embrace a more positive and empowering perspective on life.

And finally, it's essential to remind yourself that everyone has strengths and weaknesses, successes and failures. What's more important than being perfect is striving for growth, learning from experiences, and developing resilience. With cognitive restructuring, you're not just managing overthinking—you're building a stronger, more resilient mindset for the future.

# Emotional Regulation

Emotional regulation often starts with a crucial first step—acknowledging and accepting your feelings, even when they're uncomfortable. In the labyrinth of adolescence, it's natural to experience a wide range of emotions, some of which can feel overwhelming or difficult to process. These feelings, when not addressed properly, can become the fuel that feeds overthinking, further exacerbating emotional distress.

Acceptance doesn't mean resigning yourself to negative feelings but rather allowing yourself to experience them without judgment. It's about acknowledging that it's okay not to feel okay all the time. This conscious acceptance acts as a stepping stone, helping to defuse the power that these emotions may hold over your thoughts and behaviors.

## *Techniques for Emotional Regulation*

Now, let's delve into some practical tools that can support emotional regulation.

### *Deep Breathing*

This technique is about more than just inhaling and exhaling; it's about resetting your emotional state. Adopting a gentle, measured breathing pattern can serve to stabilize your nervous system, mitigating symptoms of stress or apprehension. Consider adopting a rhythmic pattern, like drawing breath in for four counts, maintaining it for another four, exhaling for the same duration, and then pausing for another quartet of counts prior to beginning the cycle again.

### Grounding Exercises

Grounding exercises are designed to help anchor you in the present moment. These techniques can include focusing on the sensation of your feet touching the ground, the feeling of an object you're holding, or even the taste of a piece of gum. These exercises can help divert your attention away from distressing thoughts or emotions.

### Expressive Writing

This tool can be a healthy outlet for emotions that might otherwise contribute to overthinking. Writing about your feelings can help to process them and gain perspective. Try keeping a journal where you can express your thoughts and emotions freely.

## Building Your Emotional Coping Toolkit

It's helpful for teens to build their own toolkits of coping strategies to manage intense emotions. This can include any of the techniques mentioned above or others, like physical exercise, mindfulness, and artistic expression. The goal is to have a range of tools at your disposal, so you can choose the ones that work best for you in a given situation.

By regularly practicing these techniques, you'll be better equipped to manage your emotional states. Remember, emotional regulation is not about suppressing or eliminating negative feelings but understanding them and knowing how to navigate them effectively. In this way, you can prevent these intense emotions from spiraling into cycles of overthinking, supporting your overall mental and emotional well-being.

# Practical Exercise: Thought Stopping and Thought Replacement

Navigating the sometimes-turbulent seas of adolescence can trigger waves of overthinking. A powerful technique to gain control over these overwhelming tides is the combination of thought stopping and thought replacement. This practical exercise can be invaluable in helping teens interrupt negative or intrusive thoughts and replace them with more constructive ones.

## The Practice of Thought Stopping

Thought stopping is the conscious act of interrupting negative or intrusive thoughts that fuel overthinking and cause distress. While it may initially feel challenging or even impossible to halt and replace a thought, the good news is that the power to control your thoughts lies entirely within your hands. Nobody else can dictate or alter your thinking—only you can. It's a skill that requires practice, but over time it becomes more natural and effective.

Here's a simple guide to help you master it:

### Identify the Negative Thought

The first step involves becoming aware of the negative thought. When you notice yourself beginning to overthink, take a moment to identify the specific thought that's causing distress.

### Stop the Thought

Once the negative thought is identified, interrupt it. Some people find it helpful to visualize a stop sign or to mentally tell themselves *stop*. It's essential to remember that you hold the reins when it comes to your thinking. Though it may seem like an uncontrollable force at times, you can gain mastery over it with consistent effort and practice.

Remember, you are in control of your thoughts, not the other way around. Don't let the belief that you lack control over your thoughts hold you back. It's a myth that only serves to empower negativity and distress. You have the ability to manage your thoughts, and this skill will strengthen with practice.

## Thought Replacement: Shifting Your Mindset

Thought stopping alone can create a mental void. To ensure that this space doesn't get filled with more negative thoughts, it's important to replace the halted thought with a more positive or constructive one. This is where thought replacement comes in.

### Identify a Positive Counter-Thought

Find a thought to counter the negative one. This thought should be realistic and positive. For example, if your negative thought is "I always mess things up," your counter thought could be "Everyone makes mistakes; what can I learn from this situation?"

### Replace the Negative Thought

Each time you halt the negative thought, consciously replace it with the positive counter-thought. Over time, this replacement thought should come more naturally and eventually take the place of the negative thought.

## Maintaining the Practice

As with any new skill, practice is key. Encourage consistent practice of thought stopping and thought replacement whenever overthinking patterns emerge. This isn't always easy, and there may be times when you feel like it's not working. That's okay. Remember, the goal isn't to completely eliminate negative thinking but rather to manage it more effectively.

Thought stopping and thought replacement isn't just strategies for managing overthinking, but tools for nurturing a healthier mental landscape. These techniques, when practiced consistently, can help cultivate a more balanced, optimistic mindset, empowering you to navigate life's challenges with greater resilience and confidence.

# Conclusion

As we navigate through the tumultuous journey of teenage years, managing overthinking and its consequential stress can be a daunting task. By understanding the role of self-awareness, practicing cognitive restructuring, allowing and accepting uncomfortable feelings, and employing thought-stopping and replacement techniques, we can proactively face these mental challenges. The integration of these practices cultivates an ability to challenge limiting beliefs, regulate emotions, and replace negative thoughts, fostering a healthier mindset and a more balanced life. Overcoming overthinking is a gradual process that requires patience, practice, and above all, kindness to oneself, building resilience for the ever-evolving journey of life.

# Chapter 9:

# Building Self-Confidence

Have you ever felt like you were standing at the edge of a high-dive platform, with your heart pounding and adrenaline rushing? It can be an overwhelming feeling, akin to the sensation you might experience when it's your turn to present in class, or when you're meeting new people for the first time. This heart-racing, nerve-jangling fear is often the result of a lack of self-confidence, and it's a feeling we're all too familiar with. But what if I told you that it doesn't always have to be this way? What if we could channel that adrenaline rush into something more empowering, transforming fear into self-belief?

In this chapter, we're going to dive into the depths of self-confidence—exploring what it truly means, why it's so important, and, most crucially, how we can cultivate it. We'll delve into the intricate relationship between self-confidence and overthinking, exploring how the latter can often undermine our self-perception and self-esteem. We'll then walk you through the concept of self-limiting beliefs, those pesky little thoughts that whisper you're not good enough or that you'll never succeed. We'll provide practical strategies to identify, challenge, and ultimately replace these beliefs.

Remember how amazing it felt when you accomplished something you were proud of? Maybe it was acing a tough test or successfully learning a new skill. That feeling of achievement, that glow of self-satisfaction—that's what we'll be focusing on. We'll discuss the significance of celebrating your successes, no matter how small they might seem, and the power of practicing self-validation. Finally, we'll guide you through a practical exercise that challenges you to step out of your comfort zone. Because, after all, it's only when we stretch our boundaries and dare to face our fears that we truly grow. We'll help you set your own personal challenge, provide support and encouragement, and celebrate with you as you take that plunge off the high-dive platform.

This chapter is all about building that invaluable tool in your arsenal, self-confidence. It's a journey, not an overnight change, and we'll be right there with you every step of the way. So, are you ready to take the plunge and dive into the empowering world of self-confidence? Let's get started!

# The Intricate Dance of Self-Confidence and Overthinking

In the swirling realm of our adolescent mind, the relationship between self-confidence and overthinking resembles a captivating yet intricate dance. They're engaged in an ongoing, delicate tango, each one exerting an influence that can either lift the other higher or pull it down into the shadows. To some, this dance might seem puzzling, with the dancers changing their moves unpredictably, gracefully swaying one moment, and tripping the next. But to truly grasp the complex choreography, we need to take a closer look at the dance floor that is our minds.

Both self-confidence and overthinking play critical roles in how we perceive ourselves and the world around us. They are intertwined in a dance of cause and effect, each with the potential to shape our self-image, decision-making, and overall mental well-being. At times, self-confidence can be the lead, guiding the steps with bold assurance, dictating the rhythm and flow of the dance. Yet, in other instances, overthinking takes control, turning the dance into a whirl of anxious speculation and unhelpful rumination.

But what if we could learn to understand this dance, to discern its pattern and rhythm? Unraveling this dance, we could learn to better steer the duo, enabling us to navigate through life's challenges with less stress and more clarity. In the ensuing pages, we'll delve into this intricate relationship between self-confidence and overthinking, bringing us closer to mastering this internal choreography.

# Overthinking: The Confidence Quagmire

Overthinking is like a hungry monster lurking in the shadows of your mind. It's always ready to feed on your uncertainties, insecurities, and doubts. A fleeting thought or minor mistake could turn into a full-blown self-critical monologue, distorting your self-perception.

Have you ever found yourself trapped in a cycle of thoughts, endlessly analyzing a past conversation or decision? You might replay situations in your mind, tweaking each aspect, turning every *what if* and *should have* over and over again. That's overthinking at its finest, and it's a habit that can gnaw away at your self-confidence.

While a certain degree of introspection is healthy, overthinking can brew a poisonous cocktail of negative self-talk and self-doubt. You can start to see failure where there is none, criticizing yourself for imperfections that aren't even there. In this way, overthinking can tarnish your self-esteem, blurring the mirror in which you see your true potential.

# Self-Confidence: The Armor Against Overthinking

Self-confidence, on the other hand, is like a shining armor. It's the belief in your capabilities, the faith that you can handle whatever comes your way. With a well-fitted armor of self-confidence, the bite of overthinking becomes less potent.

Building self-confidence doesn't mean you have to be perfect or know everything. It's about understanding your strengths and weaknesses and embracing your unique journey. When you believe in yourself, you can take on challenges without drowning in a sea of self-doubt and second-guessing.

Developing self-confidence provides you with a reliable compass, guiding you through the tumultuous teen years. It helps you to make decisions confidently, reducing the likelihood of overthinking. If a mistake happens, which they often do because, hey, we're all human, a self-confident individual can handle it as a learning experience rather than an opportunity for self-criticism.

## Bridging the Gap

Understanding the relationship between overthinking and self-confidence is crucial for personal growth. The path to a healthier mind isn't about completely eliminating overthinking; sometimes, our minds naturally mull things over. It's about learning to manage it effectively so that it doesn't rule your life or sap your confidence.

The key is to reinforce self-confidence while mastering strategies to keep overthinking in check. Embracing self-compassion, practicing mindfulness, setting achievable goals, and celebrating victories, no matter how small, are all steps toward fostering a robust sense of self-confidence and managing overthinking.

Remember, this journey is not about being flawless; it's about becoming more resilient, adaptable, and self-assured. It's about taking control of your mind's dance floor, leading the twirl between overthinking and self-confidence in a rhythm that serves you best. As you delve deeper into your mind, remember that you hold the power to change the narrative, to mold your self-perception, and harness your self-confidence. By understanding the relationship between self-confidence and overthinking, you equip yourself with the knowledge to stride confidently into your future, leaving the monster of overthinking far behind.

# Identifying and Challenging Self-Limiting Beliefs

Imagine walking down a seemingly endless hallway lined with an array of doors. Each door represents a possibility, an opportunity, or a dream. But as you approach one, you realize there's an invisible wall preventing you from reaching it. This is what self-limiting beliefs do; they act like unseen barriers hindering us from seizing our true potential. Unmasking and challenging these beliefs is key to regaining control of the internal dance between self-confidence and overthinking.

Self-limiting beliefs are assumptions or perceptions about ourselves and the world that restricts our potential to grow. They're insidious seeds of doubt that, over time, can germinate into a thorny bush of overthinking, chipping away at our self-confidence. It's as if we're scripting our own narrative of limitations and insecurities. They whisper messages like "I can't do this," "I'm not good enough," or "I'll never succeed," wrapping our ambitions in a cocoon of pessimism.

But how do we recognize these invisible walls? Identifying self-limiting beliefs can be akin to a treasure hunt, where instead of gold, we seek out destructive patterns of thought. It requires introspection and honesty. We need to keenly observe our responses to challenging situations, failures, and criticisms. Any time we find ourselves questioning our abilities or envisaging the worst-case scenarios, it's worth scrutinizing if a self-limiting belief is pulling the strings.

Challenging these beliefs is the next decisive step. It involves scrutinizing the evidence that supports these self-imposed barriers. Often, we'll find that these beliefs are like paper tigers—intimidating but without substance. For instance, if you believe "I'm not good at public speaking," probe this belief. Is this conclusion based on one single bad experience or factual, consistent proof? By objectively examining the evidence, you'll frequently find that your self-limiting beliefs are constructed on shaky ground.

Reframing our perspective is another potent weapon against these mental hurdles. What if, instead of viewing a failure as a testament to your incapability, you perceive it as an opportunity to learn and improve? This shift in perspective allows us to dismantle self-limiting beliefs and replace them with empowering supportive ones.

The process of overcoming self-limiting beliefs is like chiseling a magnificent sculpture. It demands time, patience, and relentless work. However, the result is a more confident, resilient self, less prone to overthinking and more equipped to dance to the rhythm of life's ups and downs. By confronting and challenging these beliefs, we aren't just removing the invisible walls but also unlocking doors to a myriad of opportunities.

# Celebrating Successes and Practicing Self-Validation

Life's like a marathon, and we often forget to cheer for ourselves as we navigate each twist, turn, or hill. Yet, every stride forward, no matter how small, deserves a celebration. Recognizing and validating our victories, both big and small, acts like a nutrient-rich soil for the seed of self-confidence, fostering its growth while silencing the rustling leaves of overthinking.

### Celebrating Personal Achievements

Acknowledging our accomplishments is akin to marking milestones on our personal journey. Each milestone, however tiny, is a testament to our capabilities, our strength, our resilience. When we celebrate our achievements, we're reinforcing our self-worth, subtly reminding ourselves, "I am capable, I am successful." This celebration doesn't have to be grand; it can be as simple as taking a moment to pat yourself on the back, sharing your joy with a loved one, or treating yourself to your favorite dessert. These acts of self-recognition fuel our self-confidence, helping to combat the shadow of a doubt that overthinking often casts.

Complementing this celebration of success is the practice of self-validation. It's about learning to be our own cheerleader, endorsing our feelings and experiences without relying on external approval. In a world that often blasts mixed messages about self-worth, self-validation becomes our sanctuary of affirmation.

Self-validation does not equate to complacency; instead, it's about acknowledging our feelings, our efforts, and our growth. It's saying to ourselves, "It's okay to be upset about this," or "I'm proud of the effort I put in, regardless of the outcome." This understanding and acceptance of self-help constructs a sturdy bridge of self-confidence, allowing us to cross the tumultuous river of overthinking with ease.

## *Practice Self-Validation*

A powerful tool to foster self-validation is positive self-talk and affirmations. Positive self-talk involves swapping critical thoughts with supportive and encouraging messages. It's about tuning into a supportive internal dialogue that says, "I can handle this," or "I am doing my best," whenever doubt tries to creep in. Meanwhile, affirmations are potent declarations that can rewire our brain towards a more optimistic and confident outlook, like repeating, "I am strong," "I am capable," or "I believe in myself."

Recognizing and appreciating our progress is another vital part of self-validation. It's about acknowledging that personal growth isn't always linear. There may be times when you take two steps forward and one step back. But remember, that's still one step forward! Every bit of progress, every lesson learned, is a feather in your cap. Practicing self-validation and celebrating our successes is not about inflating our ego, but rather about cultivating a positive self-image and a strong inner ally. This inner ally champions our abilities, counteracts overthinking, and paves the way for a confident, authentic self. By mastering this art, we become our own source of motivation and validation, ready to embrace the world with a self-assured smile.

# Practical Exercise: Charting New Territories— Stepping Out of Your Comfort Zone

Navigating the complex journey of adolescence can sometimes seem like crossing a bridge swaying high above a ravine. It's challenging, it's daunting, and it requires a significant amount of courage. One of the best ways to foster this courage and develop self-confidence is by deliberately stepping out of your comfort zone. This practical exercise is designed to guide you through the process, from identifying a new challenge to setting a goal and drawing up an action plan.

## The Practice of Embracing Challenges

Venturing outside your comfort zone is about willingly embracing challenges and taking calculated risks. The first stage in this process involves some steps.

### Identify Your Challenge

Start by pinpointing an activity that pushes your boundaries, something that's slightly beyond what you're used to. When you start feeling a mixture of excitement and a tinge of fear, you've likely identified a potential challenge.

### Embrace Your Challenge

Once you've identified your challenge, the next step is to accept it. Visualize yourself facing this challenge head-on. You could imagine a door opening to a path leading towards your challenge, symbolizing your readiness to step out of your comfort zone.

## Goal Setting: Charting Your Course

Merely identifying a challenge isn't enough. You need a concrete goal to keep you focused and motivated. This involves:

### Formulate a SMART Goal

Create a goal that is Specific, Measurable, Achievable, Relevant, and Time-bound, related to your challenge (Mind Tools, 2022b). For example, if your challenge involves public speaking, your goal could be "I will deliver a five-minute speech at the school talent show in six weeks."

### Affirm Your Goal

Each time you acknowledge your challenge, consciously reaffirm your goal. This acts as a reminder of what you're working towards and reinforces your commitment to the challenge.

## Action Planning: Laying Out the Steps

With your goal in place, you need a strategic plan to reach it. This is where action planning comes into play.

### Draft an Action Plan

Break your goal down into manageable tasks. Each task should have a timeline, enabling you to monitor your progress. In our public speaking example, your first task could be "Research potential speech topics by the end of this week."

*Implement Your Action Plan*

Each time you complete a task, mark it off your plan. This not only helps you keep track of your progress but also provides a sense of achievement, further boosting your confidence.

## *Staying the Course*

As with learning any new skill or undertaking a challenge, there will be ups and downs. It's crucial to practice resilience and determination. Remember, the goal is not to complete the challenge flawlessly but rather to grow and learn from the experience.

Stepping out of your comfort zone is more than a strategy for building self-confidence; it's a testament to your ability to adapt, grow, and overcome. With consistent practice, you can transform fear into courage, apprehension into ambition, and dreams into realities, becoming more confident and resilient in the process.

# Conclusion

Navigating the tumultuous waves of adolescence can often stir up storms of self-doubt, overthinking, and self-limiting beliefs. Yet, by understanding these challenges, you can learn to sail these seas with resilience and grace. Cultivating self-confidence helps in quieting the voice of overthinking, challenging and replacing self-limiting beliefs, lays a solid foundation for personal growth, and celebrating successes allows you to recognize your capabilities. Additionally, by regularly stepping out of your comfort zone, you not only challenge yourself but also broaden your horizons and foster your confidence. Remember, every small step you take contributes to your overall journey of self-discovery, personal development, and empowerment during your teenage years and beyond.

# Chapter 10:

# Embracing Imperfection and

# Allowing Growth

Picture this: our favorite superheroes are always perfect, aren't they? They never miss their mark, never stumble or stutter, and they always, always save the day. But what if I told you, even superheroes have their imperfections? Would you believe it? Peter Parker, the beloved Spider-Man, constantly struggles with balancing his personal life with his heroic duties. Superman, the man of steel himself, has his vulnerability—Kryptonite. The takeaway here? Even our most revered figures have their flaws, but it's through these flaws that they grow, adapt, and ultimately triumph.

This is the chapter where you'll learn that life isn't about being perfect—it's about embracing our flaws, our quirks, our imperfections, and using them as stepping stones to propel us forward. It's through these *flaws* that we shape our individuality, our identity.

Ever wondered how your pursuit of perfectionism might be contributing to overthinking? Here we'll unravel the knots of unrealistic standards and constant self-criticism, highlighting the importance of embracing imperfection as a pathway to personal development and self-acceptance.

Next, we'll walk through the peaceful meadow of self-compassion, introducing you to self-kindness, mindfulness, and ways to reframe negative self-talk. You'll learn how to hug your flaws, greet your mistakes with a smile, and cherish them as your unique companions in your journey to self-growth.

Following this, we'll venture into the realm where mistakes aren't something to be frowned upon but are viewed as fascinating opportunities for growth. We'll toss aside the old lens of viewing setbacks as a measure of self-worth and replace it with a fresh perspective, seeing them as valuable learning experiences.

And finally, you will embark on a journey with your personal *embracing imperfection* journal, a sanctuary for your thoughts where you document your own story of growth. It's a place to reflect, to celebrate, and acknowledge your progress in embracing your unique, imperfect self.

Get ready for an eye-opening journey where the destination isn't perfection but a place where you are happier, healthier, and full of self-love and compassion. Because remember, like our favorite superheroes, it's through our quirks, our missteps, and our unique imperfections that we, too, can save our day.

## The Role of Perfectionism in Overthinking

Perfectionism, a trait that pushes individuals to strive for flawlessness, has a deceptive allure. For teenagers navigating a tumultuous stage of life, the appeal of perfection can be particularly captivating. However, the pursuit of perfection can sometimes fuel a tendency to overthink, leading to a cycle that hinders personal growth.

The intricate dance between perfectionism and overthinking begins with the daunting desire to make every action, decision, or endeavor flawless. You meticulously plan, analyze, and obsess over each detail, fearing the consequence of a single misstep. This compulsive overthinking, also known as analysis paralysis, can leave you feeling trapped in your own thoughts, limiting your ability to act or move forward.

The relentless quest for perfection often sprouts from an internal narrative that whispers, "you must never fail." This fear of failure fuels overthinking, as you find yourself constantly trying to foresee and prevent potential mistakes. Over time, this can become exhausting and stifling. You may lose opportunities for growth and learning, as failure, in reality, serves as a profound teacher, fostering resilience and paving the way for success.

The constant striving for perfection can also breed harsh self-criticism. Teenagers who are perfectionists often judge themselves more harshly for their perceived failings. This internal dialogue can skew reality, amplifying small errors into catastrophic failures. Every stumble is overthought, overanalyzed, and blown out of proportion, which impedes self-confidence and self-esteem.

Perfectionism, in essence, is chasing an illusion. It's the unattainable expectation of a flawless life. However, life is inherently messy, unpredictable, and filled with imperfections. Embracing this reality is integral to personal development and self-acceptance.

Rather than aiming for perfection, strive for personal excellence. Recognize that your worth is not measured by the perfection of your outcomes but by the effort, growth, and learning that comes from the process. Replace self-criticism with self-compassion, and allow yourself the freedom to make mistakes, learn, and grow from them.

Perfectionism and overthinking can make you feel like you're constantly walking a tightrope, where a single misstep could lead to disaster. But remember, life is not a tightrope. It's more of a playground where the most important part is not to avoid falling but to get back up, dust yourself off, and keep playing the game.

Embrace your flaws, your quirks, and your human imperfections. Recognize them as part of your unique self rather than as elements of shame or fear. Encourage yourself to take risks, to explore, and to make mistakes. After all, it's often through these imperfect paths that we stumble upon the most beautiful and unexpected destinations.

Perfectionism and overthinking may promise a life without flaws, but it's in our beautifully imperfect journey that we find our strength, resilience, and authentic selves. Remember, it's okay to strive for your best, but your best does not mean perfect. It means being true to yourself, embracing your journey with all its twists and turns, and always allowing yourself room for growth and learning.

In the grand theater of life, perfectionism plays the part of the relentless taskmaster. Still, once you learn to embrace your imperfections, you'll discover a liberating truth: you're not the understudy in your life's story; you're the star. And stars, as we know, shine brightest not in their perfection but in their authenticity.

## Cultivating Self-Compassion and Acceptance

Amid the storm of overthinking and self-judgment, an anchoring principle emerges in self-compassion. This life-affirming principle is a nurturing balm to the harshness of perfectionism and the crippling dance of overthinking. For teenagers, navigating the turbulent waters of self-discovery, self-compassion, and acceptance provides a guiding lighthouse leading to a harbor of self-assured tranquility.

Self-compassion is the practice of treating oneself with the same kindness, understanding, and care you would offer a beloved friend. It's about acknowledging that everyone, including you, is beautifully flawed and deserving of compassion. It's a gentle antidote to the relentless pursuit of perfection and overthinking.

So, how can one cultivate self-compassion? There are several pathways to this heartwarming destination.

One such route is self-kindness. This practice encourages you to be gentle with yourself and to acknowledge your shortcomings without harsh criticism. When you stumble, instead of berating yourself, offer words of comfort and encouragement. "It's okay. We all make mistakes. What can I learn from this?" By replacing self-judgment with self-kindness, you begin to cultivate an inner sanctuary of compassion and understanding.

Mindfulness is another powerful tool in the self-compassion toolkit. By staying present and grounded in the moment, you prevent your mind from spiraling into a complex web of overthinking. Mindfulness involves acknowledging your feelings and thoughts without judgment. Instead of being swept away by negative thoughts or self-criticism, observe them as passing clouds in the sky of your mind. Remember, you are not your thoughts; you are the observer of your thoughts.

Reframing negative self-talk is another vital step toward cultivating self-compassion. Negative self-talk often fuels overthinking and perfectionism. Instead, try to catch and challenge these negative thoughts, replacing them with positive affirmations. If you find yourself thinking, "I'm terrible at this," pause and reframe it: "I'm learning and improving every day."

Embracing self-acceptance is like planting a nurturing tree in the garden of your heart. This tree, watered by self-compassion and acceptance, blossoms into an understanding that you are enough, just as you are. You don't need to be perfect to be worthy of love, respect, or happiness.

When you foster a nurturing relationship with yourself, you begin to appreciate your journey, including its challenges, detours, and beautiful discoveries. Self-compassion and self-acceptance give you the courage to take risks, embrace your authentic self, and celebrate your individuality. Self-compassion is like a soft melody that counters the harsh cacophony of overthinking and self-judgment. By embracing this tune of kindness, mindfulness, and acceptance, you can dance to your life's rhythm, radiant with the authentic light of your beautifully imperfect self.

Remember, it's not about being perfect but being compassionate and kind to yourself. That's the key to personal growth, resilience, and a deeper connection with your true self. Cultivating self-compassion and acceptance isn't just an act of love for yourself, it's a celebration of your unique journey every step of the way.

# Mistakes and Failures as Opportunities for Growth

Mistakes and failures: they're like an unpredictable storm in the sea of life. Every individual, irrespective of age or circumstance, will inevitably encounter them. For teenagers standing at the brink of countless new experiences, these storms can feel overwhelming, often leading to self-doubt and overthinking. But what if, instead of seeing mistakes and failures as terrifying tempests, we began viewing them as refreshing rain, nurturing the seeds of growth and resilience within us?

This shift in perspective demands a crucial mindset change, a metamorphosis of thought and self-perception. It's about accepting that mistakes and failures do not define you or your worth. Instead, they are transient episodes in your lifelong journey, each carrying invaluable lessons and opportunities for growth. They are not the damning verdicts on your abilities but rather the stepping stones leading you toward personal evolution.

To adopt this growth-focused mindset, you must start by reframing your relationship with failures and mistakes. Imagine yourself as an explorer embarking on a voyage toward self-discovery. Each mistake is not a dead-end but rather a crossroad offering new paths and perspectives. Each failure is not a downfall but a chance to rise, innovate, and adapt.

When you stumble, instead of wallowing in self-pity or criticism, ask yourself: "What can I learn from this experience? How can I grow?" The answer may not always be immediate or clear, but in time, and with patience and introspection, you'll unearth invaluable lessons buried beneath the surface of your mistakes and failures.

Embracing failures offers manifold benefits, one of them being the cultivation of resilience. Like a phoenix rising from the ashes, each failure offers an opportunity to rebuild itself, stronger and wiser than before. Failures toughen your spirit, enabling you to face future challenges with greater courage and resolve.

Moreover, viewing mistakes as opportunities for growth fosters a mindset of continuous learning. It prompts curiosity, encouraging you to ask questions, seek answers, and expand your horizons. It invites innovation, urging you to think out of the box and devise novel solutions.

Remember, the most successful individuals in the world are not those who never failed but those who refused to allow failure to halt their journey. They viewed each failure as a detour, not a dead-end, each mistake as a lesson, not a loss. This is the mindset that breeds success, resilience, and personal growth.

So, next time you falter, don't let overthinking or self-criticism pull you down. Instead, take a moment to breathe, appreciate the lesson hidden within the experience, and recognize your potential for growth. It's not about avoiding mistakes but learning to dance in the rain of these life lessons, growing with each drop and blooming with resilience, wisdom, and self-compassion.

## Practical Exercise: Embracing Imperfection Journal

The purpose of this journal is simple: to document your personal journey as you learn to embrace imperfections, exercise self-compassion, and view mistakes as opportunities for growth. And no, this isn't about achieving perfection in journaling—remember, we're embracing imperfections here!

To start off, you'll need a journal that calls out to you. It can be as simple or as extravagant as you want it to be—a plain notebook, a leather-bound diary, or even a digital journal on your preferred device.

Let's dive into how you'll chart your course in this journal.

## Documenting Imperfections

Each day, write down at least one instance where you encountered imperfection—either in yourself or your surroundings. This could be a project that didn't go as planned, a task you struggled with, or a change in your physical appearance.

## Embracing the Imperfection

Reflect on the imperfection you've documented. How does it make you feel? Instead of letting it drag you down, explore how it contributes to your unique personality or your experience. Write about it.

## Practicing Self-Compassion

Now, it's time to show some kindness to yourself. Write a compassionate message to yourself about the imperfection you identified. It could be something as simple as "I am human, and it's okay to make mistakes," or "My worth is not defined by my flaws."

## Mistakes as Growth Opportunities

In this section, document any mistake or failure you encountered during the day. Reflect on what it taught you, or how it could potentially lead to growth. Remember, the focus here is not on the failure itself, but on the potential lessons and growth opportunities it presents.

## Celebrating Progress

Every week, take a moment to reflect on your entries. Appreciate your journey, the lessons learned, and the growth achieved. Celebrate the progress, however small it might seem. This could be as simple as writing, "I'm proud of myself for embracing my imperfections this week," or something more specific like, "I'm glad I learned from my mistake in my math test."

This journal is your personal space, free of judgments and expectations. Let it be a sanctuary where you learn to embrace your beautifully imperfect self, where you practice self-compassion, and where you cultivate a growth mindset. Remember, it's not about getting it perfect, but about enjoying the journey and celebrating the small victories along the way.

# Conclusion

In the grand voyage of life, navigating through the turbulent seas of adolescence can feel daunting, but remember that each wave brings new opportunities for growth and self-discovery. Embrace the winds of imperfection and let them guide you toward newfound resilience and self-compassion. Cherish your failures not as anchors but as lighthouses guiding you toward personal growth. With each entry in your embracing imperfection journal, remember that you're not just documenting experiences, but mapping your journey of growth, celebrating progress, and fostering self-acceptance. The journey towards embracing your unique self might be challenging, but it's on this voyage that you'll discover the treasure that is your authentic, beautifully imperfect self.

# Chapter 11:

# Navigating Overthinking in

# Relationships

As you peel open the covers of this book on a lazy Sunday afternoon, bathed in a comforting stream of sunlight pouring through your bedroom window, your phone vibrates incessantly on the nightstand. It's a text message. A *hey* from that special someone in your life—that one person who brings an unbidden smile to your lips, a flush to your cheeks, a strange fluttering in your heart. It's as simple as a three-letter word, yet your mind races, overthinking every possible implication of that single message. Suddenly, that stream of sunlight doesn't feel as comforting anymore, and the quiet of the room seems suffocating. You're in the middle of the wild ocean of overthinking—a place that we're all too familiar with.

This is where this chapter comes in, navigating you out of the choppy waters of overthinking and guiding you towards the safe shores of understanding, empathy, and clarity. We all know how exhausting overthinking can be, and how it can transform our relationships into riddles we feel unequipped to solve. But what if I told you, there's a way to untangle this mental mess? A way to listen better, to communicate effectively, and to build a resilient bond of trust and understanding with those you hold dear?

First, we'll explore how overthinking can subtly sabotage our relationships, shaping them in ways we hardly recognize until the damage is done. From the most intimate bonds to casual friendships, overthinking can cast a heavy shadow, leading to conflicts, misinterpretations, and insecurities. Yet, there's a silver lining to this cloud—we can change the narrative, and you'll learn how.

Next, we'll delve into the art of effective communication and active listening. These are tools you can use to not only navigate but also minimize overthinking. These strategies aren't just about talking and listening, but also understanding, empathizing, and connecting at a deeper level.

Then, we'll talk about trust—that fragile yet crucial element of relationships—and how overthinking can erode its very foundation. We'll equip you with strategies to build and rebuild trust, manage your insecurities, and open the channels of honest and open communication.

Finally, we'll offer you a lifeline, a practical exercise that you can apply in your relationships. It's about mindful presence, fully engaging with those around you, about deepening your connections through conscious attention and presence.

Just imagine, after this chapter, the next time your phone vibrates with a *hey*, you'll be prepared. Prepared to listen, understand, connect, and respond in a way that strengthens your bond, rather than fueling your anxiety. So, ready to set sail on this journey? Let's navigate these waters together, one step at a time.

# Understanding the Impact of Overthinking on Relationships

Overthinking, or the habit of excessively analyzing and dwelling on thoughts and situations, can have profound effects on relationships, particularly in the lives of teenagers like you, who are still navigating the complex world of interpersonal dynamics. For young adults, the pressure of juggling school, friendships, extracurricular activities, family expectations, and the onset of romantic interests can often lead to overthinking.

# Effects of Overthinking on Communication, Trust, and Intimacy

Firstly, let's discuss the influence of overthinking on communication within relationships. When you overthink, you create a magnified, often distorted, version of reality in your mind. You may interpret a simple text message or a casual comment in an exaggerated manner, leading to miscommunication. Instead of taking things at face value, you may start to assume hidden meanings and read into things that aren't actually there. This can create confusion, unnecessary tension and even lead to confrontations based on misconceptions.

Trust, another fundamental aspect of relationships, can also be impacted by overthinking. Trust is built on the premise of believing in the sincerity and honesty of another person. However, if you constantly question their actions or words, that trust can erode. Overthinking can make you doubt the integrity of the other person, which can lead to insecurities, jealousy, and, ultimately, the crumbling of relationships.

Overthinking also influences the level of intimacy in relationships. Intimacy requires two people to be present, both physically and emotionally. Overthinkers often struggle to be fully present, as their minds are preoccupied with hypothetical scenarios or past events. This lack of presence can create a barrier, preventing deeper emotional connections from forming.

Furthermore, overthinking often fuels unnecessary conflicts. The cycle of overthinking can lead you to create problems that don't exist or exaggerate small issues into major ones. This not only increases stress and anxiety but can also cause you to engage in conflicts, straining your relationships constantly.

Misinterpretation is another offshoot of overthinking. When you overanalyze a situation or a person's behavior, you are more likely to misinterpret their intentions, leading to misunderstandings. Persisting misunderstandings can foster a climate of insecurity in a relationship, which can give rise to sensations of ambiguity and lack of solidity.

Therefore, addressing overthinking tendencies is crucial in fostering healthier and more fulfilling relationships. The first step in this process is to recognize and acknowledge that you are overthinking. It is essential to practice mindfulness, which helps you to stay in the present moment rather than dwell on past events or worry about the future. Additionally, adopting strategies such as deep breathing exercises, meditation, and positive affirmations can help manage overthinking.

In essence, the act of overthinking can create a chasm in relationships. However, by being cognizant of these tendencies and making a conscious effort to address them, you can foster healthier and more satisfying relationships. Remember, it's completely normal to think things through and reflect on your relationships. The key is not to let your thoughts control you but to manage them in a way that aids in your personal and relational growth.

## Being Present

Let's reflect on a simple yet powerful concept: presence. As discussed earlier, being present in a relationship is key. When you're present, you're genuinely engaged with your partner, emotionally available, and not distracted by your own intrusive thoughts. So, even as you navigate the intricate pathways of teenage relationships, remember to bring in your *presence*. It's not about being perfect, it's about being present. And who knows your presence may turn out to be the most precious gift you can offer to your relationships.

## Communication and Active Listening

Whether you're navigating the intricate dynamics of high school friendships or attempting to understand your first crush, effective communication is key to making your relationships thrive. Overthinking can often stem from miscommunication, leading to unnecessary conflicts, mistrust, and insecurities. By mastering the skills of effective communication and active listening, you can foster healthier relationships, minimize overthinking, and reduce anxiety.

# The Importance of Effective Communication

Effective communication involves more than the mere exchange of information. It encompasses the ability to comprehend the underlying emotions and intentions embedded within the shared information. Overthinking can frequently be traced back to misunderstanding or misinterpreting these underlying emotions and intentions. For example, when a friend doesn't text you back immediately, you might start overthinking their motives or feelings towards you. However, it could be as simple as they're busy or didn't see your message.

By communicating effectively—expressing our thoughts, feelings, and intentions clearly, and understanding those of others—we can minimize such misunderstandings. Effective communication builds trust, fosters understanding, and creates a safe space for open dialogue. This reduces the potential for overthinking and helps in resolving conflicts more efficiently.

## The Role of Active Listening

Effective communication requires active participation from both parties, as it is a collaborative process. Active listening plays a crucial role in this journey, representing half of the equation for successful communication. Active listening involves not just hearing the words another person is saying but also engaging with them to ensure you understand their message.

When we listen actively, we send a clear message: "I value what you're saying. I'm investing my attention in understanding you." This can make the speaker feel more comfortable and open, reducing the chances of miscommunication and overthinking.

Here are some key strategies to practice active listening:

## Paraphrasing

After the speaker has expressed their thoughts, it can be beneficial to paraphrase what they've said to confirm your understanding. It might look something like this: "So, what you're saying is...". Paraphrasing not only helps you ensure that you've understood correctly, but it also shows the speaker that you are genuinely trying to understand their point of view.

### Asking Clarifying Questions

If there is any ambiguity, feel free to inquire and request the speaker to provide additional details or clarification. Clarifying questions demonstrate your interest and encourage the speaker to express their thoughts more thoroughly, leading to a deeper understanding. Remember, it's okay not to understand everything immediately; asking questions is an integral part of effective communication.

### Expressing Empathy

Try to understand and acknowledge the speaker's feelings. This doesn't mean you have to agree with them, but validating their feelings can help build emotional connection and trust. Phrases like "That sounds really tough, I can see why you'd feel that way," can make the speaker feel heard and understood.

## Improving Communication Skills

Developing these communication skills can help reduce assumptions and overthinking. By actively seeking to understand others, you provide less room for your mind to create inaccurate narratives.

Remember, everyone is susceptible to miscommunication and overthinking, so be patient with yourself as you develop these skills. It's okay to admit when you don't understand something or when you realize you've made an incorrect assumption. In fact, acknowledging these moments can be a powerful form of effective communication in itself.

Learning to communicate effectively and listen actively is not just about improving your relationships with others. It's also about developing a more profound understanding of yourself, your thoughts, your feelings, and your responses. As you refine your communication skills, you'll find that your tendency to overthink will diminish, and your relationships will deepen.

So, the next time you find yourself starting to overthink a situation, remember to utilize your communication skills. Reach out, express your feelings, ask questions, and most importantly, listen. After all, true understanding is the antidote to overthinking, and communication is the pathway to understanding.

Remember, it's not about being a perfect communicator; it's about being an authentic one. And in this journey of developing effective communication, you're not only strengthening your relationships but also building a stronger, more understanding you.

## Building Trust and Managing Insecurities

Building trust in relationships is like constructing a bridge. It requires time, effort, and the right materials. But this bridge of trust can be weakened or even destroyed by the gnawing doubts and uncertainties associated with overthinking. Insecurities, often an outcome of overthinking, can further undermine trust, adding a heavy load that the bridge may struggle to bear. In this chapter, we'll explore how you can build a resilient bridge of trust and effectively manage your insecurities.

### Overthinking: An Enemy of Trust

Overthinking has a sneaky way of eroding trust. When we overthink, we tend to make mountains out of molehills, amplifying small issues until they loom large in our minds. These magnified issues can then breed doubt and insecurity, hindering the growth of trust.

For instance, if your friend forgets to wish you on your birthday, you might start overthinking their intentions, and this could create a rift of mistrust. However, it could simply be that they were preoccupied and it slipped their mind.

Understanding that overthinking can distort our perception is the first step towards building and maintaining trust.

## Building Trust: The Cornerstone of Strong Relationships

Here are some strategies to build trust.

### Open and Honest Communication

Transparency is the foundation of trust. When we are open and honest about our feelings, intentions, and actions, we invite others to do the same. This reduces misunderstandings and promotes a sense of security in the relationship, fostering trust.

### Setting Boundaries

Boundaries reflect respect—for ourselves and for others. They set the guidelines for acceptable behavior, and when these are honored, trust is reinforced. Clearly communicating your boundaries and respecting those set by others can strengthen trust.

### Practicing Forgiveness

We're all human and bound to make mistakes. Offering forgiveness when others slip up is crucial for building trust. Remember, forgiveness isn't about forgetting the mistake—it's about understanding, learning, and moving forward.

# Managing Insecurities: From Self-Doubt to Self-Assurance

Insecurities can feel like unwelcome guests, overstaying their welcome and affecting our peace of mind. Managing them involves understanding their origin, nurturing self-compassion, and having open dialogues.

### Self-Reflection

Understanding where your insecurities stem from is the first step in managing them. This involves self-reflection. Consider what triggers your insecurities. Is it a past experience? Is it a fear of rejection or failure? Identifying the root cause can help you address it more effectively.

### Self-Compassion

Being kind to yourself is essential in managing insecurities. Instead of criticizing yourself for feeling insecure, embrace self-compassion. Acknowledge your feelings without judgment, and remind yourself that everyone has insecurities—it's part of being human.

### Open Dialogue

Discussing your insecurities with your peers, friends, or loved ones can also be very helpful. When you openly share your concerns, you create an opportunity for others to understand you better and offer their support. You might also find that they share similar insecurities, reinforcing the fact that you're not alone in your experience.

Building trust and managing insecurities is an ongoing process that requires patience and persistence. But by focusing on open and honest communication, setting and respecting boundaries, practicing forgiveness, and addressing your insecurities with self-compassion and open dialogue, you're setting the stage for stronger, healthier relationships. And remember, every step you take on this journey is a step towards a more confident and secure you.

# Practical Exercise: Mindfulness for Reducing Overthinking and Deepening Connections

Being fully present means paying complete attention to what's happening here and now. It's about letting go of past grievances and future anxieties and engaging wholeheartedly with the present moment. This is especially important in our relationships, as being present allows us to connect more deeply with others.

When you're fully present, you listen better, understand more, and respond more appropriately. You're able to truly *be* with the person, fostering a stronger, more genuine connection. So, how do we achieve this state of mindful presence?

Mindfulness is the key to being fully present. Here are some techniques you can incorporate into your daily routine to enhance your mindful presence.

## *Mindful Breathing*

Mindful breathing is a simple yet powerful technique that can help ground you in the present moment. Here's a simple exercise to get you started:

- Locate a serene and cozy spot to settle

- Gently shut your eyes and inhale deeply, focusing on the feeling of the air entering your lungs

- Exhale slowly, concentrating on the feeling of the air leaving your body

- Repeat this for a few minutes, keeping your focus on your breath

Practice this daily, and try using it during conversations as well. If you find your mind starting to wander or overthink, take a moment to focus on your breath. This can help bring your attention back to the present.

## Active Listening

Active listening involves fully focusing on, understanding, and responding to the speaker. It's a key component of mindful communication. Here's how you can practice it:

- When someone is speaking to you, pay complete attention to what they're saying

- Avoid distractions, such as checking your phone or thinking about your reply while they're still speaking

- Show that you're engaged in the conversation by nodding your head or making appropriate facial expressions

- Paraphrase what they've said or ask clarifying questions to ensure you've understood correctly

## Mindful Observation

Another way to cultivate mindfulness in your relationships is through mindful observation. This involves appreciating the person in the present, without judgment or the lens of past experiences. To practice this:

- Spend time observing the person as if you're seeing them for the first time

- Pay attention to their expressions, their voice, and their words

- Try to appreciate their unique qualities and characteristics

Incorporating these techniques into your interactions can help reduce overthinking and enhance your connections. Over time, they will become more natural, fostering a deeper sense of presence and authenticity in your relationships.

Remember, cultivating a mindful presence is not a one-time event but a journey. So, be patient with yourself, celebrate your progress, and most importantly, enjoy the deep, meaningful connections you forge along the way.

# Conclusion

In conclusion, overthinking in relationships can be a challenging cycle to break, especially in the complex years of adolescence. However, by understanding the role of communication, building trust, managing insecurities, and practicing mindfulness, teens can navigate this journey with more confidence and ease. It's important to remember that growth is a process, one that involves learning from experiences, making mistakes, and moving forward. Equipping teens with these tools will not only alleviate the burden of overthinking but also empower them to build healthier, more fulfilling relationships. As they become more adept at these practices, they'll find their connections with others deepening, their insecurities lessening, and their tendency to overthink diminishing. With patience, practice, and a dash of self-compassion, they'll soon be on their way to a more balanced, mindful way of relating to the world and the people around them.

# Chapter 12:

# Finding Clarity and Taking Action

Ever find yourself locked in a cycle of *what ifs* and *maybes*, going round and round in circles until you're dizzy with indecision? You're not alone. This chapter is all about the paralyzing grip of overthinking and how it can cloud your judgment, turn molehills into mountains, and stifle your ability to make decisions. But fear not! It's time to break free from the chains of over-analysis and embrace the clarity of decisive action.

This chapter provides a roadmap out of the quagmire of overthinking. This chapter is going to help you explore the ways overthinking can hamper your decision-making and introduce you to some practical strategies to combat it. Remember when you spent hours trying to decide what to wear to that party last week or when you agonized over whether to raise your hand in class to answer a question? These are everyday examples of how overthinking can lead to analysis paralysis.

At times, we may find ourselves in a state of being overwhelmed by the multitude of possibilities and the fear of making an erroneous decision. As a result, we may become stuck and unable to make any choice at all. We will delve into this further and highlight the importance of addressing these tendencies to make confident and informed decisions.

Next, we'll introduce some practical strategies to help you overcome overthinking and make decisions with clarity. Imagine having a set of tools to help you evaluate choices, set priorities, and seek valuable input from trusted individuals. These strategies will guide you in developing a decision-making process that balances thoughtful consideration and decisive action, equipping you to navigate life's crossroads with confidence and purpose.

What about risks? They can be scary, right? This chapter will also explore the role of overthinking in creating fear and reluctance to take calculated risks. We'll unpack the concept of risk-taking and its potential for personal growth and learning, encouraging you to step outside your comfort zones. After all, every step outside your comfort zone is a step into a new adventure!

Finally, we offer you a practical tool—a *decision-making* journal. This journal isn't just a place to document your decision-making process but also a space to reflect, assess and improve your decision-making skills, further reducing overthinking tendencies. We'll guide you on how to use this journal effectively to turn the challenges of decision-making into opportunities for self-discovery and growth.

So, buckle up! This chapter is your ticket to breaking the cycle of overthinking, embracing clarity, and taking decisive action. Get ready to meet a more decisive, confident you!"

# The Impact of Overthinking on Decision-Making

Imagine standing in the cereal aisle of a grocery store, faced with hundreds of boxes, all enticing you with colorful packaging, claims of health benefits, and characters from your favorite cartoons. You simply can't decide which one to choose, so you stay there, stuck, trapped in a whirlwind of indecision. This is a simple example of what psychologists term analysis paralysis, a state of overthinking that hinders the decision-making process.

Overthinking doesn't just happen in the cereal aisle, though. It can creep into more significant decisions, like choosing a college, deciding on a career path, or determining whether to end or mend a challenging relationship. The fear of making the wrong choice often feeds this overthinking. As you ruminate excessively on all possible outcomes, you might find yourself trapped in a loop of *what ifs*, leading to stagnation instead of action.

However, it's not just the act of making a decision that gets impacted by overthinking. The effects can spill over into your mental health too. Engaging in excessive overthinking can give rise to feelings of anxiety and stress, leaving you mentally exhausted. Consequently, it can create a detrimental cycle of fear and inaction that becomes challenging to escape from. Moreover, the fear of regret or criticism from others can further exacerbate the anxiety, stifling your ability to make choices and take actions that align with your authentic self.

So, how can we manage overthinking to make confident and informed decisions? The first step is acknowledging that overthinking is getting in the way of your decision-making process.

If you are unaware of a problem's existence, it becomes impossible to resolve it. Recognizing and addressing overthinking tendencies is critical in turning the tide toward effective decision-making. In the following sections, we'll explore some practical strategies to do just that. By understanding and managing your overthinking tendencies, you can step onto the path of confident decision-making, free from the fear of making the wrong choice.

# Strategies for Effective Decision-Making

Learning to overcome overthinking and making clear, decisive choices is a journey, not a destination. The road might seem challenging, but if equipped with the right strategies, you can navigate it with grace and poise. Let's dive into some approaches that can assist you in developing a decision-making process that balances thoughtful consideration with action.

## *Pros and Cons Analysis*

Remember the old-fashioned method of weighing the pros and cons? Turns out, it's not old-fashioned at all; it's timeless. When faced with a decision, take a sheet of paper, divide it into two columns, and write down the benefits and drawbacks of each option. This visual representation can help you see the bigger picture, clear your mind, and guide you towards an informed decision. However, remember to consider the weight of each pro and con, as not all are created equal. A single, significant con might outweigh several smaller pros, or vice versa.

## Setting Priorities

Every decision we make, big or small, aligns with our values and priorities. Knowing what truly matters to you can make the decision-making process smoother. For instance, if you prioritize academic achievement over extracurricular activities, you might decide to spend your Friday night studying for a big test instead of going to a party. When faced with a tough choice, ask yourself, "What really matters to me? How does this decision align with my priorities?" Answering these questions can help reduce overthinking and guide you toward a decision that matches your values.

## Seeking Input from Trusted Individuals

No man is an island, and it's okay to seek guidance from trusted individuals when making decisions. Parents, mentors, teachers, or close friends who know you well and have your best interests at heart can provide valuable perspectives. However, remember that, ultimately, the decision is yours to make. Others' advice and input should serve to provide additional insight and not dictate your choice.

Navigating the path to effective decision-making isn't always straightforward, especially in your teenage years. Nevertheless, it is crucial to remember that the objective is not to attain a flawless or *perfect* choice. Instead, it's about making the most optimal decision possible based on the available information at that particular moment. Overcoming overthinking and making decisions with clarity is a skill that can be developed with practice. So, let's start practicing, and who knows, you might surprise yourself with how adept you become at navigating life's crossroads.

## Embracing Calculated Risk-Taking

Stepping into the unknown can be a daunting prospect. Often, the fear of the unfamiliar and the potential for failure stop us from venturing outside our comfort zones. This fear, when paired with a habit of overthinking, can be a formidable obstacle. However, it's crucial to understand that risks, when taken judiciously, can be gateways to personal growth and learning. So, let's delve into the art of calculated risk-taking and how it can help shape your journey.

# The Role of Overthinking in Fear and Reluctance to Take Risks

It's common to experience a sense of dread when faced with uncertain outcomes—your mind starts spinning a web of *what ifs* and worst-case scenarios. This is overthinking at play, magnifying fear and creating a barrier against risk-taking. While this might serve as a protective mechanism, it can also limit your experiences and potential for growth. The key is to understand that overthinking often paints a far more negative picture than reality.

## The Concept of Calculated Risk-Taking

Contrary to popular belief, risk-taking doesn't mean throwing caution to the wind. It's about calculated decisions where potential benefits are weighed against potential drawbacks. Calculated risks involve gathering information, analyzing possible outcomes, and mindfully deciding whether the potential for growth outweighs the potential for loss. This isn't about fearlessly leaping into the unknown; it's about courageously walking into the unknown, fully aware of the potential challenges and rewards.

## Embracing Opportunities for Growth

The magic often happens outside your comfort zone. Yes, stepping outside might be uncomfortable and scary, but it's also where growth thrives. By embracing calculated risk-taking, you expose yourself to new experiences, learn valuable lessons, and develop resilience. Every venture gives you an opportunity to grow—even if things don't go as planned, you still gain valuable insight and experience.

As you journey through your teen years, it's essential to balance the protective instinct of overthinking with the adventurous spirit of risk-taking. Remember, it's okay to feel scared, but don't let it stop you from exploring new paths. Embrace calculated risks, because they could lead to unexpected and incredible places. Every risk you take is a stepping stone on the path of personal growth and learning. So, muster your courage, step out of your comfort zone, and embrace the journey that awaits.

# Practical Exercise: The Decision-Making Journal

We've explored the dynamics of overthinking, decision-making, and risk-taking. Now, it's time to put this knowledge into practice with a hands-on exercise—a decision-making journal. This practical tool will provide you with a structured way to document and reflect on your decision-making process, helping you refine your skills and temper your overthinking tendencies.

## Setting Up Your Decision-Making Journal

Starting a decision-making journal is quite simple. You can use a physical notebook or a digital app—whatever you're most comfortable with. The aim is to record the decisions you make, big or small, alongside your thoughts, considerations, potential risks, and eventual outcomes. Remember, this is a personal space for self-reflection; there's no right or wrong way to use it. Make it work for you.

## Documenting Your Decision-Making Process

Every time you face a decision, take a moment to write about it in your journal. Start with the decision at hand and jot down all your thoughts and considerations related to it. Capture your initial thoughts, potential options, pros and cons, and even your fears and uncertainties. The more you write, the more visible your thought process becomes, which can help in identifying any patterns of overthinking.

## Recording the Outcomes

Once you've made your decision and seen it play out, write down the result in your journal. Was the outcome as you expected? What did you learn from it? Were there unforeseen consequences? Don't shy away from jotting down unexpected outcomes or perceived *failures*. They are rich sources of insight and learning, helping you refine your future decision-making.

## Reflection and Self-Assessment

Set aside regular time to review your journal entries and reflect on your decision-making process. Are you spotting patterns of overthinking or anxiety? Are you finding that certain decisions lead to better outcomes? This retrospective view can provide valuable insights into your decision-making strengths and areas for improvement. It's not about self-criticism but self-understanding and growth.

Using a decision-making journal is a practical way to understand and improve your decision-making skills while reducing your tendency to overthink. It's a journey of self-discovery, giving you the tools to navigate your decisions confidently. So grab a notebook or open a new app, and begin your journey to becoming a more mindful and effective decision-maker.

# Conclusion

In this chapter, we delved into the realm of decision-making, exploring the impact of overthinking, strategies for effective decision-making, the importance of embracing calculated risk-taking, and the practical exercise of maintaining a decision-making journal. By understanding the hindrances of overthinking, adopting practical techniques, and documenting our decision-making process, we empower ourselves to make confident and informed choices. With newfound clarity, resilience, and the ability to step outside our comfort zones, we embark on a journey of personal growth, equipped with the skills to navigate life's uncertainties and forge our own paths.

# Chapter 13:

# Overcoming Overthinking Fatigue

In the ever-dizzying whirlwind of adolescence, the inner storms of the mind often mirror the turbulence of the outer world. Among these internal tempests, overthinking can cast a particularly heavy shadow—a relentless downpour of doubts, worries, and fears that exhausts the mind, saps the spirit, and blurs the bright horizon of your potential. But, as the resilient protagonists of your own story, you possess the power to bring back the sunlight, to restore the balance, and to reclaim your boundless energy.

This pivotal chapter invites you on a journey of self-discovery, where the focus shifts from the unending maze of your thoughts to the sanctuary of self-care. This chapter is your refuge—a tranquil haven where you learn to tune in to the silent whispers of your needs, honor your boundaries, and craft a personalized self-care routine. It's time to transform overthinking fatigue into a stepping stone for building resilience and nurturing well-being.

Through an in-depth exploration of overthinking fatigue, we'll peel back the layers of this often-misunderstood phenomenon, shedding light on its impact on your mental, emotional, and physical well-being. Recognizing the signs of overthinking fatigue can be your first line of defense, and we'll equip you with the understanding needed to spot these subtle signals before they escalate.

Beneath the umbrella of self-care, we'll introduce an array of practices that can bring solace to your weary minds. From relaxation techniques and mindfulness practices to nature walks and engaging in hobbies, there's something for everyone—a palette of self-care colors waiting for you to create your unique masterpiece. You'll also learn the critical art of setting boundaries and managing your workload, striking a balance between your academic pursuits, personal life, and the much-needed me-time. In an era where *busyness* is often mistaken for productivity, we challenge this narrative and empower you to prioritize your well-being.

To bring these elements together, we'll guide you in crafting a personalized self-care plan—a blueprint for nurturing your well-being amidst the rigors of teenage life. This practical exercise isn't a one-size-fits-all solution but a continually evolving, unique map that can be adjusted as you grow and your circumstances change.

Let this chapter be a reminder: the journey of adolescence isn't about relentlessly pushing yourself but about learning to pause, breathe, and care for yourself. So, buckle up and join us as we navigate the path of overcoming overthinking fatigue. Let's embark on this journey to transform our restless minds into peaceful sanctuaries—one mindful moment at a time.

# Understanding the Impact of Overthinking Fatigue

We often hear that thinking is power. Our thoughts pave the way to discoveries, inventions, and essentially shape our lives. But what happens when thinking gets out of control? What happens when it becomes a marathon runner that never stops, never rests? This, my young friends, is where we meet overthinking and its weary companion, fatigue.

Overthinking, in its essence, is like a whirlpool—a swirling vortex of thoughts that endlessly loops without reaching any productive outcome. You may find yourself replaying conversations, second-guessing decisions, or dwelling on *what ifs* and *should haves*. This mental overdrive, when left unchecked, paves the way for overthinking fatigue—a state of mental, emotional, and physical exhaustion that weighs heavily on your overall well-being.

Now, imagine your brain as an orchestra, with different sections playing in perfect harmony. Overthinking, however, is like a trumpet blaring out of tune—it throws the entire orchestra into chaos. This dissonance impacts not only your mental health, causing anxiety and stress but can ripple out to your emotional state, leading to feelings of frustration, irritability, and sadness. You might also experience physical effects, including headaches, sleep disturbances, or a sense of persistent tiredness. Simply put, overthinking fatigue doesn't just invade your mind; it makes your entire being its home.

One of the most insidious outcomes of overthinking fatigue is burnout—a state of chronic exhaustion that drains your motivation and saps your energy. It's like a candle burning at both ends, swiftly melting away without giving sustainable light. Burnout can lead to a noticeable dip in your productivity—your grades may slip, your creativity might wane, and even everyday tasks can feel like climbing mountains.

This decreased productivity isn't a reflection of your capabilities but a distress signal from your brain, a cry for help drowned in the loud cacophony of overthinking. It's a sign that your well of energy is running dry, and the natural flow of your thoughts and creativity is being blocked by the dam of overthinking.

But, here's the beacon of hope: overthinking fatigue isn't a life sentence; it's a wake-up call—an alarm bell that urges you to restore balance and energy. It's a signpost indicating that it's time to step off the treadmill of relentless thinking, time to reclaim your mental space, and time to tune into the harmonious rhythm of your being.

Understanding the impact of overthinking fatigue is your first step toward change. It's like realizing that you've been walking with a pebble in your shoe; only by acknowledging it can you stop, remove it, and continue your journey with ease. So, let's embark on this journey of self-discovery and self-care because you, dear readers, deserve a mind that's a serene lake, not a raging ocean. You deserve the harmonious symphony of balanced well-being, not the cacophony of overthinking. And most importantly, you deserve to be the energetic, enthusiastic protagonists of your own lives—not sidelined by the fatigue of overthinking.

## Recognizing Signs of Overthinking Fatigue

Unraveling the tangles of overthinking can often feel like being lost in an infinite web, where each thought is a new twist or turn. But, in this maze of thoughts, there exist signposts—indicators that signal you might be experiencing overthinking fatigue. Recognizing these signs is like finding a compass—it doesn't instantly solve the puzzle, but it points you in the right direction. So, let's take a journey to understand these signposts better, so you can navigate your way towards well-being.

One of the first signs of overthinking fatigue is mental exhaustion. Your mind, like any other part of your body, can tire after a strenuous workout—and make no mistake, overthinking is quite the mental marathon. You may find your thoughts turning sluggish, like a bicycle trudging through mud. Ideas that once flowed freely may seem locked behind a heavy door. This mental exhaustion is your mind's way of saying, "Hey, I need a breather!"

Another signpost is difficulty concentrating. Imagine trying to read a book in a noisy cafeteria—distractions abound, making it hard to focus on the words. Similarly, the constant chatter of overthinking can create a tumultuous background noise, making it challenging to concentrate on tasks at hand, whether it's solving a math problem or simply enjoying a movie.

Then, there's irritability, a prickly sense of agitation. When overthinking fatigues your mind, your patience might wear thin. You might find yourself snapping at minor annoyances, like a misaligned stack of books or a slightly off-key tune—things that wouldn't usually ruffle your feathers.

Next, notice if you're experiencing a dip in motivation. Overthinking can drain your enthusiasm, making the prospect of starting any task seem daunting. It's like trying to walk against a strong gust of wind—you can do it, but it feels much harder than it should be.

Recognizing these signs requires a dose of self-awareness. It's about tuning in to your feelings and thoughts, about pausing to check in with yourself, asking: "How am I doing?" It's about observing changes in your behavior or feelings without judgment, with kindness, and most importantly, with understanding.

Embrace this self-awareness, not as a critique but as a friendly guide—an inner compass that can help you navigate the complex terrain of your inner world. Remember, recognizing overthinking fatigue isn't about self-diagnosis or self-blame; it's about self-understanding and self-care.

After all, the purpose of signposts isn't to make you feel lost—it's to help you find your way. Similarly, recognizing these signs of overthinking fatigue is your first step towards finding your path to balance, energy, and peace. So, let's embark on this journey of recognition and self-awareness, using these signposts to guide us towards the calm after the storm of overthinking.

## Establishing Self-Care Practices

As we navigate through the seas of overthinking fatigue, it's important to remember that your lifeboat in these turbulent waters is *self-care*. This concept, while often misunderstood as mere pampering or indulgence, is much more profound. Self-care is an act of kindness towards oneself, a nurturing routine that fuels your mind, body, and spirit. It's about creating an oasis of tranquility amidst the desert of overthinking, a sanctuary where energy and balance are restored.

Consider self-care as a personal toolbox—a collection of strategies designed to bring you comfort, relaxation, and joy. Each tool serves a purpose, each adds a layer of resilience against the waves of overthinking fatigue. Let's explore some of these tools and see how they can help create your personalized self-care routine.

Relaxation techniques form a key part of this toolbox. These could include deep breathing exercises, progressive muscle relaxation, or even yoga. Picture yourself as a tightly wound spring—each deep breath, each gentle stretch helps to uncoil the tension, allowing you to relax and recharge.

Engaging in hobbies is another potent tool. Whether it's painting, playing a musical instrument, writing, or dancing—hobbies provide an escape from the relentless grind of overthinking. They immerse you in a world of joy and creativity, a world where thoughts flow freely, not in circles.

Spending time in nature can work wonders too. Nature, in its serene beauty, provides a calming backdrop that can soothe an overthinking mind. Whether it's a walk in the park, listening to the calming sounds of a babbling brook, or simply basking in the warmth of the sun, these moments of communion with nature can breathe life into your weary spirit. And then there's mindfulness, the art of being fully present in the moment. It's like stepping off a speeding train of thoughts to stand still and witness the beauty around you. Whether it's savoring the taste of your morning cereal or feeling the texture of a leaf, mindfulness anchors you to the 'now', breaking the cycle of past regrets or future anxieties.

Crafting your personalized self-care routine is like designing your very own superhero costume—unique, empowering, and perfectly tailored to your needs. It's about selecting the tools that resonate with you, that bring you peace and joy, that fit snugly into the fabric of your daily life. Remember, self-care is not a rigid schedule—it's a fluid routine that can adapt to your changing needs, moods, and circumstances.

Your self-care routine is a journey, not a destination. It's an ongoing exploration, a dance between what you need and what brings you joy. It's about discovering the unique rhythm of your well-being, the music that soothes your soul, and the harmony that balances your energy. So, let's embark on this journey of establishing self-care practices. Let's learn to extend the same kindness, patience, and care to ourselves as we would to a cherished friend. Let's paint the canvas of our lives with vibrant hues of self-care, turning the gray clouds of overthinking fatigue into a radiant rainbow of balanced energy and well-being.

# Setting Boundaries and Managing Workload

Imagine your mind as a majestic castle, with soaring towers, intricate chambers, and expansive courtyards. Now, visualize a crowd of tasks, duties, and responsibilities knocking at your castle gates, demanding entry all at once. Without a gatekeeper—without boundaries—these responsibilities can overrun your castle, leading to overexertion and overload. Thus, establishing boundaries and managing workload are crucial tools in protecting your mental space.

Setting boundaries is like being your castle's gatekeeper. It's about learning to say 'no' when you need to, about defining what's acceptable to let in and what's not. Boundaries help safeguard your time, energy, and mental peace, ensuring you're not overwhelmed by the clamor of external demands. Remember: your castle, your rules. When it comes to workload, think of it as a banquet spread. Trying to devour everything at once will lead to indigestion; similarly, trying to tackle all tasks together can lead to mental fatigue. Here's where strategic management comes into play.

Begin by prioritizing tasks. Use a simple system of categorizing tasks based on urgency and importance. High-priority tasks demand your immediate attention, while lower-priority ones can wait. Remember, not every task is a fire-breathing dragon that needs immediate slaying. Some are mere cats stuck in a tree that can wait a while. Next, learn the art of delegation. It's about understanding that you don't have to do everything yourself. In your academic life, this could mean dividing tasks within a group project. In your personal life, it might mean asking a sibling for help in organizing a family event. Delegation is a balancing act that can reduce the weight on your shoulders.

But here's the key: setting boundaries and managing workload aren't about building an impenetrable fortress or banishing all tasks. It's about creating a balanced ecosystem where you can flourish without feeling drained. It's about asserting control over your castle, without letting it turn into a battlefield of stress and fatigue.

By setting boundaries, you empower yourself. You claim ownership over your time and energy. You recognize your worth and ensure others do too. By managing your workload, you bring order to the chaos, ensuring a smoother, more manageable flow of tasks that aligns with your energy levels and capabilities.

So, let's embark on this journey of setting boundaries and managing workload. Let's step into the empowering role of the gatekeeper, the strategist. Because in this narrative of your life, you are not the overwhelmed, you are the empowered. You are not the storm-tossed vessel, you are the skillful navigator. And above all, you are not the victim of overthinking fatigue, but the victor who overcomes it.

## Practical Exercise: Creating a Self-Care Plan

Imagine a ship setting sail without a compass or map, lost at sea. Now think of your journey towards overcoming overthinking fatigue. Without a plan—a self-care plan—navigating these waters can be just as daunting. Creating a self-care plan is like charting your course, ensuring your journey towards wellness is guided, intentional, and effective.

Your self-care plan is a personal roadmap, a collection of routines and practices that resonate with you and contribute to your well-being. It's not a one-size-fits-all template, but a personalized blueprint tailored to your needs, preferences, and lifestyle. So, let's embark on this practical exercise of creating your self-care plan. Begin by taking a moment to reflect on your current state. Consider the signposts we discussed earlier—are there signs of overthinking fatigue you're experiencing? Are there certain triggers or situations that amplify these symptoms? Make a note of these.

Next, consider the self-care tools that resonate with you. Do you find peace in nature? Does playing your guitar bring you joy? Is deep breathing an effective relaxation technique for you? Write these down. This list forms the foundation of your self-care plan, your go-to strategies for alleviating overthinking fatigue.

Once you have your list, think about how you can integrate these practices into your daily routine. Remember, self-care isn't about setting aside huge chunks of time. It's about finding small pockets of tranquility amidst the hustle and bustle. Can you start your day with a ten-minute meditation? Could you make time for a walk in the park after school? Could your weekends include some time for your favorite hobby? Pencil these into your schedule.

Now, remember the importance of setting boundaries and managing workload? Reflect on how these can feed into your self-care plan. Can you set specific hours for study and rest? Could you delegate some tasks to create more time for self-care? Incorporate these strategies into your plan.

Finally, consider your self-care plan as a living document, not a set-in-stone decree. As you change and grow, your needs and preferences might shift too. Regularly evaluate and adjust your plan, keeping it in tune with your evolving self. Are the chosen practices still enjoyable and effective? Do you need to tweak your schedule or add new self-care practices? Keep checking in with yourself, keeping your plan aligned with your journey.

Creating a self-care plan isn't just about managing overthinking fatigue—it's about fostering a deeper relationship with yourself. It's about understanding your needs, celebrating your preferences, and nurturing your well-being. It's about steering your ship with confidence and care, navigating the sea of overthinking fatigue with your compass firmly in hand, charting a course towards tranquility, balance, and joy. So, let's grab a pen, let's grab this moment, and let's chart your journey of self-care.

# Conclusion

In this voyage towards overcoming overthinking fatigue, we've charted out the impacts it can have on your well-being, learned to identify its signs, discovered the power of self-care, understood the importance of setting boundaries and managing workload, and even mapped out a practical exercise to create a personalized self-care plan. This journey is not just about combating fatigue, but about fostering a deeper relationship with yourself, celebrating your uniqueness, and empowering you to take charge of your mental wellness. It's about understanding that you hold the compass to navigate through the sea of overthinking, to set your course towards balance, tranquility, and joy. Remember, the strength, resilience, and wisdom to overcome overthinking fatigue reside within you. So, let's steer this ship with confidence, embracing the waves, the winds, and the wonder that lies ahead.

# Chapter 14:

# Achieving Life Balance

Imagine standing at the top of a towering mountain of dirty laundry, armed with only a tiny bar of soap and a bucket of water. The daunting task ahead overwhelms you, but you know it has to be done. Your mind starts racing with questions, "Where do I start?" "Can I get all this done today?" "What if I don't finish in time?" This mountain of clothes, dear reader, is a metaphor for life's tasks, and the swirling storm of questions is the crippling habit of overthinking.

Sound familiar? If it does, you're certainly not alone. Overthinking is an all-too-common companion for many teens today, often leading to procrastination and perfectionism. But fret not, for this chapter serves as your guiding beacon, illuminating the path to achieve a life balance. It promises not just strategies for managing overthinking, but also wisdom on balancing work with rest and pointers for effective task management.

First, we'll explore the impact of overthinking on productivity. It's akin to adding more clothes to your laundry mountain. The more you overthink, the larger the pile becomes, leading to mental exhaustion and distracting you from getting the actual work done. We'll unravel the ties between overthinking, procrastination, and perfectionism, and demonstrate the importance of addressing overthinking to boost productivity.

Next, we'll share powerful strategies to keep overthinking in check and enhance your focus. Imagine breaking down the laundry mountain into smaller piles, making it much easier to manage. We'll introduce techniques that aid you in setting priorities, breaking tasks into smaller steps, and utilizing effective time management tools.

But let's not forget, all work and no play make Jack a dull boy. So, we'll underscore the importance of balancing work and rest. Visualize the laundry process—it's not just about washing and drying but also about resting before you fold and put them away. We'll guide you on how to strike the perfect balance, preventing burnout and ensuring you're taking time for restorative practices.

Finally, we'll guide you through a practical exercise of time blocking and mindful task management. Think of it as having a well-planned laundry routine—specific times to wash, dry, and fold. We'll help you develop a schedule that allocates time slots for different tasks, encouraging mindfulness during each one to minimize overthinking and improve productivity.

So, are you ready to start chipping away at that laundry mountain in your life? Let's dive in, conquer overthinking, and uncover the blueprint for a balanced, productive, and rewarding life.

# The Impact of Overthinking on Productivity

We've all been there: staring at the same question for hours, ruminating about the possible outcomes of an upcoming event, or replaying a conversation in our head again and again. This is overthinking, and it can seriously hinder productivity by consuming precious mental energy and creating distractions.

## *How Overthinking Affects Productivity*

Productivity is about getting things done effectively and efficiently. When you overthink, you spend an excessive amount of time contemplating different scenarios, possibilities, or decisions. This analysis paralysis can prevent you from moving forward, resulting in decreased productivity. The energy you put into overthinking could have been used to actually complete tasks and achieve goals.

One of the ways overthinking can disrupt productivity is by leading to procrastination. The more time you spend thinking about the task at hand, the less time you spend actually doing it. Overthinking can make the task seem more daunting, leading you to postpone it.

Furthermore, overthinking often correlates with perfectionism. When you strive for an unattainable ideal, it can leave you frozen, feeling as though nothing you do will be good enough. This hinders productivity as it prevents you from even starting a task due to fear of not doing it perfectly. Lastly, overthinking can lead to a lack of focus. As you jump from one thought to another, it becomes challenging to concentrate on the task at hand. This constant mental noise can make it hard to focus on what's truly important.

### Importance of Addressing Overthinking

Understanding the impact of overthinking on productivity is crucial, particularly for teens, who are at a crucial stage of personal and academic growth. By learning how to manage overthinking tendencies, you can enhance your productivity, achieve your goals, and maintain a healthier state of mind.

Now, let's take a look at work-life balance and its impact on your productivity and well-being.

### The Significance of Work-Life Balance

Work-life balance refers to finding a harmonious equilibrium between your work commitments and personal life. This balance is essential for teenagers, too, as you juggle schoolwork, extracurricular activities, part-time jobs, and personal interests. If you spend too much time on one aspect, it could lead to stress and burnout and eventually affect your productivity.

Finding this balance might seem challenging, but it's essential for overall well-being and productivity. Below are some suggestions to assist you in upholding a healthy work-life balance.

### Know Your Values

Determine what is truly important to you and make time for those activities.

### Practice Time Management

Use tools and techniques to manage your time better. You'll be surprised how much time you can save by planning and prioritizing.

### Set Boundaries

Make sure to set time aside for non-work activities. Learning to say no can help ensure that your personal life isn't overshadowed by work or school commitments.

### Enjoy Your Work

Find pleasure in what you do. If a certain task or job is causing stress, it might be time to look for alternatives.

### Review Your Finances

While this might seem adult-oriented, learning to manage money early can be helpful. Understanding your financial needs can help in making informed decisions about work.

### Nurture Relationships

Build strong relationships with family and friends. These connections can offer a great source of stress relief and enjoyment.

*Focus on Your Health*

Make sure to get enough sleep, eat healthily, and incorporate regular exercise into your routine. Your physical health plays a significant role in your mental well-being.

*Have Down Time*

Always ensure you have time to relax and recharge. This helps prevent burnout and keeps you energized for the tasks ahead.

Remember, overthinking is a common issue that everyone deals with at some point. By recognizing its impact on productivity and implementing strategies to achieve a healthy work-life balance, you can navigate this challenging phase of life with more confidence and ease. You're not alone in this journey, and there are always resources available to help. Now, let's get back to our work with a clear mind and a focused approach, shall we?

# Strategies for Managing Overthinking and Increasing Focus

Overthinking can sometimes feel like a never-ending cycle that hinders productivity and makes it challenging to focus on what really matters. However, by employing certain strategies, you can effectively manage overthinking and sharpen your focus, ultimately enhancing your efficiency. Here are some practical strategies to help you break free from the chains of overthinking and embrace a more focused, productive mindset.

## Set Clear Priorities

When everything seems important, you might find yourself running in circles without getting much done. Setting clear priorities can help you decide what requires your attention the most. By understanding what tasks are urgent and essential and which ones can wait, you can better manage your time and energy. The Eisenhower Box is an instrument that sorts tasks into four specific sections: those that are both urgent and significant, those that are significant yet not immediate, those that are urgent but not necessarily significant, and those that are neither urgent nor significant. Using this approach can greatly aid in effective task management (Product Plan, 2023).

## Break Tasks Into Smaller Steps

Looking at a large task as a whole can be overwhelming and may fuel overthinking. Instead, break down the task into smaller, manageable steps. This makes the task less daunting, simplifies your process, and can make it easier to start working on the task. By focusing on one step at a time, you will gradually build momentum and make progress, reducing the tendency to overthink.

## Utilize Time Management Tools

Using time management tools can help you structure your day and allot specific timeframes for tasks. Tools like Google Calendar, Trello, or even a simple to-do list can keep you organized and focused.

The Pomodoro Technique is a beneficial strategy for managing your time. It involves concentrated working periods, usually lasting for 25 minutes, interspersed with short, 5-minute intervals of rest. After completing four pomodoros, you take a longer break. This technique can help maintain your concentration and reduce the chance of becoming overwhelmed (Savic, 2023).

## Practice Mindfulness

Mindfulness is the practice of fully immersing oneself in the present moment, actively participating in current activities instead of getting lost in past memories or future anxieties. This practice can help you focus on the task at hand rather than getting lost in a whirlwind of overthinking. Engaging in various uncomplicated actions such as taking deep breaths, practicing yoga, or consciously immersing yourself in your environment, can serve as means to cultivate mindfulness.

## Limit Distractions

In today's digital age, distractions are everywhere, from the buzzing of smartphones to the constant flow of notifications. Allocate specific times to check emails or social media and turn off unnecessary notifications. Creating a quiet, organized workspace can also help limit distractions and improve focus.

## Exercise Regularly

Physical activity can provide a mental break, reduce stress, and improve focus. Regular exercise can shift your mind away from overthinking and onto the task you're performing. Whether it's a short walk, a jog, or a bike ride, regular physical activity can help clear your mind and improve your ability to focus.

## Get Enough Sleep

Lack of sleep can contribute to overthinking and decrease focus. Ensure you're getting enough sleep every night to maintain good mental health and improve your ability to concentrate during the day. Establishing a consistent sleep schedule can aid in this.

## Practice Self-Compassion

Remember, everyone overthinks sometimes, and it's perfectly okay to have off days. Don't be too hard on yourself if you find your mind wandering or if you're struggling to focus. Recognize your feelings, remind yourself that it's okay, and take a few moments to breathe and reset.

Remember, the goal isn't to eliminate overthinking completely, but rather to manage it effectively. By utilizing these strategies, you can significantly reduce overthinking, increase focus, and ultimately become more productive. Your teenage years are a journey of growth and self-discovery, and learning to control your thoughts is part of that journey. So take a deep breath, implement these strategies, and take the reins of your mind and your productivity. You've got this!

# Balancing Work and Rest for Optimal Performance

Balancing work and rest aren't just about getting enough sleep—it's about managing your energy to boost productivity, prevent burnout, and maintain a healthy lifestyle. But before we delve into the practical strategies to achieve this balance, it's essential to understand why this balance matters.

## The Importance of Balancing Work and Rest

The secret to sustainable productivity isn't about working longer, it's about working smarter. That means knowing when to push forward and when to step back and recharge. Overwork can lead to exhaustion, reduced creativity, and eventually burnout—a state of chronic physical and mental fatigue. Furthermore, it can make you more prone to errors and reduce the quality of your work.

On the other hand, rest isn't just the absence of work. It's an active state during which vital physical and mental recovery processes occur. A well-rested mind is sharper, more focused, more creative, and more capable of learning new things.

Overthinking can rob you of this necessary rest. If your mind is constantly replaying worries or anxieties, even downtime can become stressful. This can disrupt your ability to relax and recuperate, further draining your energy and negatively affecting your productivity.

## Practical Strategies for a Balanced Life

Achieving a balanced life means incorporating restorative practices into your daily routine. Here are some effective ways to do this.

### Schedule Breaks and Downtime

Just as you plan your work or study hours, plan regular breaks throughout the day and set aside time for relaxation and leisure. This could mean using techniques like the Pomodoro, taking a walk, reading a book, or even just daydreaming. Remember, it's not wasted time; it's an investment in your future productivity.

### Incorporate Mindfulness Practices

As previously discussed, mindfulness emphasizes the importance of being completely absorbed and active in the present moment. By incorporating habits such as meditation, deep respiration routines, or yoga into your daily regimen, you can assist in calming your mind and minimizing excessive contemplation.

### Prioritize Sleep

Your sleep is a powerful restorative process, crucial for memory consolidation, mood regulation, and physical recovery. Try to establish a regular sleep schedule, create a calming pre-sleep routine, and ensure your sleep environment is conducive to quality rest.

### Invest in Self-Care

Self-care isn't indulgent; it's necessary. This entails maintaining your physical well-being, emotional stability, and mental health. That could mean eating nutritious meals, getting regular exercise, spending time with loved ones, journaling, or pursuing a hobby.

### Set Boundaries

In today's interconnected world, it's easy to let work, school, or social demands infringe on your rest time. Set clear boundaries between work and rest. This might mean turning off email notifications after a certain hour, keeping work or study activities out of your bedroom, or setting aside specific times when you are unavailable for non-emergency requests.

## Striking a Balance: A Continuous Process

Achieving equilibrium between labor and relaxation is not a singular accomplishment, but rather an ongoing process that demands frequent care and modification. It requires conscious decision-making, discipline, and sometimes even saying *no* to demands that encroach on your rest and relaxation time.

Remember, the aim is not to have equal parts of work and rest—different periods in your life might demand more work, such as during exams, or more rest, like during a vacation. The goal is to find a rhythm that suits your current situation, understanding that your needs will change over time.

# Practical Exercise: Time Blocking and Mindful Task Management

Overthinking, losing focus, struggling to juggle multiple tasks—sound familiar? Let's try an exercise called time blocking coupled with mindful task management, a strategy that can help you maintain your focus, manage your time better, and prevent overthinking.

## Step 1: Time Blocking

Time blocking involves dividing your day into chunks or blocks of time, each dedicated to a particular task or activity. Here's how to get started.

### List Your Tasks

Make a list of all the tasks you need to accomplish. This can include schoolwork, chores, hobbies, relaxation time, and even social activities.

### Estimate Time Needed

Next to each task, estimate how long you think it will take to complete it. This doesn't have to be perfect, just a ballpark figure.

### Schedule Your Blocks

Now, take out your calendar (physical or digital) and start assigning each task to a specific block of time in your day. Make sure to include blocks for rest and leisure, too—these are just as important as your work-related tasks.

### Stay Flexible

Remember, this is not a rigid plan. The aim is to have a guide that helps you structure your day, but things can (and will) change. Be ready to adjust as necessary.

## Step 2: Mindful Task Management

Once you have your time blocks set, it's time to focus on mindful task management. This simply means fully engaging with the task at hand during its allotted time and not letting your mind wander to other tasks or concerns. Here's how you can practice this.

### Set Your Intentions

Before you start each task, take a moment to set your intention. This could be as simple as saying to yourself, "For the next hour, I am fully focused on studying for my math test."

### Minimize Distractions

Create an environment conducive to concentration. This could mean clearing your workspace, putting your phone on silent, or using noise-canceling headphones.

### Take Mindful Breaks

After each block, take a short break—but do it mindfully. This might be a quick walk, a moment of quiet reflection, or a few deep breaths. The idea is to let your mind reset before diving into the next task.

*Practice Self-Compassion*

If you find your mind wandering during a task, gently bring your focus back without self-judgment. Remember, the goal is progress, not perfection.

That's it! You've now completed your first session of time blocking and mindful task management. Over time, you'll get a better understanding of how long tasks take and how you work best. Remember, the purpose of this exercise is to provide a structure that helps you manage your tasks and reduce overthinking. Feel free to tweak the process to suit your personal style and needs better.

# Conclusion

In today's fast-paced and demanding world, finding effective strategies to manage our time, overcome overthinking, and maintain a healthy work-life balance is crucial. Through the exploration of concepts like time blocking, mindful task management, and prioritizing rest and self-care, we have uncovered practical tools to enhance productivity, reduce stress, and achieve our goals. By implementing these strategies and adopting a mindful approach to our daily tasks, we can cultivate a sense of control, focus, and balance, which empowers us to thrive academically, personally, and professionally. Remember, it's never too early to start building these habits, and with practice, they can become valuable lifelong skills. So, take the first step towards a more productive and fulfilling life today.

# Chapter 15:

# Finding Support and Seeking Help

Navigating the uncertain waters of adolescence can often be a formidable undertaking. The tides of change surge with relentless intensity, prompting us to question ourselves, our relationships, and the world around us. In this chapter, we shine a lantern on this intricate journey, illuminating a key element of self-discovery and personal growth: the quest for support and help. Comprising approximately 2,200 words, this chapter pledges not merely to encourage you to seek support but also to guide you in building your own distinctive network of assistance, a collective that resonates with your unique needs and aspirations.

This chapter embarks on the significant issue of overthinking, a common trait among teenagers. We unravel the often-misunderstood need for seeking support to cope with this tendency, breaking the chains of the stigma that still tightly grip the topic of mental well-being. From here, we draw your attention to the diverse range of supportive individuals and resources accessible to you. We help you identify this network within your life, which may include family, friends, mentors, or even the unseen yet reassuring voice at the end of a helpline. We broaden your horizons to the manifold resources available, ranging from support groups to online communities and counseling services. Each is tailored to be in sync with your unique needs.

As we navigate this journey, we underscore the role of communication in fortifying this support structure. We aim to equip you with the skills necessary to express your needs, fears, and emotions effectively. We explore the importance of setting boundaries and inspire you to seek out active listeners within your network. More importantly, we strive to empower you to advocate for yourself, to muster the courage to ask for the support you require, reminding you that it's okay not always to be okay.

We also delve into the realm of professional help, exploring the potential benefits of therapy and counseling. In doing so, we challenge common misconceptions and demystify the process of seeking professional assistance. We provide information on various therapeutic approaches, lending you the tools necessary to find the one that best fits your needs.

Finally, this chapter culminates with a practical exercise: creating your support plan. We walk alongside you as you identify your support network, resources, and strategies for seeking help. Regular reviews and adjustments are encouraged, mirroring the dynamism of your evolving needs.

This chapter, therefore, serves as a compass, steering you toward a better understanding of the significance of seeking support while also equipping you with practical tools to create and maintain your support network. As we embark on this enlightening journey, remember that every brave step you take towards seeking support is a step towards stronger mental well-being and personal growth. Buckle up, for the voyage to understanding and embracing the world of support and help begins here.

## Seeking Support for Overthinking

Overthinking can often seem like an internal battle, a mental tug-of-war that teems with tangled thoughts and unresolved emotions. If you're a teenager, you might already be familiar with this struggle. Your mind can become filled with worries about grades, friendships, relationships, and your future vying for your attention, often amplifying the pressure you feel. This is why it's so crucial to seek support when overthinking starts to consume your daily life.

The act of reaching out, though simple, holds power to untie the knots of anxiety and create a clearer path toward healthier mental habits. Unveiling your vulnerabilities may seem intimidating. However, it's essential to remember that seeking assistance doesn't demonstrate weakness. Instead, it bears witness to your courage and self-consciousness.

The world of psychotherapy, as discussed in the previous articles, offers a broad range of treatments and techniques that can help manage overthinking. CBT, for instance, can help you become aware of harmful thought patterns, teaching you how to question them and shift towards healthier ways of thinking. Other therapies might focus on stress-coping strategies, mindfulness, and even tracking emotions to understand their impact on your behavior. This means there's always a technique that can be tailored to your unique needs.

Yet, many adolescents hesitate to reach out due to the unfortunate stigma surrounding mental health assistance. This stigma can distort the reality of therapy, painting a picture of it being something only for those with severe mental disorders. The truth, however, is quite the contrary. Just as you would visit a doctor for a physical ailment, visiting a therapist for mental health is equally important, if not more so. Our minds, after all, govern our perception and experience of the world.

Engaging with a professional in the field of mental health can offer a secure environment where you're free to articulate your emotions and thoughts devoid of any judgment. The therapist's experience and understanding can guide you toward managing overthinking more effectively. Bear in mind that therapy is a collaborative effort—your therapist will cooperate with you to comprehend your thoughts and emotions and assist you in establishing efficient strategies for coping.

Besides professional help, seeking support from family and friends can be incredibly beneficial. Sharing your struggles with overthinking can not only unburden you but also increase awareness among your loved ones, thereby fostering a supportive and understanding environment. Suppose you're not yet comfortable discussing this with your immediate circle. In that case, there are countless communities and support groups, both online and offline, that offer a space for shared experiences and mutual encouragement.

Goal setting, another method we've explored, can also be a powerful tool to combat overthinking. By setting specific and achievable goals, you provide your mind with a concrete focus, reducing its tendency to wander into the realms of worry and uncertainty.

In conclusion, overthinking might be a challenge, but it's not an insurmountable one. It's okay to need help; seeking it is a courageous step toward better mental health. Reach out to a mental health professional, connect with loved ones, and remember that your thoughts don't define you—you have the power to shape them.

# Building Your Support Network

The labyrinth of teen years is easier to navigate when you're not walking alone. You need companions—individuals who extend their support, lend an ear, and encourage you when the paths get tough. Furthermore, you need resources and tools that equip you to handle the trials of your journey. This chapter will help you identify supportive individuals and resources that align with your needs and preferences.

Every teenager has a unique support network already in place, even if you haven't yet recognized it. This network consists of individuals who genuinely care about your well-being. These can be friends who cheer you up, family members who offer wise counsel, mentors who guide you, or trusted professionals who provide expert advice. Identifying these individuals is the first step in understanding and leveraging your support network.

Friends and family are often the first port of call. They know you best, they care about you, and they want to help. Be open about your feelings of overthinking with them. You'd be surprised how understanding and supportive they can be. However, remember that it's equally important to respect their boundaries and understand that they may not always have the capacity to provide the support you need.

In addition to your personal circle, consider expanding your network to include mentors and trusted professionals. Teachers, coaches, school counselors, and community leaders can offer objective advice and guidance. These individuals have experience and wisdom that can help you navigate your challenges effectively.

At the same time, mental health professionals like therapists and counselors play a crucial role. Therapists offer a secure, unbiased environment to delve into your emotions and thoughts, aid you in creating successful coping mechanisms, and steer you toward enhanced mental well-being. Remember, reaching out to these professionals is not a sign of weakness; it is an act of self-care and strength.

But what if you're not yet ready to open up to someone in your personal life, or professional help seems daunting? That's where resources like helplines, support groups, and online communities come in. Helplines offer anonymous, immediate support at the end of a phone call. Support groups, both online and offline, bring together individuals facing similar challenges, creating a platform for shared experiences and mutual encouragement. Online communities, forums, and apps provide 24/7 accessibility to resources, advice, and camaraderie.

Educational resources, such as self-help books and informative websites, can also be a valuable addition to your toolbox. They can provide insights into overthinking, offer practical tips, and help you feel less alone in your experience.

Remember, building a support network is not a one-size-fits-all process. It's about finding the right combination of individuals and resources that work best for you. Take your time, explore your options, and remember that it's okay to ask for help. Your support network is a testament to your resilience and your proactive approach towards better mental health. So, reach out, connect, and remember, you don't have to navigate your journey alone.

# Opening Up: Mastering Effective Communication and Expressing Your Needs

If overthinking is a locked door, effective communication can be the key that opens it. It's not always easy, but learning to express your needs, concerns, and emotions related to overthinking is vital for mental well-being. This chapter will offer strategies to help you convey your thoughts and feelings, set healthy boundaries, and actively seek the understanding and support you need.

Communication isn't a one-way street. It's about expressing yourself and also about being heard. When it comes to overthinking, your feelings can sometimes be like a tangled ball of yarn—hard to unravel and even harder to explain. But just as a knotted thread becomes manageable once you find the end, your thoughts, too, become more understandable when you start voicing them.

Begin by articulating your experiences of overthinking to yourself. Journaling can be an excellent tool for this. Once you understand your own feelings, you're better prepared to explain them to others. Try to be as honest and clear as you can. Use "I" statements to express your feelings, such as "I feel overwhelmed when I overthink," rather than "You don't understand me."

Remember, everyone's experience with overthinking is unique. Don't be discouraged if people don't understand right away. Patiently explain that overthinking isn't a choice but a struggle you're facing, and their support is essential to you.

It's equally important to set healthy boundaries while communicating. Just as you have a right to express your feelings, you also have a right to protect your mental space. Let your network know what kind of support you need and when you need it. This could look like saying, "I appreciate your advice, but right now, I just need someone to listen," or "I'm feeling overwhelmed. Can we talk about this later?"

Active listening is a crucial part of effective communication. Encourage your support network to listen attentively, ask clarifying questions, and refrain from offering unsolicited advice. When they understand your experiences better, they can provide more meaningful and effective support. Lastly, remember that advocating for yourself isn't selfish—it's necessary. It's okay to ask for what you need. Whether you need a quiet moment, a shoulder to lean on, or professional help, it's essential to make your needs known. Expressing your needs can be empowering. It shows that you are taking charge of your mental well-being and actively seeking ways to manage overthinking.

Effective communication is a skill that takes practice, but it's worth the effort. It bridges the gap between your internal world of thoughts and the external world of support, helping you find understanding, compassion, and help. So, take a deep breath, gather your thoughts, and open the door to a conversation.

## Professional Help and Therapy Options

As we explore our minds, it's not uncommon to encounter twists and turns that leave us feeling lost and overwhelmed. Overthinking is one such challenge, and it can often feel like you're trapped in a never-ending cycle of thoughts. But there's good news: you don't have to navigate this maze alone. Professional help, such as therapy or counseling, can act as a guiding light, helping you to manage overthinking effectively.

However, before we delve into the world of therapy, let's dispel some misconceptions. Some believe therapy is only for severe mental health issues or crises. Others may think that seeking professional help is a sign of weakness. But these notions couldn't be further from the truth. Therapy is a valuable resource for anyone who wants to improve their mental well-being, regardless of the nature or intensity of their challenges. Taking care of oneself by seeking help or support is not indicative of weakness. On the contrary, it demonstrates courage and a commitment to self-care.

Seeking professional help provides a secure and non-judgmental environment where you can freely explore your thoughts and emotions. Trained therapists are equipped with tools and strategies that can help you manage overthinking. They can help you understand why you overthink and guide you toward healthier thought patterns. Their external perspective can provide fresh insights into your experiences and help you see things in a new light.

Now, let's talk about the different therapy options available. The therapeutic landscape is diverse, offering various approaches tailored to individual needs and preferences. CBT is one such approach, which is particularly effective for overthinking. CBT focuses on challenging and changing unhelpful thought patterns, thus giving you more control over your thoughts.

Mindfulness-based therapies, such as mindfulness-based cognitive therapy (MBCT), have shown potential for providing beneficial effects. These therapies teach you to focus on the present moment instead of getting lost in your thoughts. They encourage acceptance of your thoughts without judgment, helping you break free from the cycle of overthinking.

You might also consider group therapy, where you can connect with others who are facing similar challenges. The sense of shared experiences can provide validation and support. Choosing the right therapy and therapist can be a process of trial and error. You might need to try different therapists or therapy types to find the right fit. It's important to find a therapist with whom you feel comfortable and safe, as a strong therapeutic relationship can significantly enhance the effectiveness of therapy.

Remember, reaching out for professional help isn't a sign that you've failed to manage overthinking on your own. It's a proactive step towards understanding yourself better and acquiring tools to manage your thought processes effectively. So, consider turning on that guiding light as you navigate the maze of your mind—you might find it leads you to clearer thoughts and greater peace of mind.

# Practical Exercise: Creating a Support Plan

A journey through the complexities of your mind, particularly when you're wrestling with overthinking, can sometimes feel like a solo expedition. But it doesn't have to be. In fact, building a support plan is like assembling your personal expedition team, equipped with resources, strategies, and people who can provide guidance and understanding when the terrain gets tough. Ready to begin? Let's plot your route.

## Identifying Your Support Network

Just like every great expedition team, your support network should consist of a variety of individuals, each offering unique strengths. These might be trusted friends who understand your struggle with overthinking, family members who provide comfort, mentors who offer wisdom, or professionals like therapists who can equip you with effective strategies. Draw a mind map of your potential support network.

## Exploring Your Resources

The right resources can make your journey easier. Perhaps there are books that offer insights into overthinking, online forums where teens share their experiences, or helplines you can call when things get overwhelming. Make a list of these resources, and don't hesitate to explore new ones as you find them.

## Developing Your Strategies

Now that you've got your team and resources, it's time to work out how you'll seek their help when overthinking strikes. What will you say? How will you express your needs? Draft a few conversation starters or scripts that you can use to communicate your feelings.

## Scheduling Check-Ins

Even the best plans need revisiting. Life changes, and so will your needs and support network. Regularly review your support plan, and don't be afraid to make adjustments. This could be as simple as a monthly journal reflection or a semi-annual chat with your therapist or mentor.

Keep in mind that your personal support plan is not rigid or unchangeable. It is a dynamic document that can and should adapt as you grow and evolve. The process of creating this plan is just as important as the plan itself. By consciously considering your needs and resources, you're taking proactive steps to manage your overthinking.

This journey might seem daunting, but remember, every explorer experiences moments of uncertainty. With your support plan at hand, you're well-equipped to navigate through thoughts and find your way toward clearer thinking and peace of mind.

# Conclusion

In the expedition of life, it's essential to remember that you don't have to traverse the terrain of overthinking alone. By identifying your support network, exploring your resources, and crafting your strategies for communication and help-seeking, you're setting up your personal toolkit for navigating the twists and turns of this journey. It's crucial to understand that everyone's path is unique, and thus, your toolkit will and should evolve with your experiences. With your adaptable and robust support plan in hand, you can confidently face the challenges of overthinking and embrace a healthier and more balanced mental landscape. Your thoughts may be intricate and complex, seemingly entwined in a knotted web, but remember, there's always a way to disentangle these knots. By understanding the tendencies to overthink and breaking free from its unproductive grip, you're setting the first steps towards clarity. Armed with the aid of your support network and the right resources, you're more than equipped to illuminate the path to understanding and navigate your way out of this mental maze.

# Conclusion

As we reach the final stretch of our journey through this book, it's important to reflect on the ground we've covered. We began with an exploration of the concept of overthinking, its impacts, and why it's particularly relevant for you as a teenager. We have delved deep into the mind, examining how patterns of overthinking emerge, and how they can distort our perception of ourselves and the world around us. Our journey has led us through the process of understanding, recognizing, and managing overthinking, with the shared goal of empowering you to lead a more balanced and fulfilling life.

Let's look back and remember that one of our initial discoveries was that overthinking is not a personal failing or a character flaw; it's simply a habit of the mind, one that can be altered. Just as paths in a forest become more prominent and easier to traverse the more they are used, so too does the mind create patterns. The more we indulge in overthinking, the more it becomes our default mode. But this analogy carries with it a hopeful message: just as we can forge new paths in a forest by choosing to walk differently, we can reshape our mental landscape through consistent practice and patience.

A significant part of reshaping this mental landscape involves embracing imperfection and allowing for growth. We've discovered that perfection is an illusion, an unattainable ideal that can often fuel overthinking. In its place, we've explored the value of self-compassion and acceptance, replacing harsh self-judgment with kindness and understanding. By viewing our mistakes and failures as opportunities for growth, we can break free from the cycle of overthinking and self-blame. And, with the help of practical tools like the Embracing Imperfection Journal, we've started creating tangible records of our progress and positive mindset shifts.

One area where overthinking often rears its head is in the realm of relationships. Through this book, we've understood how overthinking can strain connections and cause unnecessary confusion and misunderstandings. However, we've also discovered ways to navigate overthinking in relationships. Effective communication and active listening techniques, paired with trust-building strategies, can help us foster more meaningful and fulfilling relationships.

The chapters about finding clarity and taking action, and overcoming overthinking fatigue have equipped us with further tools for handling overthinking. We've learned to see risk-taking as an avenue for growth and decision-making as an opportunity for learning rather than a source of stress. We've also discussed how crucial it is to establish self-care practices, not only as a way of managing overthinking, but as a means of cultivating overall well-being.

Lastly, we've explored how to achieve balance in life, through strategies for enhancing productivity, managing workload, and balancing work and rest. In this technologically-driven era, where distractions are numerous and expectations are high, finding balance is more essential than ever before. Equipped with practical tools like time blocking and mindful task management, we are now better prepared to handle the demands and pressures of teenage life.

While this book has provided you with an array of strategies, tools, and perspectives to handle overthinking, it's vital to remember that change takes time. Altering entrenched patterns of thought is not an overnight process, and there will likely be moments of struggle. It's okay if progress seems slow, or if you falter and fall back into overthinking from time to time. What's important is to keep coming back to the practices that encourage mindfulness and growth.

We end this book on a note of encouragement and hope. The final chapter underscores the fact that you're not alone in this journey. There are many resources available, both online and offline, and you're encouraged to reach out, to seek support, and to keep learning and growing. Remember, each day is a new opportunity to move beyond overthinking and closer towards your authentic, mindful self.

Even as we close this book, remember that your journey towards overcoming overthinking continues. Carry forward the insights you've gained, and continue to apply the strategies you've learned. Be patient with yourself and remember that transformation takes time and practice.

As you move forward, it's my hope that this book serves not as a set of strict rules or a rigid blueprint, but as a map to guide you through your unique journey. I hope it acts as a reminder that there is no *perfect* path, and that it's okay—in fact, it's necessary—to stumble, learn, and grow. It is in the process of overcoming, not in the absence of challenges, that we truly discover our strengths and potential.

May you continue to forge your path, empowered with a greater understanding of your mind and a toolbox full of strategies to manage overthinking. Remember, you are more than your thoughts, and you hold the power to shape your mental landscape. Embrace your growth, cultivate mindfulness, and strive for balance. Remember that it's okay to be a work-in-progress. After all, aren't we all?

Thank you for embarking on this journey with me. I look forward to hearing about your continued adventures in overcoming overthinking, embracing growth, and navigating the exciting, sometimes tumultuous, but always rewarding journey of teenage life.

# References

Ackerman, C. (2017, April 12). *28 benefits of gratitude & most significant research findings*. PositivePsychology https://positivepsychology.com/benefits-gratitude-research-questions/

Arnold, P. D., Zai, G., & Richter, M. A. (2004). Genetics of anxiety disorders. *Current Psychiatry Reports*, *6*(4), 243–254. https://doi.org/10.1007/s11920-004-0073-1

Berjot, S., & Gillet, N. (2011). Stress and coping with discrimination and stigmatization. *Frontiers in Psychology*, *2*(33). https://doi.org/10.3389/fpsyg.2011.00033

Mind Tools. (2022). *SMART goals*. https://www.mindtools.com/a4wo118/smart-goals

Product Plan. (2023). *Eisenhower matrix | prioritization framework | definition and examples* https://www.productplan.com/glossary/eisenhower-matrix/

Savic, D. (2023, June 9). *The pomodoro technique: How it can help you manage your time better*. https://trick-tack.com/pomodoro-technique-time-management/

US News. (2023, May 17). *What are the best ways to stop overthinking and reduce anxiety?* https://health.usnews.com/wellness/mind/articles/proven-strategies-to-stop-overthinking-and-ease-anxiety-now

World Health Organization. (2021). *Mental health of adolescents* https://www.who.int/news-room/fact-sheets/detail/adolescent-mental-health

Wtop News. (2021, July 13). *12 proven strategies to stop overthinking and ease anxiety now.* https://wtop.com/health-fitness/2021/07/12-proven-strategies-to-stop-overthinking-and-ease-anxiety-now/

Printed in Great Britain
by Amazon

44218685R00106

A tragedie of Abraham's sacrifice written in French by Theodore Beza, and translated into English by Arthur Golding. Ed., with an introduction, notes and an appendix containing the Abraham sacrifiant of Theodore Beza

Théodore de Bèze, Malcolm William Wallace

University of Toronto Studies
Philological Series

# GOLDING'S
# A TRAGEDIE OF ABRAHAMS SACRIFICE

WRITTEN IN FRENCH BY THEODORE BEZA
AND TRANSLATED INTO ENGLISH BY
ARTHUR GOLDING

EDITED WITH AN INTRODUCTION, NOTES AND AN APPENDIX
CONTAINING THE ABRAHAM SACRIFIANT OF THEO-
DORE BEZA, BY MALCOLM W. WALLACE, PH.D.,
LECTURER IN ENGLISH, UNIVERSITY COLLEGE, TORONTO

UNIVERSITY OF TORONTO LIBRARY
MCMVI

EDITION LIMITED
TO 650 COPIES

Entered according to Act of the Parliament of Canada in the office of
the Minister of Agriculture, by the Librarian of the University of Toronto,
in the year of our Lord one thousand nine hundred and six

# PREFACE

*A Tragedie of Abrahams Sacrifice* is a translation by
Arthur Golding of the *Abraham Sacrifiant* of Théodore de
Bèze, the eminent French theologian and reformer. The
translation, which was finished in 1575, was published at London by Thomas Vantroullier in 1577, and has never been
reprinted. The volume has become exceedingly rare; a copy
is in the Bodleian Library, but I have not been able to learn of
the existence of any other. The Bodleian copy, which was
once in the possession of Malone, contains a manuscript note
signed by him to the effect that it was bought at the sale of
Mr. Forster's books in November, 1806, for £10 4s. od. The
*Biographia · Dramatica* says : " This piece, which is
rarely met with, sold for 20 guineas at a sale in King's
auction room, a few years ago." Lowndes also notes,
" Forster 1166, 10£. 5s. King and Lochée's, in 181–, 21£."
Collier refers to a manuscript copy of the play which is in the
collection of the Duke of Devonshire (*Annals*, II, p. 250).

In the present edition I have attempted to reproduce as
accurately as possible the copy which is in the Bodleian (black
letter, 18mo.) except in one particular, viz. the abbreviated
words are written in full. The capitalization, punctuation,
paging and line arrangement, both in the introductory matter
and in the play proper, have been preserved. The original
title-page in fac-simile faces the title-page of this edition, and
the pages on which illustrations appear have been reproduced
to face the corresponding pages of the reprint.

These illustrations would seem to be original with Golding's
edition, although the workmanship is decidedly superior to
that found in contemporary English wood-cuts. A copy of the
1552 edition of Beza's play in the Bibliothèque Mazarin, and
a copy of the 1553 edition in the Bibliothèque de l' Arsenal
contain no illustrations, and the detailed descriptions of Beza's
other editions given by Rothschild make no reference to illustrations before 1669 (v. *Le Mistére du Viel Testament*, II,
pp. xlix-lxiii) Moreover it is hardly possible that Golding
reproduced the wood-cuts of any of the earlier French versions.

A, B, C and D contain no illustrations of the Abraham and Isaac story; F, the version followed most closely by Beza, contains one crude wood-cut which is reproduced by Rothschild, and which he rightly describes as " un bois grossier" (vol. I, p xxix); it bears no similarity to any of Golding's illustrations. Of the four wood-cuts in E, which, like F, was published in 1539, the only one which might possibly bear any resemblance to those of Golding's edition is that found on the title-page, and which is described as " un petit bois, qui représente Abraham levant son glaive sur la tête d'Isaac." Two wood-cuts reproduced in the 1833 edition published at Florence of Feo Belcari's *Rappresentazione e Festa d'Abraam e d'Isaac suo Figliuolo* bear no resemblance to those of Golding's. The presence of the devil in two of the four illustrations of Golding's edition is practically conclusive evidence that they were made either for Beza's play or for Golding's translation, and since none of the sixteenth century editions of the former are illustrated we may conclude that the wood-cuts were made for the latter. It is still just possible, of course, that they are not English workmanship.

I have not thought it desirable in the Introduction to say anything of Beza's life or work, for the subject has been already treated by many writers. The first of these was Hieronymus Bolsec, who in 1582 made a bitter attack on Beza in his *Historia de vita, moribus, doctrina, et rebus gestis Theod Beza,* etc.—" faict pour aduertir & diuertir les Catholiques de ne se laisser abuser par . doctrines mortiferes." Extracts from this work are included in a republication of the author's life of Calvin which appeared at Lyons in 1875 Other early accounts of Beza's life are that of Jacobus Laingeus—*De vita et moribus Theodori Beza*, etc., Paris, 1585, and that of Antonius Fayus (Antoine de la Faye)—*De vita et obitu D Theodori Beza*, Geneva, 1606, 4°. Baum's *Theodore Beza nach handschriftlichen Quellen* (3 vols. Leipzig, 1843-1852) is by far the most exhaustive work that has appeared on the subject, but it follows the course of Beza's life only down to the year 1563 Professor Henry M. Baird's *Theodore Beza, the counsellor of the French Reformation, 1519-1605* (Heroes of the

Reformation, N. Y. and Lond. 1899, 8vo.) is a popular account of Beza's life and work. A detailed bibliography of Beza's publications is appended to Dr. Heinrich Heppe's *Theodore Beza: Leben und Ausgewählte Schriften*, which forms the sixth part of Hagenbach's *Leben der Väter und Begründer der reformirten Kirche* (Elberfeld, 1861, 8vo.) Two valuable critical estimates of Beza's work are A. Sayous' study in his *Études Littéraires sur les Écrivains François de la Reformation*, vol. I, and *Théodore de Bèze à Lausanne, Étude par Auguste Bernus* (Lausanne, 1900).

It is a pleasure to acknowledge here my indebtedness to Mr. H. H. Langton, Librarian of the University of Toronto. As general editor of the UNIVERSITY STUDIES he has been indefatigable in his efforts to eliminate textual errors, and his kindly interest in the volume has extended to the making of many valuable suggestions which I have been glad to incorporate in the introduction.

M. W. W.

UNIVERSITY COLLEGE, TORONTO.
May 5, 1906.

# TABLE OF CONTENTS

# INTRODUCTION

## THE LIFE OF ARTHUR GOLDING

In *Notes and Queries* (vol. x., p. 115) a correspondent seeks for fuller information than we now possess concerning the life of Arthur Golding. " It seems very strange," he says, " that such a celebrated man, and one who had such influential friends and connexions, and was also the owner of such extensive properties, should have suddenly disappeared, and that there should be no record of where he was buried or if he left any family." And yet, in this respect the fate of Golding was not different from that of the great majority of his literary brethren of the Elizabethan age. Unless manuscript sources at present inaccessible should some day throw more light on the subject, it would seem that there is little chance of adding very much to the confessedly scanty details of the life of one of the most important translators of an age when translation was esteemed almost as highly as original composition. The present study cannot pretend to furnish any very important contributions to the subject ; its purpose is rather to bring together details from various printed and manuscript sources, and to present them in a more amplified form than has hitherto been attempted.

Arthur Golding was the descendant of a prosperous family which had resided in the County of Essex since the time of the Conquest, for in the Doomsday Book we find among the holders of lands in the hundred of Colchester " Goldinc 1 house."[1] The place-name Goldingham—" the town of the Goldings "— occurring as it does in the immediate vicinity of the extensive lands held by the family for many generations, would seem likewise to denote the antiquity and importance of the family.[2] In the reign of Edward I. we have record of a certain Warin Golding, of the town of Halsted, and in 1306 John Golding, of the same town, was witness to a deed of William de St. Martin.[3]

---

[1] *The Victoria History of the Counties of England—The County of Essex* vol i.

[2] "Goldingham" is also a family name in Essex. V. Fuller's *Worthies of England*, vol. i, p. 360.

[3] Morant's *Essex*, vol. ii, p. 328—Hinckford Hundred—Belchamp St. Pauls.

From the reign of Edward II. on, the name appears frequently in public documents. In a paper dated July 6, 1345, " de protectione pro quibusdam personis, qui cum Rege in obsequium suum ad partes transmarinas profecturi sunt," we find the name of Thomas Goldyng.[1] Another document which bears the date 1374 " de marinariis arestandis pro navibus et bargeis Regis " has the following item: " Johannes Goldyng, magister navis Regis vocatæ La Mighel de Hull, ad sexaginta et decem marinarios in comitatibus Suffolc' et Essex'.[2] Toward the close of the fifteenth century Thomas Golding of Grays, in Cavendish, Suffolk, and of Beauchamp St. Paul in Essex, married Agnes, daughter of Edm. Lutton.[3] On her death he " married Elizabeth, one of the daughters and co-heirs of John Worthie [or Wortley?] of Blamsters in Halstead, Esq.,........and had by her John Golding, Esq. of Pauls Belchamphall and Halstead."[4] This was Arthur Golding's father, and the following quotation from Morant regarding the lands which he held shows that he was a very prosperous gentleman; " He held a tenement here called Spicer's, 2 acres of arable in Chapel-feild, and several parcels of land of the Dean and Chapter in socage. He had also estates in Beauchamp Otton and Beauchamp St. Ethelbert and in Halsted, Worthies Place, Blomsters Maner, Aylewards Place, Pascalls, Picherds, Wynde Wells, etc., in Hempsted, a messuage called Blagden, and 86 acres of arable, 15 of meadow; in Bumpsted-Helion the maner of Boblowe. (t)

(t) Inquis. 2 Ed. vi., Nu. 78."[5]

John Golding's possession of such extensive properties is the more noteworthy in view of the fact that his elder brother, Roger, had been Thomas Golding's heir.

John Golding's first wife, Elizabeth, widow of Reginald Hamond of Ramsden Belhouse, was the daughter of Henry Stowe, Knt., and heiress of West Malling in Kent. She died on December 26, 1527, leaving to John Golding four children—

---

[1] Rymer's *Foedera*.

[2] *Ibid.*

[3] Hunter's *Chorus Vatum* on the authority of a Harleian MS.

[4] Morant, *op. cit.*

[5] *Ibid.*

Thomas, William, Elizabeth, and Margaret. His second wife was Ursula, daughter and co-heir of William Merston of Horton, Surrey, by whom he had four sons—Henry, Arthur, George and Edward, and three daughters Mary, Dorothy and Frances.[1] John Golding became one of the auditors of the Exchequer, and the prominent position which several of his children came to occupy in later years was no doubt due in part to the father's successful career. He died on November 28, 1547.

Sir Thomas Golding, John Golding's eldest son and heir, owned valuable lands in Essex, some of which he is said to have secured by questionable means while acting in his capacity of Commissioner for certifying the Chantry lands. He was Sheriff of Essex and Hertfordshire in 1561,[2] and of Essex alone in 1569.[3] His wife was one of the daughters and co-heirs of Thomas Royden of Peckham in Kent, and had been previously married to ———— Twisden.

Sir Thomas' eldest sister, Margaret, married John de Vere, sixteenth Earl of Oxford, and about 1545 she became the mother of Edward, the seventeenth Earl, whose name is a familiar one to all students of Elizabethan literature. He was a great favourite of Queen Elizabeth, and the story of his insult to Sidney on the tennis court is well known, for when the Queen forbade the duel which had been arranged as a result of Sidney's challenge to the Earl, the former withdrew to Wilton, and busied himself in composing the *Arcadia*. Edward de Vere died in 1604. His only sister, Mary, who had married Peregrine Bertie, Lord Willoughby of Eresby, and after his death, Charles Tyrrell, Esq., had died in 1568.

None of the other members of John Golding's numerous family attained to the high worldly place occupied by his eldest son and eldest daughter. William, the second son, married Elizabeth, one of the daughters and co-heirs of Edmund West of Cornard, in Suffolk (she was the widow of John Bukenham, Esq.), and had two children—Edmund and Dorothy. His

---

1 Morant, from whom these facts are chiefly derived, makes no mention of the daughter, Mary. References to her are based on Hunter's *Chorus Vatum*.

2 Fuller, *Worthies of England*, vol. i, p. 368—Tho. Golding, mil.

3 *Ibid.*—Tho. Golding, Knt.

sister Elizabeth married Roger Wingfield of Norfolk. Of Arthur Golding's own brothers, Henry, who was heir to his mother, and who died on December 6, 1576, leaving a wife, Alice, the daughter of Clovill of Hemingfield in Essex, and George, who died on November 24, 1584, also leaving a wife, Mary, were both possessed of considerable property in Essex, to the greater part of which Arthur Golding succeeded at their deaths. Of his sisters, Mary became the wife of Anthony Broke, of Reading; Dorothy of Edmund D. Dockwra or Dockwather, by whom she became the mother of " 2 memorable sons," Arthur and Henry; and Frances, of Mathew Bacon of Shelfhanger in Norfolk.[1]

The year of Arthur Golding's birth is fixed for us by a legal document quoted in Morant's *Essex*. In connection with the fact that Henry Golding, who died in 1576, was possessed at that time of the manor of East Thorp and other lands in the Lexden Hundred we find the statement: " Arthur, his brother and next heir, then aged 40, succeeded him,(q)

(q) Inquis. 19 Eliz. Feb. 7."[2]

Accordingly we may set down 1536 as the year of his birth. Both Warton and Phillips say that he was a native of London. Of his education we know nothing definite, for although he is said to have been a member of Queen's College, Cambridge,[3] his name does not appear in the records of the College. Malone says that he was a fellow-commoner of Jesus College, Cambridge in 1552.[4] His famous nephew, the Earl of Oxford (then Lord Bulbeck) who was Golding's junior by only nine years, entered Queen's as a fellow commoner in November, 1558. It is practically certain, however, that Golding did not take a degree, or his name would not have appeared on the title-pages of his numerous books simply as " Arthur Golding, gentleman." Before the year 1563 we have no accurate information regarding his life. Hunter says that " it would seem that the poet was in the service of Sir Henry Sydney by the

---

[1] Hunter (*op. cit.*) says that she married Montfaucon of Shassinger in Norfolk.

[2] Morant, *op. cit.*, vol. ii, p. 180.

[3] V. Cooper's *Athenæ Cantabrigienses*, vol. ii, p. 431.

[4] Hunter, *op. cit.*

M.S. in Heber Library No. 1523; but this is doubtful."[1]    Mr. Sidney Lee tells us that "in 1549 he was in the service of Protector Somerset, who wrote, 5 Oct., requesting him to solicit the aid of the Earl of Oxford's servants in repressing rebellion."[2] The letter in question reads as follows :

"We commend us unto you.    And for the confidence we have in you, being our servant, we will and require you to solicit and give order for our very good Lord the Earl of Oxford's things, servants, and ordinary power, that he himself, and the same also, be in good readiness, whatsoever shall chance to require his service for the King's Majesty; whereof, if any occasion shall chance, we will signify by our letters. Thus we commit the order of the whole unto your good discretion, and will you to use herein convenient secrecy.    From Hampton Court the 5th October, 1549.

Your loving Lord and Master,

"E. SOMERSET."

"To our loving servant,

——— Golding, Esquire."[3]

I do not know upon what authority it has been assumed that this letter was addressed to Arthur Golding, but surely that assumption is a mistake.    In the copy of the letter which is here reproduced there is a blank before the name 'Golding.' If we remember that at this time Arthur Golding was just thirteen years of age, is it not absurd to think of the Protector's writing to him on such high matters, and referring to "the confidence we have in you" and "your good discretion"? The fact, however, that the services of a Golding are bespoken with the Earl of Oxford makes it inherently probable that the letter was addressed to a relative of Margaret Golding, wife of the sixteenth Earl.    We can hardly be far wrong in assuming that her brother Sir Thomas, at this time a young man nearly thirty years of age, is the Golding in question; at any rate we may dismiss the idea that the letter was addressed to a lad of thirteen years.

---

1 *Op. cit.*

2 V. article on "Arthur Golding" in *Dictionary of National Biography.*

3 "Somerset to Golding.    Orig. St. P. Off. Domestic, 5th Oct. 1549." Quoted in P. F. Tytler's *England under the Reigns of Edward vi. and Mary.*

In 1563 Arthur Golding was receiver for his nephew Edward de Vere, Earl of Oxford, at that time a young man eighteen years of age, who had succeeded to the earldom during the previous year. The Earl was in ward to the Queen, and was now living with Sir William Cecil, master of the wards; it seems probable that Golding resided with his nephew for some time at Cecil's house in the Strand, for on April 2nd, 1563, he dedicated his translation of *The historie of Leonard Aretine* to Sir William Cecil, Knight, from Cecil-house in the Strand. The dedication of *The Histories of Trogus Pompeius*, i. e. Justin's *History*, is dated December 23, 1564, and is also from Cecil-house; at Cecil-house, too, is dated the dedication to the first four books of Ovid, which was written in 1564, although it did not appear until the following year.

For the next two or three years Golding seems to have devoted himself assiduously to the work of translating Cæsar and Ovid,—the work which was to give him his real claim to a place in literary history, for the great majority of the voluminous translations of his later life were of a religious character, and of more or less ephemeral interest. It was a period of great activity in rendering accesible to English readers the classics of the ancient world, and the boundless curiosity of the Elizabethans regarding the literature of the past assured the translator an appreciative audience, who would display no over-niceness in their critical estimate of his work. In 1562 Thomas Twine had completed the translation of the *Aeneid* which Thomas Phaer had already (between 1555 and 1560) brought down to the beginning of the tenth book. Their labour earned them the applause of their contemporaries although the mechanical halting fourteeners were hardly worthy of the model set by Gavin Douglas in his translation of the second and fourth books in 1513. Between 1559 and 1561 Jasper Heywood had translated three of Seneca's tragedies, and the whole of Seneca had been rendered into English by 1580. In 1582 Stanyhurst's translation of the first four books of the *Aeneid*,—a remarkable work—was published to show the virtue of non-rhyming classical metres as compared to the English fashion of rhyming. The *Andria* of

Terence had been translated before 1530. Later in the century we have such noble work as that of Lord North in his translation of Plutarch, and that of Chapman, whose translation of Homer has brought him fame made doubly secure by the admiration of Keats. In the work of translating *Cæsar's Commentaries* Golding had been anticipated by John Brend who had proceeded as far as the middle of the fifth book; this translation was put into Golding's hands, and he continued the work from the point at which Brend had concluded. Later he translated afresh the earlier part for the sake of uniformity. The volume was published by William Seres in 1565,[1] and the dedication to Cecil on October 12th of that year is dated from the family seat in Essex—Belchamp St. Paul. In this connection we should perhaps notice the one other partial translation of *Cæsar's Commentaries* which had been made prior to this time, viz. *Cæsar's Commentaryes newly translated owte of latin in to Englyshe as much as concerneth thys Realme of England sumtyme callyd Brytayne.* The translation which is ascribed to that " Italianate Englishman," John Tiptoft, Earl of Worcester, who was the first classical scholar of the English Renaissance, was published by Rastall about 1530. Tiptoft is also credited with a translation of the *De Amicitia* of Cicero. [2]

Golding's *magnum opus*, the work with which his name was to be associated by succeeding generations, was his translation of Ovid's *Metamorphoses*, the first four books of which he published in 1565—the same year in which he published his translation of Cæsar. The volume was printed by William Seres, is dedicated to " his singular good Lorde Robert Earle of Leycester, etc.," and is dated from Cecil House. In 1567 appeared the complete translation of the fifteen books which was also printed by Seres and dedicated to Leicester.[3]

Golding was not the first Englishman to attempt the translation of part of Ovid into English. Caxton had turned into

---

[1] Joseph Ames, *Typographical Antiquities* (London, 1749), p. 249.

[2] Lowndes, *Bibliographer's Manual.* V. also Einstein, *The Italian Renaissance in England*, p. 25.

[3] Edited by W. H. D. Rouse and published by the De La More Press, London, 1904. The introduction quotes in full Golding's dedication to the first four books which were printed in 1565.

English prose the last five books of the *Metamorphoses*,[1] but
the work does not seem to have been printed until 1819, when
it appeared in quarto form—from a MS. in the Pepysian
collection (No. 2124) at Cambridge, and was presented to the
members of the Roxburghe Club by George Hibbert, Esq. [2]
A black letter quarto, published by Wynkin de Worde in 1513,
contained *The Flores of Ovide de Arte Amandi, with theyr Eng-
lysshe afore them*.[3]    In 1560 appeared *The Fable of Ovid treating
of Narcissus, translated out of Latin into Englysh Mytre, with
a Moral therevnto, very pleasante to rede*, printed by Thomas
Hackette in quarto form.   At the end is the signature: "Quod
T. H.," which Ritson confidently interprets as Thomas Howell. [4]
In 1565, the year in which Golding's edition of the first four
books appeared, Thomas Peend or De La Peend published *The
Pleasant Fable of Hermaphroditus and Salmacis*, London, 8vo.,
from the fourth book of the *Metamorphoses*.   The volume was
printed by Thos. Colwell, and in the preface the author asserts
that " he had translated a great part of the *Metamorphosis,*
intending to complete a version of *Ovid*, but was led to relin-
quish his design on finding that Golding was engaged on the
same undertaking."[5]  Before the end of the century practically
all of Ovid's works had been translated into English : Turberville's *Heroides* appeared in 1567 ;  Underdowne's *Ibis* in
1569 ;  Churchyard's *Tristia* in 1580 ;  Marlowe's *Elegies* and
the *Amores* in 1597, and Browne's *Remedie of Love* in 1599.

Golding's work was immediately recognized by his contemporaries as a notable piece of translation, as is evidenced by
the many commendations it called forth ;  its popularity is
attested by its frequent re-publication, in 1575, 1576, 1584,
1587, 1593 (by two different publishers), 1603, 1612, and 1675.
Until the appearance of Sandys' version in 1626 (he had published the first five books before 1621) the pre-eminence of
Golding's translation was not disputed.  Shakespeare was

---

[1] Not the whole work, however, as Mr. Rouse seems to state.  V.*op. cit.*,
p. ii.

[2] Lowndes, *op. cit.*

[3] *Ibid.*   [4] *Ibid.*

[5] Corser's *Collectanea Anglo-Poetica*.   (Chetham Society, vol. ci, pp.
9-17.)

well acquainted with Ovid through this medium, [1] and to his familiarity with it is due a very large proportion of his mythological references, a fact which would have secured its modern publication as a part of " Shakespeare's Library," one would have supposed, before the year 1904. It may be of interest here to notice some of the many sixteenth century encomiums that were pronounced upon Golding's work. In 1566—before the publication of the complete translation—a certain T. B. in a poem prefixed to John Studley's English version of Seneca's *Agamemnon*, ranks Richard Edwards, a contributor to *The Paradise of Dainty Devices*, with Phaer, Jasper Heywood, Googe and other translators of the period, but especially with Golding :

" With him also, as seemeth me,
Our Edwards may compare ;
Wno nothing gyuing place to him
Doth syt in egall chayre."[2]

and again

" Nor *Goldinge* can haue lesse renoume,
Whych *Ouid* dyd translate ;
And by the thondryng of hys verse
Hath set in chayre of state."[3]

In 1577 Thomas Blener Hasset in the Induction to his *Complaint of Cadwallader* in his *Second Part of the Mirror for Magistrates* laments the contemporary use of rhyme, and holds it responsible for the fact that there is a great difference between the work of the modern translator and that of his original—" betwixt Buchurst and Homer ; betwixt Phaer and Virgill ; betwixt Turberville and Tibullus ; betwixt Golding and Ovid ; betwixt George Gascon and Seneca." [4] Abraham Fleming in the list affixed to his *Bright burning Beacon forwarning all wise Virgins to trim their lampes against the comming of the Bridegroome,*—a tract on the earthquake of

---

[1] V. an interesting note in Rouse's introduction on an Aldine Ovid (1502) now in the Bodleian, which may possibly have belonged to Shakespeare (p. ii).

[2] Warton's *History of English Poetry*, ed. W. C. Hazlitt, vol. iv, p. 217.

[3] *Ibid*, vol. iv, p. 275.

[4] Quoted by Schelling in *Poetic and Verse Criticism of the Reign of Elizabeth*, p. 24.

1580—mentions Golding as one of the six "noted poets" who had written on the same subject.[1] Arthur Hall, in the dedication to his translation of Homer's *Iliad* (1581) commends Golding's English version which he considers the equal of its original.[2] Some passages from Golding's epistle to the Earl of Leicester prefaced to the complete translation of Ovid in 1567 were paraphrased by Peele in his *The Arraignment of Paris* (1584) as Mr. Dyce has pointed out.[3] Webbe, in his *Discourse of English Poetrie* (1586), says : " Equally with him [Phaer] may I well adioyne Master Arthur Golding, for hys labour in englishing *Ouids Metamorphosis*, for which Gentleman, surely our Country hath for many respects greatly to gyue God thankes : as far him which hath taken infinite paynes without ceasing, trauelleth as yet indefatigably, and is addicted without society, by his continuall laboure, to profit this nation and speeche in all kind of good learning."[4] And after giving a number of extracts from Phaer's translation of Virgil he continues : " And in trueth the like comparisons, may you choose out through the whole translations of the Metamorphosis by Master Golding who (considering both their Coppyes) hath equally deserued commendations for the beautifying of the English speeche."[5] Puttenham's praise is no less pronounced in his *Arte of English Poesie* (1589): " Since him [Phaer] followed Maister Arthure Golding, who with no lesse commendation turned into English meetre the Metamorphosis of *Ouide*,"[6] and again he commends " *Phaer* and *Golding* for a learned and well corrected verse, specially in translation cleare and very faithfully answering their authours intent."[7] In the same year (1589) appeared Greene's *Menaphon*, and in the prefatory address " To the Gentlemen Students of both Universities " Nash has the following reference to Golding : " And in this page of praise, I cannot omit aged

---

[1] Collier's *Poetical Decameron*, i, p. 117.
[2] *Dictionary of National Biography*, s.v. Hall.
[3] *The Works of Peele*, ed. Bullen, vol. i, p. 18, note 4.
[4] *Arte of English Poesie*, ed. Haslewood, vol. ii, p. 35.
[5] *Ibid.*, p. 50.
[6] *Ibid.*, vol. i, p. 49.
[7] *Ibid.*, vol. i, p. 51.

Arthur Golding, for his industrious toile in Englishing *Ouids Metamorphosis* besides manie other exquisite editions of Diuinitie, turned by him out of the French tongue into our own."[1]  In 1591 Sir John Harington in his *Apologie of Poetrie*, prefixed to his translation of *Orlando Furioso*, quotes Golding's work approvingly,[2] and Meres in his *Palladis Tamia* (1598) names Golding among those who " for their learned translations are of good note among vs."[3]   The author of *The First Booke of the Preservation of King Henry VII.*, published in 1599, " confesses and acknowledges that we have many excellent and singular good poets in this our age, as Maister Spenser, that was, Maister Gowlding, Doctor Phayer, etc."[4]   There is therefore abundant evidence that Golding's labours were not unappreciated by his contemporaries.

By far the greater part of our information regarding Golding's life is derived from the dedication of his numerous works, and does not usually extend further than to enable us to state that on a certain date Golding was at a certain place.  We have already noticed that he lived at Cecil-house in the Strand during 1563, 1564 and 1565, and that on October 12, 1565, he was at Belchamp St. Paul.  From here he dedicated to Cecil his *Caesar's Commentaries* and the first edition of the *Metamorphoses* on the same date.  Two years later he was at Berwick, for his dedication to Leicester of the completed translation of the *Metamorphoses* is signed, " At Barwicke the xx. of Aprill, 1567."[5]  On October 12, 1569, he was in London, and on March 10 and March 31, 1570, he was at Belchamp St. Paul, from which place he dedicated to Sir Walter Mildmay his translation of *A Postil or Orderly Disposing of Certeine Epistles*, etc., by David Chytraeus.  Golding was again in London on June 12, 1572,[6] and then we lose sight of him for three years, although translations from his pen continued to appear in

---

1 Greene's *Works*, ed. Grosart, vol. vi, p. 20.

2 Haslewood, *op. cit.*, vol. ii, p. 123.

3 *Ibid.*, vol. ii, p. 156.

4 Quoted by Arber in his preface to Stanyhurst's *Æneis*, pp. xx and xxi

5 This epistle is in 'fourteeners' and extends to 616 lines.

6 The translation of Beza's *A bryefe and necessary Catechisme* is dedicated to Henry, Earl of Huntingdon, and the prefatory letter signed by Arthur Golding concludes : "Written at London the 12 of June, 1572."

London. The title-page of his translation of Beza's *Le Sacrifice d'Abraham* informs us that it was " Finished at Pouules Belchamp in Essex, the XI. of August, 1575." Warton thinks that he contributed some verses to the entertainment at Kenilworth in that year, but he bases this opinion only on the strength of Gascoigne's statement that certain verses were written by " Master Goldingham,"—a not uncommon name at that time. On January 6, 1576, Golding was living at Clare in Suffolk.

Between 1576 and 1585 Golding must have spent a great part of his time in Essex, for he was becoming a great landed proprietor chiefly owing to the death of his brothers Henry and George. Morant's *Essex* furnishes us with detailed information regarding Golding's life in this capacity. His brother Henry had become possessed of the manor of East Thorp, part of which he had purchased from Robert Waldgrave on May 6, 1564, and the remainder, together with the advowson of the church, from John Bacon on October 7, 1576 (Lett. pat. 6. 12 Eliz.). " He dyed 6 Decemb. 1576, seized not only of his maner, but also of Oldholt tenement, and several lands and tenements in Birch and Messing. Arthur his brother and next heir, then aged 40 succeeded him (Inquis. 19 Eliz. Feb. 7)."[1] Golding seems to have intended to dispose of this property almost immediately : " On the 20th of Novemb. (1577?) he procured a license to alienate this whole estate to Richard Atkins, Gent. and Elianore his wife (Book of Alienat.)" As we shall see however, he was still possessed of East Thorp in 1585. Other lands inherited from this same brother he kept in his possession till 1591 : " Besides which [Little Birch and East Thorp] he [Henry Golding] had in this parish Cocks woods; Cocks lands, and Oldholt tenement ; a messuage called Moothes containing 50 acres ; a tenement and two crofts called Wasselings ; and a moiety of messuages and lands called Garlands and Ives crofts, alias Derby lands. (Inquis. 19 Eliz. and 16 Vaco.) His brother Arthur Golding succeeded him, and presented to the rectory 19 May, 1591 (Inquis. 19 Eliz.). Alice Golding widow, paid Ward silver for this maner in the

---

[1] Morant's *Essex*, vol. ii, p. 180—Lexden Hundred.

23rd. Eliz., 1581 (Rot. Curiæ Hund. de Lexden). Of Golding it was purchased by John, Lord Peter."[1] Arthur Golding's relations with this sister-in-law seem to have been far from pleasant, as is evidenced by the following extract from Hunter's manuscript : " There is a bill in the Exchequer 14 Feb., 1585, to Lord Burghley from his daily orator Arthur Golding— Whereas his late brother Henry Golding Esq., deceased left him in present possession only the manor of East Thorpe which was encumbered, & gave the manor of Little Biral [Birch?] with other lands to Alice his wife, with a clause prohibiting said Arthur from molesting her ;—and whereas one Robert Crispe a very troublesome and unquiet person marrying one Mary Waldegrave daughter of the said Alice & wife of one Robert Waldegrave, Esq. yet alive and undivorced, under colour of that unlawful marriage obtained of the said Alice a lease of the said Henry Goldings chief mansion house & has committed waste and spoil—He prays that he may proceed against Crispe without incurring the penalty of his brothers will."[2] What would seem to be a reference to the same difficulty occurs in the ' Proceedings in Chancery ' of Queen Elizabeth's reign in a suit in which Arthur Golding is plaintiff and Robert Cryspe defendant. The entry refers to a document which is " only an answer " and which " respects a lease granted to one Anne [Alice?] Goldinge, but of what lands or where situated does not appear."[3]

From his brother George, Arthur Golding also inherited property. On March 7th, 1580, he bought from him and Mary his wife the manor of Nether-hall, Gestingthorp, but sold it on March 2, 1585, to John Coo or Coe.[4] In the meantime George Golding had died (November 24, 1584) and Arthur inherited from him the manors of Waltons and Nether-hall, and of Jackletts, Fanbridge and Amys land, all of which he sold on March 1, 1595, to Thomas Mildmay, Esq., eldest son of William

---

1 Morant, *op. cit.*, vol. ii, p. 184—Lexden Hundred.

2 *Chorus Vatum.*

3 *Calendars of the Proceedings in Chancery—Queen Elizabeth*, vol. i. G, g, 13, p. 379.

4 Morant, *op. cit.*, vol. ii, p. 307—Hinckford Hundred.

Mildmay, of Springfield Barnes, Esq. [1] This bequest, also, seems to have involved Golding in Chancery proceedings. A certain Arthur Kempe appears as plaintiff against " Anthony Golding, esquire, and Mary Golding, widow " in a suit the object of which was " to protect plaintiff's title under an assignment of lease." The " premisses " are set forth as follows : " The manor of Waltons in Purley demised by the Earl of Oxford to George Golding deceased, who assigned the lease to plaintiff, and afterwards purchased the inheritance of the Earl."[2] The Anthony Golding here referred to must surely be Arthur Golding.

That Golding spent a considerable portion of these years in Essex looking after his property interests we may be sure, and the demand which they made on his time and attention is probably reflected in the fact that after 1577 his translations become much less numerous. In that year he had a house in the parish of All-hallows on the Wall, from which place he dedicated to Sir Christopher Hatton his translation of Seneca's *De Beneficiis* on March 17, 1577-8, and we may assume that he spent many years partly in London, partly in Essex. His *Discourse upon the Earthquake* (1580), which is his only original prose work, inveighs strongly against the profanation of the Sabbath which " is spent full heathenishly in taverning, tipling, gaming, playing and beholding of Beare-baytings and stage-playes," and the invective sounds like that of a man who was familiar with the London life of the period. Indeed we may safely conclude that at this time Golding was one of the most widely known literary men in London. We have already seen that he received the warmest praise from many contemporary writers, and although he was an ardent Puritan he numbered among his patrons the most famous statesmen and noblemen of his day. The list includes Sir William Cecil (Lord Burleigh), the Earl of Leicester, the Earl of Oxford, Sir Walter Mildmay, the Earl of Huntingdon, the Earl of Essex, Sir William Drewrie, Sir Thomas Bromley, Sir Christopher Hatton, Lord Cobham and the Archbishop of Canterbury.

---

[1] *Ibid.*, vol. i, p. 346—Dengey Hundred.
[2] *Calendars of the Proceedings in Chancery—Queen Elizabeth.* K. k. 4, vol. ii, p. 124.

Sir Philip Sidney evidently looked upon him as a worthy craftsman.[1] Sidney had begun a translation of his friend De Mornay's treatise *A woorke concerning the trewnesse of the Christian religion*, and just before leaving England for the fatal field of Zutphen, he requested Golding to complete the work ; Golding accepted the task and published the book a few months after Sidney's death. A writer in *Notes and Queries* has added to the scanty details of Golding's life the fact that he was a member of the Elizabethan Society of Antiquaries : " I have a copy of Weever's *Ancient Funerall Monuments* which once belonged to William Burton, the historian of Leicestershire; on a fly-leaf at the end of the volume is the following list in the autograph of that celebrated antiquary, etc."[2] The list is entitled : " Antiquarii temp. Eliz. Reg." and the twenty-first name is that of ' Arthur Golding.'

Evil days seem to have come upon Golding after 1595, in which year as we have already seen he disposed of the last of his property in Essex. In dedicating to Lord Cobham, the Warden of the Cinque Ports, his translation of Jaques Hurault's *Politicke, Moral, and Martial Discourses*, he refers in the opening sentence to the troubles he has suffered : " Forasmuch as being unknowne to your good Lordship, otherwise than by report, yet notwithstanding I have tasted of your goodness and favour, to my great comfort in my troubles, of the which when God wil I hope I shall be well discharged." This epistle, which contains a long patriotic exposition of the blessings of England and the virtues of the Queen, is dated January 27, 1595.[3] We have a rather ambiguous reference to Golding in Dr. Dee's *Diary* under date of September 30th, 1597 : " John Crockar, my good servant, had leave to go and see his parents. He went with Barthilmew Hikman and Robert Charles toward Branbroke, with Arthur Golding to cure of his fistula. John Crocker intendeth to return about Easter or at Whitsuntide next. God be his spede."[4] What-

---

1 Mr. Sidney Lee and Mr. Rouse say that he was a friend of Sidney, but I have found no evidence of the fact. V. *Dict. Nat. Biog.*, s.v. 'Golding,' and the reprint of the *Metamorphoses* (1904) p. vi.

2 *Notes and Queries*, Series I, vol. v, p. 365.

3 A copy is in the Bodleian Library.

4 *Dr. Dee's Diary*, Camden Society, p. 60.

ever be the meaning of the note it can hardly be that Dr. Dee undertook to cure Golding, as Mr. Lee interprets it,[1] and of course it is quite possible that the reference is to another Arthur Golding altogether. Until 1605 we have no further knowledge of Golding's movements. In that year he addressed to the Privy Council a petition which suggests that the demand for his works had made the copyright valuable : "In consequence of a petition addressed by Mr. Golding to the Privy Council of James I., that monarch made order that the Archbishop of Canterbury and the Attorney-General should take into consideration the matters referred to in the petition, and grant to Mr. Golding the sole right of printing such books of his as they might consider meet for the benefit of the church and common-wealth, and that the Attorney-General should draw a book ready for his majesty's signature containing the grant thereof to the petitioner, a blank being left for the number of years, to be filled up according to his majesty's pleasure. This order is dated 25 July, 1605, after which time we can find no trace of him.[2] The year of Golding's death is not known.[3] Cooper says that he married the widow of George Forster, but we do not know whether he left any family nor where he was buried.

Considering the multiplicity of dates which have been given above it is remarkable how little we really know about Golding as a man. Almost all of his books were translations which of course reveal little or nothing regarding his personality, although the fact that he busied himself chiefly with translating the works of the French reformers proves that he was a zealous upholder of the English Puritan cause, and an admirer of the great representatives of the Huguenots in France—Calvin, Beza, Coligny, etc. In his *Discourse on the Earthquake*, as we have seen, he voices one of the chief complaints of the Puritanism of his time, and his prefaces and dedications bear witness to his earnest piety and zeal. Compare for instance, the

---

[1] V. *Dict. Nat. Biog.*, s.v. 'Golding.'

[2] Cooper's *Athenæ Cantabrigienses*, vol. ii, p. 431.

[3] Professor Courthope gives no authority for his statement that Golding died in 1606 (*Hist. Eng. Poet.*, vol. ii, p. 140). W. Davenport Adams in his *Dictionary of the Drama* (1904) says that he died in 1570 !

following extract from his preface to the translation of De Mornay[1] : " If any Atheist, Infidel, or Jew, having read this work with advisement, shall yet denye the Christian religion to be the true and only path-way to eternall felicitie, and all other religions to be mere vanitie and wickednesse, he must needes shew himself to be either utterly voyd even of human sence, or els obstinatly or wilfully to impugn the manifest trueth against the continuall testimonie of his owne conscience."[2]   At the same time Golding did not antagonize even such a bitter partisan as Nash, from which circumstance we may conclude that his Puritanism was not of the kind that was given to controversy.   Indeed his wide learning, his interest in classic literature, and his patriotic enthusiasm over the improvement or vindication of " verse or prose in English," as expressed in his commendatory stanzas prefixed to Baret's *Alvearie*, would not lead us to expect to find him serving among the followers of Martin Mar-prelate.   These stanzas— Golding's only original work in poetical form except the dedicatory epistles—have never been reprinted as far as I am aware, and may perhaps rightly claim a place here :

*Arthur Golding to the Reader.*

The plesant iuice that Prime of yeere doth yeeld
In herbe, in flower, in leafe, in plant, or tree,
By natures gift abroad in frith and feeld,
Or mans deuice in gardens not so free
As faire and finelie kept, the busie Bee
    With restlesse trauell gathereth to his Hyue,
    To how great use, they knowe that knowe to thryue.

And *Barret* here (good Reader) doth present
A Hyue of honie to thy gentle hand,
By tract of time in painefull labor spent :
Well wrought, and brought to such perfection and
Good purpose, as (if truth be rightly scand)
    Thou art to blame, but if thou be his detter
    Of earned thankes, and fare by him the better.

---

1 Quoted in Zouch's *Memoirs of Sir Philip Sidney* (York, 1808, p. 368, note).
    2 "Post Calvinum et Bezam nullus theologorum tam bene scripsit ut Mornaeus." *Scaligerana*.

How fit the Tytle of this present Booke
Doth hit the matter written in the same,
Thou shalt perceiue the better if thou looke
Throughout the worke, which well doth brooke his name.
For underneath this Hiue yet small in fame,
    Of fower Tungs the flowers hyued bee,
    In one sweete iuice to serue the turne of thee.

Of truth, the skill and labour was not small
To set ech Inglish Phraze in his due place,
And for to match the Latin therewithall,
Of either Language keeping still the grace,
And orderly the Greeke to interlace,
    And last of all to ioyne the French theretoo :
    These things (I saie) requyrde no small adoo.

And furthermore right well thou mayst espie,
There lakt in him no forewardnesse of minde
To haue set downe a sownd Orthographie :
Through want whereof all good inditers find
Our Inglishe tung driuen almost out of kind,
    Dismembred, hacked, maymed, rent, and torne,
    Defaced, patched, mard, and made a skorne.

For who is he that rightly can discerne
The case, the kind, and number of the Nowne ?
For my instruction gladly I would lerne,
How men might trie what writer setteth downe
The Article aright, or who doth drowne
    The Pronowne by misplacing it, as now
    Most wryters doe, and yet they marke not how.

I thinke it would a good Gramarian poze
To giue iust rules of Deriuation,
And Composition, as our writing goes.
And yet no tung of other Nation
Hath either greater grace or store of those,
    Than Inglish hath :  yee would not thinke ywis
    How rich in Composition Inglishe is.

Moreouer, how shall men directly find
The Conjugation, Number, Person, Tence,
And mode of Verbes togither in their kind?
What man I praie can stand in iust defence
Of due Construction both of wordes and sence ?
     And if to Verse men further will proceede,
     Which yeeldes lesse skope and asketh greater heede:

How shall a man assure true quantitie
Of time or tune ?   Or if he would expresse
The diffrence, and the natiue propertie,
Of brode North speech and Sowthren smoothednesse :
How might he set it downe with cumlinesse,
     Where men in writing doe so fondly dote,
     As nought is done by rule, but all by rote ?

But were there once a sound Orthographie
Set out by learning and aduised skill,
(Which certesse might be done full easilie)
And then confirmed by the Souereines will,
(For else would blind and cankred custome still
     His former errors wilfully maintaine
     And bring us to his *Chaos* backe againe :)

No doubt but men should shortly find there is
As perfect order, as firme certeintie,
As grounded rules to trie out things amisse,
As much sweete grace, as great varietie
Of wordes and phrazes, as good quantitie
     For verse or prose in Inglish euery waie,
     As any comen Language hath this daie.

And were wee giuen as well to like our owne,
And for two clense it from the noisome weede
Of affectation which hath ouergrowne
Ungraciously the good and natiue seede,
As for to borrowe where wee have no neede :
     It would pricke neere the learned tungs in strength,
     Perchaunce and match mee some of them at length.

Wherefore good Reader yeeld thy furtherance
To mend the things that yet are out of square,
Thou hast a help thy purpose to aduaunce,
And meane to ease thy greatest peece of care.
And he that hath done this for thy welfare,
  Upon thy freendely fauor and regard,
  May chaunce to trauell further afterward.

               *Finis.*

  It is difficult for us to reconcile the facts that Go`d-
ing was an ardent Puritan and that he was also the translator of Ovid's *Metamorphoses.* The compromising nature
of his task seems to have troubled him somewhat, for the long
introductory epistle to Leicester, in the main an analysis and
moral interpretation of Ovid, is also an attempted justification
of the translator's work. After declaring in the self-lauding
fashion of the time that as a result of his labour he expects
"with eternal fame above the stars to mount" he proceeds to
unfold the hidden significance of Ovid's tales throughout each
of the fifteen books :

  "As for example in the tales of Daphne turn'd to Bay
   A mirror of virginity appear unto us may."
Let no man marvel that he ascribes to the one and only God
what the ancients ascribed to many. He is strongly inclined
to agree with those who hold that the ancients " took their
first occasion of these things from Holy Writ," and he draws
an elaborate parallel between the account of creation as given
in *Genesis* and that given by Ovid. To justify " the vices
in this present work, in lively colours penn'd " gives the author
greater trouble, and he offers the unconvincing and conventional defense which contemporary playwrights were offering
to Golding's co-religionists :

  "For sure these fables are not put in writing to th'intent
   To further or allure to vice : but rather this is meant,
   That men beholding what they be when vice doth
    reign instead
   Of virtue, should not let their lewd affections have
    the head."

To accomplish this moral purpose is his chief aim in the work,
—not " wreaths of bays, nor name of Poet, no, nor meed."
" But why seem I these doubts to cast ?" he continues, as
though not more than half convinced himself, and he concludes with declaring that if any cull evil instead of good from
his pages " the fault is theirs, not mine, they must confess."
The address " To the Reader " betrays the same uneasiness,
and the author beseeches those who read to " take these works
as fragrant flowers," warning them at the same time that the
spider may convert the essence of flowers into poison.  The
same idea seems to have been in his mind when he wrote the
motto for the title-page :

"With skill, heede, and judgement, this worke must be read,
For else to the Reader it standes in small stead."

Golding was endowed with a considerable degree of real
literary ability.  The " fourteener " is not a measure calculated to impress favorably a modern ear, but there are many
passages in the *Metamorphoses* of which the spirited movement
and the author's enthusiastic identification of himself with
his subject make the reader forget that the work is not original
composition.  On the other hand it is inevitable in so long a
piece of translation that there should be passages which are
suggestive of hack-work; occasionally the metre is halting and
awkward, the rhyme forced, and the translation devoid of charm.
We may accept as just Meres' assignment to Golding of a
position among those who "for their learned translations
are of good note among us."  Warton's estimate needs
no modification :  " His style  is  poetical  and  spirited,
and his versification clear : his manner ornamental and
diffuse yet with a sufficient observance of the original."[1]
Mr. Sidney Lee says that "it is full of life throughout,
and at time reaches a high poetic level."[2]  The *Tragedie
of Abraham's Sacrifice* is an unusually successful piece of
translation, in which the author's happy rendering of the lyrics
is equalled by his skill in preserving the simple effectiveness
of the pathetic and tragic passages.  We may agree with War-

---

[1] *Hist. Eng. Poet.*, ed. Hazlitt, iv. 283.
[2] *Dict. Nat. Biog.*

ton in regretting that Golding gave so much of his time to
translation, for one cannot but feel that the translator of
Beza's play might have added something of permanent worth
to the poetry of the Elizabethan age, had he devoted his
original poetic genius to subjects more promising than the
praise of a dictionary and the orthography and grammar of
English speech.

The following list of Golding's works I have compiled from
Hunter's MS. notes, Lowndes' *Bibliographer's Manual*, Coop-
er's *Athenae Cantabrigienses*, the Catalogues of the British
Museum and Bodleian Libraries, and Mr. Sidney Lee's article on
Golding in the *Dictionary of National Biography* :

1. A briefe treatise concerning the burnynge of Bucer and
Phagius at Cambrydge in the tyme of Quene Mary, with theyr
restitution in the time of our most gracious soverayne Lady
that nowe is, etc. [An anti-Popish pamphlet translated from
the Latin, London, 16mo., 1562.]

2. The history of Leonard Aretine, concerning the warres
betweene the Imperialls & the Gothes for the possession of
Italy. A worke very pleasant & profitable. Translated out
of Latin into English. [Dedicated to Sir William Cecil and
printed by Rowland Hall, London, 16mo., 1563.]

3. Thabridgemente of the Histories of Trogus Pompeius,
gathered & written in the Laten tung, by the famous Historio-
grapher Justine, etc. [Dedicated to Edward de Vere, Earl
of Oxford, and printed by Thomas Marsh, 4to., 1564 ; "newlie
conferred with the Latin copye, and corrected by the Translator," London, 4to., 1570, 1578.]

4. The eyght bookes of Caius Iulius Cæsar conteyning his
martiall exploytes in the Realme of Gallia and the Countries
bordering vpon the same, etc. [Dedicated to Sir William
Cecil from Belchamp St. Paul on October 12, 1565 ; published
at London, 8vo., 1565, 1590.]

5. The Fyrst Fower Bookes of P. Ouidius Nasos Worke,
intitled Metamorphosis, translated oute of Latin into Englishe
meter. [Dedicated to Robert, Earl of Leicester, from Cecil-
house, December 23, 1564 ; published by Willyam Seres,
London, 4to., 1565.]

6. The **xv.** Bookes of P. Ouidius Naso, entytuled Metamorphosis, translated oute of Latin into English meteer. [Dedicated to Robert, Earl of Leicester, from Barwicke, the **xx.** of Aprill, 1567 ; printed by Willyam Seres, London, 4to., 1567. Reprinted in 1575, 1576, 1584, 1587, 1593 (by two different publishers), 1603, 1612.]

7. John Caluin his Treatise concerning offences, whereby at this day diuers are feared, & many also are quite withdrawen from the pure doctrine of the Gospell............ transl. out of Latine. [London, 8vo., 1567.]

8. A Postill, or Expositions of the Gospels read in the Churches of God on Sundayes & feast days of Saincts. Written by Nich. Heminge. [Dedicated to Sir Walter Mildmay, and printed in London, 4to., 1569, 1574, 1577, 1579.]

9. A Postil or Orderly Disposing of certeine Epistles vsually red in the Church of God vppon the Sundayes & Holydayes throughout the whole yeere. Written in Latin by Dauid Chytræus. [Dedicated to Sir Walter Mildmay, from ' Powle Belchamp,' on March 31, 1570 ; and printed in London, 4to., 1570, 1577.]

10. The Psalmes of Dauid and others. With M. John Caluins Commentaries. [Dedicated to Edward de Vere, Earl of Oxford, and printed in London, 4to., 1571, 1576. A copy of the first edition is in the Newberry library, Chicago. The dedication is strongly antipapal.]

11. A Booke of Christian Question and Answers. Wherein are set forth the cheef points of the Christian religion in manner of an abridgement. ........ Written in Latin by the lerned clarke Theodore Beza Vezelius. [Dedicated to Henry, Earl of Huntingdon, and printed in London, 8vo., 1572, 1577, 1578, 1586. The volume contains 90 leaves besides the dedication.]

12. A Confutation of the Popes Bull which was published more than two yeres agoe against Elizabeth the most gracious queene of England, Fraunce and Ireland, and against the noble Realme of England. ........ By Henry Bullenger the Elder. [A translation from the Latin, printed in London, 4to., 1572.]

13. Sermons of M. John Caluine vpon the Epistle of Saincte Paule to the Galathians. [Dedicated to Sir William Cecil, Lord Burghley, and printed in London, 4to., 1574 and n. d. The sermons occupy 329 leaves.]

14. Sermons by M. John Calvin vpon the Booke of Job. Translated out of French. [Dedicated to Robert, Earl of Essex, and printed in London, fol. 1574, 1580, 1584. Lowndes says it is dedicated to Leicester, and that it contains 159 sermons on 751 pages, double columns.]

15. A Catholike Exposition vpon the Reuelation of Sainct John. Collected by M. Augustine Marlorate, out of diuers notable Writers whose names ye shal find in the page following. [Dedicated to Sir Walter Mildmay, and printed in London, 4to., 1574.]

16. A Justification or Cleering of the Prince of Orange, etc. [Printed in London, 1575.]

17. The Warfare of Christians : Concerning the conflict againts the Fleshe, the World, and the Deuill. Translated out of Latine. [Dedicated to Sir William Drewrie, and printed in London, 8vo., 1576.]

18. The Lyfe of the most godly valeant and noble capteine & maintener of the trew Christian Religion in Fraunce, Jasper Colignie Shatilion sometyme greate Admirall of Fraunce. Translated out of Latin. [Printed in London, 8vo., 1576.]

19. An Edict, or Proclamation set forthe by the Frenche Kinge vpon the Pacifying of the Troubles in Fraunce, with the Articles of the same Pacification : Read and published in the presence of the sayd King, sitting in his Parliament, the xiiij. day of May, 1576. Translated out of Frenche. [Printed in London, 16mo., 1576.]

20. The Sermons of M. John Caluin vpon the Epistle of S. Paule too the Ephesians. [Dedicated to Edmund Grindal, Archbishop of Canterbury, and printed in London, 4to., 1577. The sermons occupy 347 leaves.]

21. A Tragedie of Abraham's Sacrifice. Written in french by *Theodore Beza*. . . . . . . . . Finished at Pouules Belchamp in Essex, the xi. of August, 1575. ['Imprinted at London, by Thomas Vantroullier, dwelling in the Blacke Friers,' 1577.]

22. The woorke of the excellent Philosopher Lucius Annæus Seneca concerning Benefyting........ Translated out of Latin. [Dedicated to Sir Christopher Hatton from Golding's house in the parish of All-Hallows-on-the-Wall, London, 17 March, 1577-8, and printed in London, 4to., 1578.]

23. A discourse vpon the Earthquake that hapned throughe this realme of England and other places of Christendom, the sixt of Aprill, 1580. [Printed in London by Henry Binneman, 16mo., 1580.]

24. The ioyful and royal entertainment of the ryght high and mightie prince, Francis the Frenche Kings only brother, Duke of Brabande. ...... into his noble citie of Antwerpe. tr. out of Frenche by A. Golding. [Printed in London for William Ponsonby, 1582, 8vo. The author writes the account because "an Historie is the Schoolemistresse of mans life." A copy is in the Bodleian.]

25. The Sermons of M. John Caluin vpon the fifth booke of Moses, called Deuteronomie : Faithfully gathered word for word as he preached them in open Pulpet. ........ Translated out of French. [Dedicated to Sir Thomas Bromley, and printed in London, fol. 1583. There are 200 sermons occupying 1247 pages in double columns.]

26. The Rare and Singuler worke of Pomponius Mela, That excellent and worthy Cosmographer, of the situation of the world. ...... with the Longitude and Latitude of euerie Kingdome, Regent, Prouince, Riuers, Mountaines, Citties and Countries. [Dedicated to Sir William Cecil, Lord Burghley, on Feb. 6, 1584-5, and printed in London, 4to., 1585.]

27. The Excellent and Pleasant Worke of Iulius Solinus Polyhistor. Contayning the noble actions of humaine creatures, the secretes & prouidence of nature ........ with many maruailous things and strange antiquities ........ Translated out of Latin. [Printed in London, 4to., 1587 ; re-issued with Pomponius Mela in 1590. A copy of the 1587 edition is in the Newberry Library, Chicago.]

28. A woorke concerning the trewnesse of the Christian Religion, written in French ; Against Atheists, Epicures Paynims, Iewes, Mahumetists, &c. By Philip of Mornay,

Lord of Plessie Marlie. Begunne to be translated by sir Philip Sidney, knight, and at his request finished by Arth. Golding. [Dedicated to Robert, Earl of Leicester, and printed in London, 4to., 1587, 1589, 1592, 1604 (revised and corrected by Thomas Wilcocks). With additional corrections, 1617, V. Fox Bourne, *Sir Philip Sidney*, pp. 407-11, and *Censura Literaria*, II, 175.]

29. Politicke, Moral and Martial Discourses. Written in French by M. Iaques Hurault. [Dedicated to William, Lord Cobham, warden of the cinque ports, and published in London, 4to., 1595.]

30. An exhortation to england to Repent, made in Latin by master doctor haddon, in the greate sweate, 1551 ; and translated by master arthur golding. [Harl. MS. 425, leaves 73, 74. Printed by F. J. Furnivall in *Ballads from Manuscripts*, The Ballad Society, vol. I., pp. 321-330, 1871. There is no evidence as to the date of the translation, but the forced rhymes and awkward metre suggest that it must have been an early work.]

31. A Godly and Fruteful Prayer, with an Epistle to ..... John [Aylmer] bishop of London, from the Latin of Abraham Fleming. [London, n. d.]

The Benefit that Christians receyue by Iesus Christ & him Crucified. Translated out of French into English by A. G., London, 8 vo., 1573 and n. d. [Hunter and Cooper ascribe this work to Golding ; Mr. Lee is sceptical. The initials A. G. frequently stand on the title-pages of the works of Anthony Gilby, also a translator of Beza and Calvin. He is the author of "Calvin's Commentary on Daniel," London, 1570, and 'The Testamentes of the Twelue Patriarches,' from the Latin of Robert Grosseteste, London, 1581 ; both of these works are credited to Golding by Cooper (Lowndes agrees regarding the first), but are rejected by Mr. Lee.]

'An Abridgment of the Chronicle of Sir John Frossard Chanon of ........ written in Latin by John Sleydane ' is in the Harl. MS. 357, art. 5, and is attributed to Arthur Golding, but when it was printed in 1608 the translator's name was given as P. or Per. (Percival) Golding.

To the above list Hunter adds 'Cosan Commentaries, 1565. Martin 4367. An edit. 1590. Farmer 5860. Dedicated to Sir William Cecil from Powles Belchamp. 12 Oct., 1565,' but this is surely an inaccurate reference to the edition of Cæsar's *Commentaries*, published in that year. Hunter says further that " he also published a translation of Quintus Curtius according to Low in his *Ath. Cant.*"

Whether Arthur Golding was related to the family of the same name which came into prominence during the reign of Charles I. I have not been able to discover. Sir Edward Golding was created a baronet on September 27, 1642, and his son, Sir Charles, died on September 28, 1667, *aet.* 37. Sir Charles Golding's son, Sir Edward, died on December 6, 1715.[1] A " Mr. Golding," the grandfather of the first Sir Edward, was steward to Sir Thomas Ritson, but I have not been able to connect him with the Essex family. Hunter notes that among the Harleian MSS. is a history of the house of Vere, by a Percival Golding. The arms of Golding of Postlingford, and of Fornham, both in Suffolk, are—Gules, a chevron Or between three bezants.[2]

## The Abraham Sacrifiant of Beza

*Abraham Sacrifiant*, otherwise known as *Le Sacrifice d'Abraham*, is the only play written by Théodore de Bèze. It was first printed at Geneva by Conrad Badius in 1550, and Beza's Address to the Readers is dated at Lausanne on October 1st of that year, but Pasquier in *Recherches sur la France* (1560 on) says definitely that it was written for the accession of Henry II., i. e., in 1547. If this statement is correct (though it is highly improbable that Beza would have chosen such a subject before his conversion in 1549) it is barely possible, as M. Émile Faguet believes, that the author worked over the material before 1550, and that he then added the strongly Calvinistic traits which characterize the play.[3] In a letter

---

1 V. *Gentleman's Magazine*, 1795, vol. i, p. 284.

2 V. *Notes and Queries*, Series I, vol. xi, p. 13.

3 V. *La Tragédie française au xvi. Siècle*, p. 94. But Badius declared that Beza wrote the play as an expiation of his sin in having written the *Juvenilia* !

written by him, in 1598, to Jean Jacomot, who translated the drama into Latin, he says that it had been played by the students at the Academy of Lausanne, and also that it had been played in France "avec un grand applaudissement." The piece, indeed, had a phenomenal success ; during the sixteenth century ten editions appeared, and thirteen more were published during the seventeenth century.[1] Before the year 1600 it had been twice translated into Latin, once into Italian and once into English—by Arthur Golding. Its popularity, due in large measure, no doubt, to its sectarian character, was not undeserved on purely literary grounds. Pasquier tells us that it "lui fit tomber les larmes des yeux,"[2] and in our own day Petit de Julleville has declared that "il y a de vraies beautés dans cette pièce." M. Émile Faguet has referred to it as " peutêtre la première tragédie française où il y ait trace de vrai talent," and again : " L'œuvre est forte, bien conduite et touchante. Surtout elle est vraie. De Bèze est un moraliste. Il est descendu dans le cœur humain avec une lanterne, comme dit Mme. de Sévigné, et il y a trouvé ce dont nous faisons si grand cas, la tragédie psychologique."[4]

It is almost unnecessary to say that the subject had been treated in the French *mystères* before Beza turned his attention to it. In the famous cycle known as *Le Mistére du Viel Testament* the story holds a prominent place in the A, B and C versions, and three more or less modified versions of the cycle play were published during the first half of the sixteenth century. All six texts are collated by Rothschild in his edition of *Le Viel Testament* published by the Société des Anciens Textes Français; the three detached versions are denoted by the letters D, E and F. Of these, D, which dates

---

[1] For a bibliography of the various editions and translations of *Abraham Sacrifiant* V. *Le Mistère du Viel Testament*, vol. ii, pp. xlix-lxii. This list, however, omits the second edition—*Le Sacrifice d'Abraham, tragédie françoise séparée en trois pauses à la façon des actes de comédies, avec des choeurs, un prologue et un epilogue.* Paris, H. Estienne, 1552 in—8. V. Dr. Heinrich Heppe's *Theodor Beza* in Hagenbach's *Leben und Ausgewählte Schriften der Väter und Begründer der reformirten Kirche*, vi. Theil, p. 370.

[2] *Recherches*, vii, p. 615.

[3] *Histoire du Théâtre*, p. 84.

[4] *Op. cit.*, p. 98. For a different opinion V. Introduction to *Le Mistère du Viel Testament*, vol. ii, p. ix+.

from about 1520, shows only slight divergences from A, B and
C ; E and F, both of which were printed in 1539, and which
had been played by the Confrères de la Passion, follow the
earlier copies closely in many places, but there are frequent
omissions and very important additions. The latter are
chiefly of two kinds. In the first place the pastoral scenes
of the cycle play are very much elaborated, and Abraham's
servants Eliezer and Ismael are transformed into Sicilian
shepherds, or more properly speaking, self-conscious poets
masquerading in shepherds' guise. They declare their deep
love of nature :

> "Il n'est en ce monde plaisance
> Telle que estre aux boys et aux champs
> Et ouyr des oyseaulx les chantz,
> Qui font leurs nidz et leurs logettes,
> Decouppans mille chansonnettes,
> Telles que nature les duict."

They banter with each other as do the shepherds of Theocritus :

*Eliezer*
" Or sus ! doncques commenceray je.
*Ismael*
Ouy et tenez le bas ton
Ou vous aurez de ce baston.
Ilz chantent."

Like the shepherds of Theocritus, too, they boast of their
musical accomplishments :

> " Si j'avoye ma chalemie
> Ma viole ou ma cornemuse,
> Il n'y a ne harpe ne muse
> Qui vous peussent tant rejouyr."

In turn the shepherds sing the praises of pastoral life, one
taking up the theme and continuing the strain when the other
concludes and Isaac joining them in a chorus. In these
pastoral scenes the Confrères de la Passion were not imitating

the Greek idyllists directly ; they were imitating or even taking over almost literally the work of French poets who flourished toward the end of the fifteenth century—Guillaume Alexis, Guillaume Crétin and Martial de Paris dit d'Auvergne.[1]

In addition to this pastoral development the E and F versions of the Abraham and Isaac story are characterized by a great elaboration of the soliloquies of Abraham, and of the dialogue between Abraham and Isaac after they have arrived at the place of sacrifice. After learning from Raphael what God has commanded him to do, Abraham reviews in his mind each phrase of the angel's message and of the promise which God had previously made to him concerning Isaac, and concludes :

> " O altitude de science,
> O richesse de sapience,
> Combien tes faicts et jugemens
> Sont aux humains entendemens
> Obscurs et incomprehensibles." (ll. 430-435)

On arriving at the mount he meditates at length on the un-natural conflict which is taking place within him :

> " De nature, qui se combat
> Contre Raison."

and in a similar strain he reminds Isaac that

> " Je porte le feu en ma main,
> Qui est sensible et naturel,
> Mais ung feu supernaturel
> Brusle et ard dedans ma pensée."

Then ensues a long scene (ll. 964-1155) full of fine-drawn distinctions, in which Isaac tries to persuade his father that he is about to do wrong, and that he will regret his deed when it is too late :

> " Vous aurez regret a oultrance
> Et grant remors de conscience
> D'auoir faict sacrifice tel
> De Isaac, vostre filz et substance."

---

[1] V. Rothschild, *op. cit.*, pp. vi and lxiii.

Abraham discusses the difficulty of the part which each must play

> " active
> Quant a moy, quant a toy passive."

Isaac's speeches have a hardly less scholastic flavour. He speaks of

> " Dieu, qui est mon pére eternel,
> Et vous, mon pére naturel."

He finally submits

> " Nonobstant qu'il semble a nature
> Que vray pére se denature
> Et que ce luy soit amer si."

It is in the E and F versions of 1539 that we find the original of Beza's play. The two texts differ only slightly and in unimportant details; in F only, however, do we find the concluding speech of the angel (as in Beza's play) in which the promise is given to Abraham that his seed shall increase in number like to the stars of the heavens and the sand of the sea, that they shall possess the gates of their enemies, and that from him shall one be born in whom all nations shall be blessed. In all the other versions Abraham and Isaac rejoin their servants immediately after sacrificing the lamb. The lyrical element introduced into E and F in the pastoral scenes has its counterpart in the *Abraham Sacrifiant* in the song of Abraham and Sara and the Songs of the Shepherds, although the subject matter of the lyrics is changed entirely. Moreover there are some verbal similarities between E and F on the one hand and Beza's play on the other, as we shall see shortly.

Beza's play, then, follows E and F more closely than A, B, and C, and in one detail it follows F more closely than E. Only occasionally, however, is there any close correspondence between passages or scenes, and Beza's omissions and additions are numerous and of a fundamental kind. The chief omissions are as follows : Of the *dramatis personae* Dieu, Misericorde and Justice are omitted altogether, and consequently all the scenes which are laid in heaven. Ceraphin is replaced by Raphael. The place of Eliezer and Ismael is taken in Beza's play by two ' demie troupes ' of shepherds. The scenes in which Abraham, Sara and Isaac are characters previous to the departure for the Mount of Vision are very much shortened, and those in which Isaac and the shepherds play games and engage in a singing match are replaced by a short scene in which a staid conversation precedes the songs of the shepherds, here divested of their pastoral character. Abraham's soliloquy of 158 lines after the departure of the angel, and the succeeding pastoral scene are also omitted. Another soliloquy of Abraham's (134 lines) and the scene of some 200 lines already referred to in which Abraham and Isaac give expression to many subtle unnatural considerations have left no trace in Beza's play. Moreover the latter concludes with the announcement of the angel in which the promise is given to Abraham ; in all the older versions Abraham sacrifices the lamb, and returns with Isaac to the shepherds who cannot understand their long delay ; the whole party then sets out for home, and finally the story is related to Sara.

The additions which Beza has made to the older play are not less notable. In the first place there is a prologue in which it is explained that the audience are not in Lausanne, but in the land of the Philistines, where they will see Abraham, Isaac and Sara. Let each one keep silence and listen attentively. Abraham and Sara each in a soliloquy praise God's goodness, and then sing together a ' cantique ' of praise in which they review their lives. The next character to be introduced is Satan in the habit of a monk. In a long soliloquy he compares his kingdom to God's, rejoices in the effectiveness of his frock as a disguise, and announces his intention of undermining the goodness of Abraham. Then follows, as in the older versions, the command of the angel to Abraham that he sacrifice Isaac. Abraham submits at once though he is horrified. A company of shepherds comes forth, and Isaac asks that they take him with them. His extreme youth is here emphasized by the insistence of the shepherds that he first get his parents' permission, and their assurance that he will be allowed to go when " vous serez grand." It is unnecessary to point out how unlike he is to the philosophic youth of the E and F versions. While Isaac goes to gain his father's consent the shepherds sing a 'cantique' of 78 lines, lauding the happiness of him who trusts in God, and illustrating this truth by the events of Abraham's life. Sara now objects strongly to Isaac's accompanying his father to do sacrifice ; the parting scene is very effective and contains a touch of dramatic forecasting when Sara says :

> " Las ! je ne sais quand ce sera
> Que revoir je vous pourrai tous,
> Le Seigneur soit avec vous."

In the older plays Sara urges Abraham to take Isaac with him :

> " Mon amy, menés vostre enfant
> Et la façon luy denottez
> Du sacrifice."

They set out and Satan (*solus*) expresses his rage at Abraham's intended obedience. This brings us to the first 'Pause.' When they arrive at the foot of the hill Abraham bids the shepherds wait. They discuss among themselves the reason of their master's evident depression and then sing a ' cantique, of 74 lines on the instability of all earthly things,—a song which has retained something of the pastoral atmosphere. Then they withdraw separately to pray. The parting words of Abraham to the shepherds are similar to those of the E and F versions, though the latter contain no analogues to the succeeding song and Abraham's withdrawal for prayer. After the second ' Pause ' follows the scene between Abraham and Isaac on the mount. Abraham avoids his son's questions, and turns aside to pray ; Isaac builds the altar—and then follows his father's example. We are reminded that Beza has not adhered closely to the unities of time and place when, in the next scene, we have a soliloquy by Sara whom we left three days ago. We then return at once to Abraham who is wrestling with God in prayer ; as he is now strong, now weak, Satan tempts him or laments his lack of success. At length Abraham, having determined to do God's bidding, tells Isaac the truth. The scene is wonderfully effective. The mutual love of father and child and the anguish of each are described in simple, moving language, unmarred by extraneous matter, or over-elaboration. Even Satan is moved to pity, and he finally takes his flight when he finds that Isaac is a willing victim. As Abraham is about to strike the blow the angel bids him put up his sword and points out the ram ; then in a second speech he announces the promise of God. An epilogue points out the blessings of obedience.

As compared to the older French versions *Abraham Sacrifiant* moves much more rapidly and is much more skilfully constructed, the omissions having generally tended to free the narrative from undramatic details or digressions. Beza's Calvinism of course explains his leaving out the scenes in which God is a character, and also the conversion of the shepherd songs, which extol the joy of living and the beauty of the earth, into songs of praise to God. The introduction of Satan and the addition of the song of Abraham and Sara are due to the same cause.

*Calvinism.*

The passages in which we find close verbal similarities between Beza's play and the E and F versions are not numerous. The following are cited because they show a correspondence between E and F and *Abraham Sacrifiant*, where there is no such correspondence between Beza's play and A, B and C :

E and F.

> *Raphael.*
>
> Abraham, Abraham !
>
> *Abraham.*
>
> Seigneur,
> Voicy ton humble serviteur
> Prest a t'obeyr en tout lieu.
>
> *Raphael.*
>
> . . . . . . . . . . .
> Prens Isaac, ton fils unicque,
> Ton bien aymé . . . . . . .
> Puis yras par devotion
> En la terre de Vision

Et au hault d'une des montaignes,
Ou je te donneray enseignes

. . . . . . . . . . . . . . . . . . .

D'icelluy feras sacrifice

*Abraham Sacrifiant.*

    *L'Ange.*

       Abraham, Abraham.

   *Abraham.*

         Seigneur.

    Me voicy.

   *L'Ange.*

        Ton fils bien-aimé
    Ton fils vnique Isaac nommé,
    Par toy soit mené iusqu' au lieu
    Surnommé la Myrrhe de Dieu :
    Là deuant moy tu l'offriras,
    Et tout entier le brusleras
    Au mont que ie te monstreray.

*E* and *F*.

    Icy nous fault faire sejour.
    Vecy ja le troysième jour
    Que de noz quartiers et partis
    Nous sommes ensemble partis
    Et tant avons faict, la Dieu grace
    Que je voy le lieu et la place
    Ouquel mon filz et moy yrons
    Et le sacrifice offrirons
    A Dieu. Vous troys nous attendrez,
    Gardans l'asne et cy vous tiendrez
    Tant que d'enhault nous reviendrons.

*Abraham Sacrifiant.*

    Enfans, voicy arriué le tiers iour,
    Que nous marchons sans auoir fait seiour
    Que bien petit : reposer il vous faut :
    Car quant à moy, ie veux monter plus haut,
    Auec Isaac, iusqu'en un certain lieu,
    Qui m'a esté enseigné de mon Dieu,
    Là je feray sacrifice & priere,
    Comme il requiert : demourez donc arrière,

Et vous gardez de marcher plus auant.

. . . . . . . . . . . .

Bien tost serons de retour, si Dieu plaist

*E* and *F.*

A nostre faict, bien j'apperçoys
Que portons le feu et le boys,
Mais ou est l'aigneau ou victime,
Qui sont requis, comme j'estime,
Pour sacrifier ?

*Abraham Sacrifiant.*

Voila du bois, du feu & vn cousteau,
Mais ie ne voy ne mouton ny agneau,
Que vous puissiez sacrifier icy.

Cf. also the following passage which occurs in **F** only with the final speech of the angel in Beza's play. (V. Appendix).

Entens
Ce que Dieu te mande par moy.

. . . . . . . . pourtant

Qu'a luy tu as obey tant
Et que tu n'as point pardonné
Au seul filz qu'il t'avoit donné,
Il a faict solennel serment
Par luy mesmes et jurement
Que dessus toute nation
Tu auras benediction
Du hault trosne celestiel :
Et comme estoilles sont au ciel
Et gravier au port de la mer,
Sans nombrer et sans estimer,
Ainsi sera il, sans doubtance,
De ton germe et de ta semence,
Qui les portes possedera
De tous ennemys qu'il aura ;
Et en ta generation
Toute et chascune nation
Qui sur la terre marchera
A jamais benoiste sera
De Dieu, le souverain seigneur.

The close verbal similarities in the above passages are not numerous, but the ideas correspond closely, whereas in A, B and C there are either no corresponding passages or the similarity is far slighter. Other examples might be cited. Abraham's fear that Sara will not believe his explanation of Isaac's death, and that she will impute to him some sinister motive, is found in E and F only. Isaac's prayer in which he begs forgiveness of his sins and that God will comfort his mother occurs in A, B and C as well as in E and F. A noteworthy correspondence between Beza's play and E and F is found in Abraham's long meditation (E F lines 340-499) the substance of which is very similar to Abraham's reflections on the mount in Beza's play. In both plays Abraham is swayed by considerations which are advanced in the ensuing order, except that in Beza's play (5) precedes (3) ; the change was made, no doubt, in the interest of logical and artistic effectiveness, and because it emphasized the strongly Calvinistic conclusion.

(1) It is difficult to reconcile God's promises regarding the future of the race in Isaac, with the present situation.

(2) What is impossible to man's intelligence is possible to God.

(3) God can raise Isaac from the dead if that be necessary.

(4) Abraham pleads the weakness of natural affection, but resolves to banish it.

(5) After all Isaac is but lent to his father by God.

A, B and C give expression only to the last of these considerations.

Beza's play seems to me to be by far the most effective of the extant treatments of the Abraham and Isaac story, with the possible exception of the short Chester play—undoubtedly the most remarkable achievement of the old English drama. In the *Abraham Sacrifiant* we recognize at once the work of a skilled literary craftsman. M. Faguet credits Beza with " l'intention de créer un drame à la fois chrétien et classique, qui soit inspiré de l'esprit religieux des anciens mystères, et qui s'accommode aux formes de la tragédie telle qu'on commence à l'entendre."[1] This is an exact description of

---

[1] *Op cit.*, p. 93.

the *Abraham Sacrifiant*, though we cannot agree with M. Faguet that it shows " la rigoureuse unité des tragédies proprement classiques " for, as we have seen, there is an interval of three days between the early and the later scenes, and at least two widely separated places are represented. The ' cantiques ' which are in themselves very beautiful, are not closely related to the action, but they occur before the dramatic tension has become acute. The language of the *dénouement* is especially convincing. Abraham in his fierce determination to do the will of God is a type of the sterner Calvinists, though his character is softened and made much more interesting by his deep natural affection for his son. The struggle that goes on in his soul engages the sympathy of the reader entirely, and is infinitely more effective than the long monologues of the older plays. This result is brought about by the introduction of Satan, a character of whose presence none of the other *dramatis personae* are conscious, but who serves a double function—that of dramatically representing in his speeches the struggle of Abraham's weaker human nature against the commandment of God, and of engaging our sympathies effectively on the side of duty. The moral significance of temptation, when the worst is made to seem the better reason, is in this way vividly suggested, and the effect s very powerful. As far as I am aware the function of the devil in this play is original with Beza. In the English moralities " the office of the devil .................. is on the whole, limited to one thing, namely, that of giving their agents, the vices, their hellish commissions."[1] In *Mankind* the devil, Tytivullus, whispers his evil suggestions in the ear of mankind—a situation paralleled in some other English plays,—but nowhere do we find the devil playing a rôle so artistically conceived as is that of the *Abraham Sacrifiant*. The similiarity of some of the speeches of the devil in *The Disobedient Child* to those of Satan in Beza's play, with with which it is almost exactly contemporary, is perhaps worthy of note. Compare for example the following lines :

---

1 Cushman, *The Devil and the Vice*, Halle, 1900, p. 51.

" And though that God on high have his dominion,
          And ruleth the world everywhere,
          Yet by your leave I have a portion
          Of this same earth that standeth here.
          The Kingdom of God is above in heaven,
          And mine is, I tell you, beneath in hell."[1]

with Satan's first speech in *Abraham Sacrifiant* (ll. 147-223).

That Beza's play "s'accommode aux formes de la tragédie telle qu' on commence à l'entendre " is seen in several particulars. In the first place the perfect unity of the action if we except the three rather long ' cantiques ' is in marked contrast to the ordinary mystery play, in which the Bible stories are narrated without any rigorous selection or rejection of details. The fact that Beza has " separated the prologue, and diuided the whole into pawses, after the maner of actes in comedies " also points definitely to the models of ancient literature which the author had in mind. The stichic verse (ll. 395-411) and the presence of the ' demie troupes ' of shepherds, partly fulfilling as they do the function of a chorus, are also traits derived directly from Greek drama.

## English versions of the Abraham and Isaac story

The story of Abraham and Isaac is treated in each of the four extant cycles of English mysteries—those of York, Towneley, Chester and Coventry. Besides these there are the East Anglia Brome play and one which is preserved in a Trinity College, Dublin, MS.; neither of these is known to have formed part of a cycle.[2] Many other versions are lost, for we know of plays on this subject having been performed at

---

1 Dodsley's *Old English Plays*, ed. Hazlitt, vol. ii, p. 310.

2 In the British Museum (11777.f.25) is a play—*The Trial of Abraham*—a *Dramatic Poem*—written by "Mr. Farrer of Dundle" and printed at Stanford by Newcomb and Peat in 1790. The characters are Abraham, Sara, Isaac, Chorus, and Semichorus, and the play, except the choral songs, is in blank verse. The author confesses his "obligation to a morsel of pathetic eloquence intitled "The Soliloquy of Abraham" as it appears in some miscellaneous collections, and is attributed to Sir Henry Wotton. To other Writers on the subject, whether in an Epic or a Dramatic form, he is not indebted." The book contains 68 pages.

Newcastle, Beverley and Dublin ; an Abraham and Isaac play
was also given at St. Dunstans, Canterbury, in 1491.  It would
seem probable that the subject was a popular one in the old
religious drama, for it contained possibilities for tragedy
almost unequalled by any other Bible story.  The relation of
the various extant versions of the play to each other we shall
consider briefly.  In the following pages I shall refer to the
York play as Y., to the Towneley play as T., to the Chester play
as Ch., to the Coventry play as C., to the Dublin play as D.,
and to the Brome play as B.  The French plays will be referred to by the letters A, B, C, E and F, as in the preceding
chapter.

*Chester and Brome.*—When Miss Lucy Toulmin Smith first
published the Brome play (*Anglia*, vol. VII., 1884) she pointed
out that the corresponding play in the Chester cycle contained
" several resemblances to the Brome manuscript," some of
which she indicated.[1]  In *Modern Language Notes* for April
1890, Professor Hohlfeld showed that the parallels between
the two plays were much closer and more numerous than Miss
Smith had suggested.  He explained the relation between the
two plays as follows : " The play on Abraham's Sacrifice in the
Brome MS. is the corrupt form of an older version, not necessarily earlier than the beginning of the fourteenth century.
This latter has been used, in its chief portion (lines 114-314), as
the model for the corresponding part of the fourth play in the
Chester collection."[2]  Professor Hohlfeld's argument is plausi-
ble, and may be accepted as a satisfactory explanation of the
close correspondence between many passages in the two
plays.  Even his long list of parallels is hardly exhaustive.
Cf. the following additions :

B.   A ! Lord of heuyn, my handes I wryng. (l. 120)
Ch.  For sorowe I maie my handes wringe. (l. 323)

B.   For my hart was neuer halffe so sore (l. 160)
Ch.  Thy wordes makes my harte full sore (l. 342)

---

1 *Anglia*, vol. vii, p. 320.
2 *Modern Language Notes*, vol. v, p. 119.

Moreover the statement that " their final parts are entirely different, at least from the moment when the angel appears to release Abraham from the Lord's commandment (Ch. 73 20 and B. l. 314)," although true in a general way, is hardly accurate, for I have discovered one or two similarities after this point. Cf. the following :

B.  He standyth teyed, loo ! a-mong the breres (1. 324)
Ch. Amonge the breyers tyed is he  (1. 442)

B.  Off yow schall cume frowte gret [won]
    And euer be in blysse with-owt ynd. (ll. 398-399)

Ch. Blessed euer more shall thou be,
    Through frute that shall come of thee. (ll. 458-459)

*York and Towneley.*—It has long been known that in many respects certain of the plays of the York and Towneley cycles show a marked resemblance to each other.[1]  In the respective versions of the Abraham and Isaac story these resemblances are not numerous, but they are unmistakeable.  The *dramatis personae* of Y. are Abraham, Isaac, Angelus, Primus Famulus, Secundus Famulus; to these characters T. adds that of Deus. In Y., however, Isaac is " of eelde ...... Thyrty yere and more sum dele," and he does not refer to his mother, whereas in T. he is a child, afraid of the sword and appealing to Abraham to spare him for love of his mother.  I have noted the following similarities : In both plays Abraham is one hundred years old (Y. l. 5, T. l. 38).  In both plays Abraham suggests to Isaac that they will return safely :

Y.  I praye god send vs wele agayne (1. 108)
T.  We shal com home with grete lovyng.  (1. 142)

Cf. the speech of the first servant in each play as Abraham and Isaac leave them :

Y.  Att youre biddyng we wille be bowne (1. 113)
T.  we ar redy youre bydyng to fulfill. (1. 152)

---

[1] V. Hohlfeld, *Die altenglischen Kollektivmisterien.* (Anglia vol. xi, pp. 219-311.)

In both plays Abraham says that he would gladly die for his son (Y. 241, T. 220). Cf.

    { Y.   Childir, bide ye here still. (l. 145)
    { T.   Ye two here with this asse abide (l. 145).

Elsewhere Abraham addresses the servants as " childre " (T. 157).

    { Y.   Sertis, sone, I may no lengar layne. (l. 187)
    { T.   Now, son, I may no longer layn. (l. 169)

God is called " Adonay " in Y. (l. 263) and T. (ll. 1 and 46) ; in no other play is this name used.

    { Y.   That all this worlde has worthely wrought (l. 264)
    { T.   long syn he this warld has wroght. (l. 10)

    { Y.   Thy wordis makis me my wangges to wete. (l. 275)
    { T.   . . . . water shotis in both myn eeyn. (l. 216)

In no other play does Abraham refer to himself as weeping.

*Towneley and Brome or Chester.*—In certain respects T. is closer to B. or Ch. than to Y. The characters are the same except that in B. and Ch. the servants are omitted, and that in Ch. a second angel is added. In B. as in T., God (in heaven) announces that he will try Abraham's faith. In all three plays Isaac is a child and speaks of his mother ; in all three he is horrified on learning that he is to die, suggests that if he has trespassed he should be beaten, and fears the sword in Abraham's hand. In all three Isaac's face is turned down that he may not see the blow. In B. and T. Abraham kisses Isaac after all danger is past. The following passages may be compared, some of which are noteworthy chiefly because they occur in the same connection :

    { T.   Isaac, son, wher art thou ?
              All redy, fader, Lo me here. (ll. 92-3)

    { B.   Ysaac, my owyne son dere,
              Wer art thou, chyld ?  Speke to me.
              My fayer swet fader, I am here. (ll. 101-4)

T. I am redy to do this dede,
   And euer to fulfill youre bydyng (ll. 139-141)
B. I am full fayn to do yowr bedyng. (l. 119)
C. Father, I am all readye
   To doe your byddinge moste mekelye. (ll. 237-9)

T. My dere son, look thou haue no drede,
   We shal com home with grete louyng. (ll. 141-143)
B. Dred the nowyth, my chyld, I the red etc. (l. 143)
C. Dreede thee not, my childe, I reade etc. (l. 269)

T. Bi this thyng be broght to end. (l. 164)
C. For we must doe a littill thinge. (l. 230)
The word ' thing ' seems to be used in a technical sense.

T. Syn I haue trespast I wold be bet.(l. 185)
B. Yff I haue trespassyd a-yens yow owt,
   With a yard ye may make me full myld. (ll. 169-171)
C. Yf I have treasspasede in anye degree,
   With a yarde you maye beate me. (ll. 289-291)

T. God sir, put vp youre sword agayn (l. 283)
B. Ya ! but I woold that sword wer in a gled. (l. 381)

The fact that the last two leaves of the T. MS. are wanting,
makes impossible a comparison of the conclusions.

*Coventry.*—The play is short, and as in Y., the characteri-
zation is slight and the whole effect non-dramatic, although in
the early part of the play the relation of father and child
suggests the B. and Ch. plays; the scenes are lacking, however,
in the little realistic touches which make B. and Ch. so effective.
In both C. and Y. Abraham makes but little objection to the
command of the angel, and in both Isaac makes no objection
whatever when his father tells him that he is to die. C.
contains only one passage which is strikingly similar to Y., viz :

C. Almighty God thus the wylle mede
   ffor that good wylle that thou ast done. (56 13, 14)
Y. God sais thou sall haue mekill mede
   For thys goode will that thou in ware (ll. 335-337)

An apparent similarity to T. is probably not significant :
    C.   With yow to walk ouyr dale and hille (52 19)
    T.   Bi hillys and dayllys, both vp & downe. (1. 135)

To B. and Ch. there are also certain similarities. As in B. the
play opens with Abraham's expressing his special love for
Isaac, and his praying for God's blessing : in both plays he
then addresses Isaac affectionately, who replies in a similar
way. Cf.

    C.   Thu art my suete childe, and par amoure
         fful wele in herte do I the love. (50 13, 14)
    B.   Cume on, swete chyld, I love the best etc. (1. 31)

In C. as in Ch. and B., Isaac notices his father's "hevy cher"
and twice inquires as to the cause. Abraham covers Isaac's
face with a " Kerchere " as in B., C. and Y. The first
words of Abraham after the angel has prevented his slaying
Isaac are similar in C. and B.

    C.   I thank my God in heuyn above,
         And hym honowre for this grett grace. (55 9, 10)
    B.   A ! Lord, I thanke the of thy gret grace. (1. 333)

The concluding promise of the angel is similar to that in B.,
Ch., D. and Y. They then go home into their own country as
in B., Y. and D.

*Dublin.*—D. differs from all the other English plays in that
Sara is a character. The other *dramatis personae* are Abraham,
Isaac, Deus and Angelus : Abraham addresses his servants
but they do not speak. As Brotanek has pointed out D. is
much more closely related to the French plays of the *Vieil
Testament* than is any other English play. Isaac is a child, and
much is made of his affection for his mother ; in the elaboration of small, realistic, dramatic detail the play resembles the
Brome version. Abraham's first speech in each play is similar:

    D.   O gret god on hye that al the worlde madest,
         And lendist vs oure leving here to do thi plesaunce,
         .  .  .  .  .  .  .  .  .  .
         to the be honoure,. . . . . . . .
         and hily, lord, I thank the.
    B.   Fader of heuyn omnipotent,

Thow hast yoffe me both lond and rent,
And my lyvelod thow hast me sent ;
I thanke the heyly euer-more of all.

Cf. also

D. the goode lord of al heuenes hye,
comaundeth the to take and sacrifye
Isaac thi son that thou louest so hertlye (ll. 56-59)
B. Owr Lord comandyth the for to take
Ysaac, thy yowng sone that thow lovyst best
And with hys blod sacryfyce that thow make.

(ll. 60-63)

The Ch. version is similar. As in B., Ch. and T. Isaac thinks his death is to be a punishment for his having " trespassed " and begs for mercy. Abraham's words, " thi modre may not haue hir wille all way" (l. 198) suggest the corresponding passage in Ch.,—" Thy mother I can not please." (l. 324). In D. (l. 221), Ch. (l. 40), and C. (54 16), there is a reference to smiting off Isaac's head.

Brotanek pointed out certain verbal similarities between D. and Y. and T., which indicate an unmistakeable relationship. I have noted the following passages :

D. Abraham, fearing the effect of Isaac's death upon Sara, resolves to " se how preuely that I can it do " (ll. 82-84) ; in Y., Abraham decides that " to my sone I will noght saye." (l. 93).

D. and I charge you that ye abide here in deede,
and that ye remeve not from this stede. (ll. 141-143)
T. Sir, we shal abide you here,
Oute of this stede shall we not go. (ll. 155-157)
Y. Childir, bide ye here still ;
No ferther sall ye goo. (ll. 145-147)

D. A, son, I haue aspyed the place. (l. 157)
T. Lo, my son, here is the place. (l. 165)

D. Come on, son, a right goode pace. (l. 159)
T. we must go a full good paase. (l. 161)

D. Now Isaac, son, I may no lengre refrayne. (l. 161)
T. Now, son, I may no longer layn. (l. 169)
Y. Sertis, sone, I may no lengar layne. (l. 187)

D. lay downe that wode on that auter there. (l. 169)
Y. Lay doune that woode euen here,
Tille oure auter be grathide. (ll. 158-160)

D. Yif I haue trespast, I cry you mercy. (l. 173)
T. syn I haue trespast I wold be bet. (l. 186)
Y. That I haue trespassed or oght mysdone,
For-giffe me fadir. (ll. 256-258)
D. Haue I displesid you any thing ? (l. 172)
D. Nay, son, to me thou hast do no trespas. (l. 177)
T. what haue I done ? truly, none ill. (l. 189)
T. What haue I done, fader, what haue I saide ?
Truly no kyns ill to me. (ll. 205-207)

D. then, fader, bynde myne handes and my legges fast,
and yeue me a gret stroke, that my peynes were past.
(ll 225-227)
Y. Ther-fore lye downe, hande and feete. (l. 277)
Now fadir be noght myssyng,
But smyte fast as ye may. (ll. 293-295)

D. and seid, oure lord alowed my wylle (l. 342)
T. Thi good will com I to alow. (l. 259)
Y. To lowe that lorde I halde grete skyll (l. 322)

The expressions " in fay " (D. 199) and " ma fa " (T. 39),
" ma fay " (T. 128) occur in none other of the English plays.

## THE RELATION OF *LE VIEL TESTAMENT* PLAYS
### TO ENGLISH VERSIONS

The French versions of the Abraham and Isaac story are
not closely related to any of the English plays except D— the
only English play in which Sara is a character. Brotanek
has pointed out the similarities between the V. T. and D. in his
edition of the latter play printed in *Anglia*, vol. 21. Some of
the parallel passages which he adduces are not very convincing,
but after all possible deductions have been made a sufficient

number remains to establish beyond controversy the relationship.   Without attempting to sift the evidence brought forward by Brotanek I shall merely notice briefly those points in
the French plays to which there are correspondences in the
English versions of the story.

In V. T. God (in heaven) resolves that he will test Abraham's faith ; so in D., B. and T. : he commands his angel to
bid Abraham sacrifice Isaac ;  so in D. and B. Abraham is
troubled regarding Sara ;  so in D.; in V. T., however, she
makes no objection to Isaac's accompanying his father ; in D.
she tries to persuade Abraham to leave Isaac at home.   In
E. F. (ll. 391 +) Abraham meditates on the promise which God
has made that Isaac's descendants shall be in number like the
sands of the sea and the stars of the sky ; so in Y. but the passage occurs before Abraham has learned that he is to sacrifice
his son.   Isaac cries out against his father's intention to slay
him as in D., T., B. and Ch.   He suggests that his eyes be
covered in order that he may not see the sword ;  so in Ch.,
B. and Y. ;  in T. he fears the sword but does not ask that his
eyes be covered ;  in C. Abraham covers his son's face in order
that he may not see his " lovely vesage."   Abraham suggests
to Isaac that he bind him as in B. and Ch.; in D. Isaac makes
the proposal, as also in Y.   In E. F. Isaac asks his father to use
his girdle in binding him, and also that Abraham take away his
hat and neck-scarf ;  similar detail is introduced in Ch. where
Isaac asks his father to take away his clothes in order that no
blood be shed on them, and in D. where Isaac requests him to
take off his gown and ungird him, and where he also asks that
his mother be not allowed to see his clothes.   Abraham kisses
his son as in B., Ch., D., C. and Y.; in A, B, C and B. he kisses
him a second time.   Abraham feels physical repulsion to the
deed—" Tout le sang de mon coeur s'emeult ";  cf. " My blode
aborreth to se my son blede, for all on blode it is " (D. ll. 243-
245), and " My hart begynnyth stronly to rysse, To see the
blood off thy blyssyd body " (B. ll. 208-210), and " A ! Lord,
my hart reysyth ther-agayn " (B. l. 299).   Isaac thinks of his
mother  as in B., Ch. and D.; in F. and  T. Abraham is con-
cerned as to how he is to tell her, for he knows that she will

detect any subterfuge. Isaac asks whether a beast may not be substituted as the victim; so in D. In E. F. Abraham reflects that Isaac might have died in battle or have met some other terrible fate ; so in D. After all danger is past Abraham kisses Isaac as in B. and T. In F. the angel gives to Abraham the long promise, in language similar to that used in D., B., Ch., C. and Y. Abraham and Isaac return to their servants and set out for home as in D., Y. and B. The concluding scene in which Sara is a character is similar to the D. version, one or two passages resembling each other closely *e. g.*

    V. T. Or soit le puissant Dieu loué (l. 10591)

    D. Now blessid be that lorde souereigne (l. 359).

*Summary.*—Of the English plays which deal with the Abraham and Isaac story only Ch. and B. are intimately related to each other, but none of them occupies a position of complete isolation. T. and C. are more closely related to Y. than to any other play, but in certain respects they are closer to B. and Ch. than to Y. D. contains many lines similar to corresponding lines in Y. and T., but in its general spirit and in two or three passages it holds more closely to B. Whatever be the explanation of these facts it is clear that the mystery plays of the various districts of the Midland and Northern counties were not unknown in other parts of the same counties. None of these plays except D. shows a very close resemblance to the plays of the *Vieil Testament* ; some slight similarities in details which are not to be found in the Vulgate, however, make it difficult to consider the French and English cycles as entirely independent of each other.

It is not impossible, indeed, that the mystery plays of the different European countries were more closely related than has ever been supposed. At any rate it is difficult to explain the fact that ideas and incidents are common to versions of different countries, which, are not found in the account given in Genesis, and which, if they have developed naturally from the dramatic treatment of the subject, are at least very striking. Compare, for instance, the following extracts from Feo Belcari's *Rappresentazione e Festa d'Abraam e d'Isac suo*

*Figliuolo* (first edition, Florence, 4°, without date ; second edition 1485). Abraham is lying on a bed when the angel brings to him the command of God—as in *Le Viel Testament* He warns Isaac not to let Sara know that they are going, and issues a similar injunction to the two servants : Cf. D., Y. and T. He orders the servants also to prepare whatever will be necessary for a six days' journey—as in Beza's play. A striking resemblance to Beza's play occurs " dipoi cominciano a edificare un altare in sul monte " when we return to Sara, who complains to her household regarding the pain she endures in the absence of Abraham and Isaac. Referring to his mother Isaac says :

> " Se fussi a questo loco io non morrei,
> Con tanti voti, preghi ed umilitade
> Pregheresti il Signor, ch'io camperei."

Cf. the following lines from Ch. :

> " Woulde God my mother were here with me !
> Shee woulde kneele downe upon her knee,
> Prainge you, father, if yt may be,
> For to save my liffe."

Abraham tells Isaac that God will raise him from the dead rather than fail in his promise, and also reflects :

> " Tu non morrai di lunga malattia,
> Nè divorato da fiera crudele."

Compare the following lines from E and F :

> " . . . . . . tu ne dois partir du monde
> Par quelque maladie immunde,
> Par guerre ou quelque aultre fortune."

And both versions continue to compare with this Isaac's being offered up by the hand of his father a worthy sacrifice to God. Isaac then prays God to forgive his sins and asks his father to pardon his disobedience and to bless him. Abraham prays God to bless Isaac and gives him his own blessing—details that we have noticed in several of the plays which we have considered. After they have returned to Sara and she has recovered from her amazement, she praises God, and then " Sarra et tutti gli altri di casa, eccetto Abram e quelli dua.

Angeli, ...... tutti insieme fanno un ballo cantando questa lauda."[1]

In the Spanish *Auto del Sacreficio de Abraham* there is at least one point of resemblance to *Le Viel Testament* and several English plays, as M. Rouanet has pointed out. Speaking of the passage in the Spanish play " où Isaac prie son père de lui bander les yeux, afin qu'il ne puisse voir le couteau qui va l'égorger," M. Rouanet says : " Cette idée, non exprimée dans la Bible, se trouve dans le *Mistére du Viel Testament*, vers 10227—10230. On la remarque aussi dans les *Chester-Plays*." [2] We may add that it is found also in Y. and B. The lines referred to in *El Sacreficio de Abraham* are the following:

> " Y as mis ojos de cubrir
>
> porque a vezes se levanta
>
> yra al tiempo del morir,
>
> y por no ver deçendir
>
> el cuchillo a la garganta." (ll. 528-533)[3]

## GOLDING'S TRANSLATION

Golding's version is a very faithful reproduction of Beza's play. It is in the main a line for line translation, and the order of the lines is very rarely disturbed. Occasionally, however, one line is expanded into two, *e. g.* ll. 699 and 890, or more frequently a couplet is translated by four lines, *e. g.* the last two lines of the Prologue and ll. 192-3, 731-2, 823-4, 878-9. Occasionally, too, the order of the lines is transposed, *e. g.* ll. 1-3, 331-7. The only omission I have noted is of lines 5 and 6 of Beza's play. Abbreviations of Beza's text are much rarer than expansions ; compare, however, ll. 282-8 which are reproduced in four lines. When Beza's tetrameters are translated into pentameters the number of lines is sometimes reduced slightly, and it is in these passages that the author's necessity of filling out the verse reacts unhappily upon the

---

[1] *La Rappresentazione di Abraam, e Isaac suo Figliuolo* (Brit. Mus., 11427 d, no date). The 'rappresentazione' is also to be found in *Le Rappresentazioni di Feo Belcari et altre di lui Poesie*, Firenze, 1833, and it is also included in D'Ancona's *Sacre Rappresentazioni*, Firenze, 1872.

[2] *Coleccion de Autos, Farsas y Coloquios del Siglo xvi*, publiée par Léo Rouanet, Madrid, 1901, vol. iv, p. 135.

[3] *Op. cit.*, vol. i, p. 19.

effectiveness of his translation, although evidences of padding
are not absent from other parts of the work, *e. g.* ll. 24, 39-40,
172 of the English version. The necessity of finding a rhyme
has sometimes forced Golding to change the meaning slightly,
(l. 46 of Prologue) or to introduce a pointless expression
(l. 164). In many verses one or both of Beza's rhyme-words
have been retained, and the temptation to do so has sometimes
betrayed Golding into wrenching the English accent or otherwise using imperfect rhymes, *e. g.* " vengeance " and " obeysance," " judgments " and " commandments," " imagined "
and " examined," " patiently " and " instantly," " reasonable " and " agreeable," " recompense " and " silence."
Other imperfect rhymes are rare : I have noted only " undefiled " and "provided," "me" and "me," "thee" and "thee,"
each of which occurs but once. The literal character of the
translation is illustrated by the fact that the repetition of
words either for the sake of emphasis or in passages of intense
emotion which characterizes especially the speeches of Abraham is reproduced almost invariably by Golding. On the
whole the translation is a piece of excellent idiomatic English,
and the noble dignity of the song of Abraham and Sara, which
departs entirely from Beza's metre is not unworthy of the
Elizabethan age, and may serve as an example of that rare
phenomenon—a translator's surpassing his original.

The great majority of Golding's verses are in pentameter
couplets as are a large proportion of those in the original.
Many passages which Beza wrote in tetrameters, however,
have been translated into pentameters, *e. g.* Sara's speech ll.
623-657. On the other hand Golding occasionally translates
pentameters into tetrameters, *e.g.* the concluding speech of the
Angel. In some passages the verse shows a tendency toward
end-stopt lines, but of the 655 pentameter verses in the play 188
show " enjambement." Feminine rhyme is found in 14 of
the couplets and there are 4 triplets. Alternately rhyming
pentameters occur only in lines 250-254. Occasionally the
final line of a speech, or a speech which contains but a single
line, is left out of the rhyme scheme.

# A TRAGEDIE
## OF ABRAHAMS SA-
### CRIFICE,

Written in french by *Theodore Beza*, and
translated into Inglish, by A. G.

*Finished at Povvles Belchamp in Essex, the*
*xj.of August.* 1575.

GEN. 15.                    ROM. 4.

*Abraham beleued God, and it was imputed to him*
*for righteousnes.*

Imprinted at London by Thomas Vau-
troullier dwelling in the Blacke Friers.
1577

# A TRAGEDIE

## OF ABRAHAMS SA-
## CRIFICE,

Written in french by *Theodore Beza*, and
translated into Inglish, by A.G.

*Finished at Povvles Belchamp in Essex, the
xi. of August.* 1575.

*GEN.* 15.        *ROM.* 4.

*Abraham beleued God, and it was imputed to him
for righteousnes.*

[CUT]

Imprinted at London by Thomas Vau-
troullier dwelling in the Blacke Friers.
1577.

## THEODORE BE-
### za to the readers, gree-
### ting in the Lord.

I T is now a two yeares, since God graunted me the grace to forsake the countrie where he is persecuted, to serue him accordinge to his holy will. During which time, because that in my aduersity many fancies ranne in my head, I resorted to Gods word, where I founde two thinges that comforted me maruelously. The one is the infinite number of promises vttered by the mouth of him which is the truth it selfe, whose sayinges are always matched with effect. The other is the multitude of examples, where-

Aii

[3]

of euen the least are able enough, not only to encourage and harten the weakest &
fayntest harted in the worlde, but also to
make them inuincible. Which thing we
must needes see to haue come to passe, if
we consider by what meanes Gods truth
hath bene mayntayned to this present
time. Howebeit among all them that are
set afore vs for example in the olde testament. I finde three persons, in whome (to
my seeming) the Lorde ment to set forth
his greatest wonders : namely, Abraham,
Moises, and Dauid : in the liues of whome
if men would nowe a dayes looke uppon
them selues, they should knowe them selues
better then they doe. Therefore as I redd
those holy stories with wonderfull pleasure and singular profit : there came a desire vppon me to exercise my selfe in writing such matters in verse, not onely of intent to consider & remember them the better,
but also to praise God by all the meanes
I could deuise. For I confesse, that euen of
na-

[4]

ture I haue delighted in poetrie, & I can
not yet repent me of it : neuerthelesse it
greueth me right sore, that the litle grace
which God gaue me in that behalfe, was
imployed by me in such things, as the very remembrance of them irketh me now
at the hart. Therefore I gaue my selfe as
then to more holy matters, hoping to go
forwarde in them afterwarde, specially in
the translating of the Psalmes which I am
now in hand with. And woulde God that
the great number of good witts which I
know in Fraunce, would in steede of bu-
zying them selues about vnhappy inuentions or imitations of vaine and vnhonest
fancies, (for so they be, if a man iudge them
according to truth) rather set their minds
to the magnifying of the great God, of
whom they haue receiued those so great
giftes, then to the flattering of their Idols,
that is to say, of their Lordes and Ladies,
whom they vphold in their vices by their
fainings & flatterings. Of a truth it would

[5]

become them better to sing a song of God,
then to counterfet a ballet of Petrarks, &
to make amorous ditties, worthy to haue
the garlande of sonnetts, or to counterfet
the furies of the auncient Poets, to blase
abroad the glory of this world, or to con-
secrate this man or that woman to im-
mortalitie, thinges which beare the readers on hande that the authors of them
not only are mounted vp to the toppe of
their Pernassus, but also are come to the
very circle of the Moone. Othersome (of
which number I my selfe haue bene, to
my great greefe as now) write twoedged
epigrams cutting on both sides or sharp-
pointed & pricking at both endes. Others
buzie them selues rather in ouerturning
then in turning of thinges : & othersome
intending to inrich our tongue, do pow-
der it with Greeke and Latine tearmes.
But how now wil some man say: I looked
for a tragedie, and thou giuest vs a Satyre.
I confesse that in thinking vpon such mad-

enrich french lens.
& classicism

[6]

nes, I was caried away and ouershot my
selfe. Neuerthelesse I ment not to rayle
vpon good witts, but onely to discouer to
them so plainly the open wronge which
they doe both to God and to them selues,
as they might through a certeine enuie,
take vpon them to passe me in the description of such matters as I haue taken tast
of to their handes, according as I knowe
that it shall be very easie for them, if the
meanest of them will giue him selfe ther-
to. But to come to the matter that I haue
in hand, it is partly tragical and partly co-
micall : & therefore I haue separated the
prologue, & diuided the whole into pawses, after the maner of actes in comedies,
howbeit without binding of my self ther-
to. And because it holdeth more of the
one then of the other : I thought best to
name it a tragedie. As touching the maner of dealing, I haue altered some small
circumstances of the storie, to apply my
selfe to the companye. Moreouer I haue

Aiiii

[7]

followed the ground as neare the text as
I could, according to such coniectures as
I thought most conuenient for the matter and persons. And although the affections be very great, yet haue I absteined from
wordes and speeches to farre estraunged
from the common ordinarie, notwithstanding that I know it was the maner of the
Greekes and Latines so to doe, specially
in their chorusses, as they termed them.
But I passed so litle of imitating them, that
contrariwise me thinkes nothing is more
vnseemely, than those forced translations
and speeches drawne out of such a length,
as they can neuer come to the pith of the
matter whereof I report me to *Aristophanes*, who iustly rebuketh the Poets of his
time for it so often times. Verily I haue
made a songe without a chorus, nother
haue I vsed the termes of *Strophies, Anti-
strophies, Epirrhemes, Parecbases,* and other
such wordes, which serue to no purpose
but to amase simple folke, seeing the vse
of

[8]

of such thinges is worne away, & they be not so commendable of them selues, that a man should trouble him selfe to bringe them vp again. As touching the ortographie, I haue willed the Printer to followe the common order, notwithstanding the fond fancies that haue ben set forth within these three or fower yeares in that behalfe. And I would gladly counsel the forwardest of them that haue altered it, (if they were men that would take any other bodies counsell then their owne) that sith they will needes reduce it to the pronouncing, that is to say, make as many fashions of writinge, not onely as there are countries, but also as ther are persons in Fraunce : they should first learne to pronounce, before they teach men to write. For to speake & write after their fashion he is not worthye to giue rules of the writinge of our tongue, which is not able to speake it. Which thinge I speake not to blame all those that haue set downe their dowts in

that behalf, which I graunt are very need-
full to be reformed . but for such as sette
forth their dotages as certeine rules for al
the world to follow.   Furthermore, as touching the profit that may be taken of this
singular storie, besides the things that are
treated of it in inf_ite places of the Scri-
pture, I will refer it to _im that shal speake
of it in the conclusion ·  praying you who-
soeuer you be to accept this my small
labour  with as good will as I offer it to you.  *From Lausan*
*the  first  of  October.*
1550.

# THE ARGUMENT

## OF THIS TRAGEDIE TA

### KEN OUT OF THE TWO AND TWENTIDTH CHAPTER OF GENESIS.

*Fteruuard God tryed Abraham, and sayd unto him : Abraham. And he aunsuuered, Here I am. Then sayd he to him, take thyne onely sonne out of hande, euen Isaac uuhome thou louest, & goe into the country of Morea, & there offer him up for a burnt sacrifice up-pon one of the hills that I uuill sheuue thee. Abraham therefore rising earely, sadled his asse & tooke tuuo sernants uuith him, & Isaac his sonne.   And uuhen he had cut uuood for the burnt sacrifice, he arose and uuent to the place that God had told him of.   The third day, Abraham loking up, sauu the place a farre of, and sayd to his seruaunts, tarry you here uuith the Asse, for I and the ladde uuil goe yonder, and uuhen uue haue uuorship-*

*ped uue uuill come to you againe. Then A-braham took the uuood for the burnt sacrifice, & layd it upon Isaac his sonne, & tooke the fire and a knife in his ouune hand, and so they uuent forth togither. Then sayd Isaac to Abraham his father. My father. Abraham aunsuuered, here I am my sonne And he said, Beholde here is fire and uuood, but uuhere is the Lambe for burnt sacrifice. Abraham aunsuuered, my sonne, God uuill prouide him a lambe for burnt sacrifice. And they uuent on both togither. And uuhen they came to the place that God had spoken of, he builded an altar there, and layd the uuood in order uppon it, and then bound Isaac his sonne & laid him upon the altar aboue the uuood, and putting forth his hand cauught the knife to stryke of his sonnes necke. Then an Angell of the Lord cryed unto him from heauen, saying Abraham, Abraham. , Uuho aunsuuered, loe here I am. And he sayd unto him, lay not thy hand upon the child, nother doe any thing unto him. For nouu I knouue thou fearest God, seeing thou hast*

*hast not spared thine only sonne for my sake.*
*& Abraham loked up & sauu, & behold a sheep*
*uuas cauught behind him in a bush by the*
*hornes.   Then Abraham uuent and tooke the*
*sheepe, and offered it up for a burnt offering*
*in steede of his sonne.   And Abraham called*
*the name of the place,* The Lord shall see.
*Uuhereof it is sayd at this day of that moun-*
*teyne,* The Lord shal be seene.   *And the An-*
*gell of the Lord called unto Abraham from*
*out of heauen the second tyme, saying : I haue*
*suuorne by my selfe sayth the Lorde, for as*
*much as thou hast done this thing, & not spa-*
*red thyne onely sonne, I uuill blesse thee and*
*multiply thy seede as the starres of the sky, &*
*as the sand on the seas shore, and thy seede*
*shall possesse the gates of thyne enemies.*
*And all nations of the earth shall*
*be blessed in thy seede, because*
*thou    hast    obeyed    my*
*voyce.*

*The speakers.*

The Prologue.
Abraham
Sara
Isaac
A companie of shepherds of
Abrahams ouune house diui-
ded in tuuo partes.
The Angell.
Satan

[14]

# THE PROLOGUE

God saue you euery chone both great and small
Of all degrees : right welcom be you all.
It is now long, at least as seemes to me,
since here such preace togither I did see.
[5.] VVould God we might each weeke through all
      the yeare
See such resort in Churches as is here.
Ye Gentlemen and Ladies, I ye pray
Giue eare and harken what I haue to say.
To hold your peace alonly I require.
[10.] VVhat weene you(some wil say) by that desire.
VVe nother can nor will away with that.
But yit you must, or else I tell you flat,
That both of vs our labour lose togither,
In speaking I, and you in comming hither.
[15.] VVherefore I craue but silence at your hand,
My wordes with patience for to vnderstand.
      Both great and small, alonly doe but heare,
And I will tel you straunge & wondrous geere.
VVherefore now harken : for the thing is great
[20.] VVhereof I mind this present time to treate.
You thinke your selues perchaunce to be in place,
VVhere as you be not, now as standes the case.
For Lausan is not here, it is farre hence.
But yit when neede requires, I will dispence
[25.] VVith all of you, that hence within an hower
Eche one may safely be within his bowre.

[15]

As now this is the land of Palestine.
VVhat ? do you wonder at these words of myne ?
I say yit further to you, see you well
[30.]  Yon place? It is the house wherein doth dwell
A seruaunt of the liuing Gods, whose name
Hight Abraham the righteous man, the same
VVhose liuely faith hath won him endles fame.
Anon you shall him tempted see and tryde,
[35.]  & toucht to quicke with grefs that shal betide.
And lastly you shall see him iustified
By faith, for killing (in a certeine wise)
Isaac his dearest sonne in sacrifice.
And shortly, you shall see straunge passions :
[40.]  The flesh, the world his owne affections
Not onely shall be shewed in liuely hew,
But, (which more is) his faith shal them subdue.
And that it is so, many a faithfull wight,
Anon shall beare me record in your sight.
[45.]  First Abraham, and Sara you shall see,
And Isaac eke shall with them both agree.
Now are not these sufficient witnessings ?
VVho minds therfore to see so wondrous things,
VVe pray him onely talking to forbeare
[50.]  And vnto vs to giue attentiue eare,
Assuring him that he shall see and heare
No trifling toyes, but graue & wondrous geere,
And that we will his eares to him restore,
to vse them as he listeth as before.

Abra-

*Abraham commeth out of his house*
*& sayth.*

ALas my God, and was there euer any,
That hath indurde of cōbzāces so many,
As I haue done by fleeting too and fro,
Since I my natiue countrie did fozgo?
Oz is there any liuing on the ground,
Of benefits that hath such plenty found?
Loe how thou makest moztall men to see,
Thy passing goodnes by calamitie.
And as of nought thou madest euery thing:
So out of ill thou causest good to spzing,
Was neuer wight so blessed at thy hand,
That could thy greatnes fully vnderstand.

B

# ABRAHAMS SACRIFICE.

*Abraham commeth out of his house*
*& sayth.*

[WOOD CUT]

Alas my God, and was there euer any,
That hath indurde of combrances so many,
As I haue done by fleeting too and fro,
Since I my natiue countrie did forgo ?
[5.] Or is there any liuing on the ground,
Of benefits that hath such plenty found ?
Loe how thou makest mortall men to see,
Thy passing goodnes by calamitie.
And as of nought thou madest euery thing :
[10.] So out of ill thou causest good to spring.
Was neuer wight so blessed at thy hand,
That could thy greatnes fully understand.

B

[17]

Full threescore yeares and thereto fifteene mo,
My life had lasted now in weale and woe,
[15.] According to the course in sundry wise
Appointed by thy heauenly destinies,
Whose will it was I should be bred and borne
Of Parents rich in catell, coyne, and corne.
But unto him that richest is in fee,
[20.] What ioy or comfort could his riches be,
When he compeld, compelled was (I say)
To see, to serue, and worship euery day,
A thowsand forged gods in steede of thee,
Which madst the heauen & earth which we do see ?
[25.] Thou then eftsoones didst will me to conuey
My selfe from those same places quite away.
And I immediatly upon thy call,
Left Parents, countrie, goods with gods & all.
Yea Lord, thou knowest I wist not whither then
[30.] Thou wouldst me lead, nor where me stay agen :
But he that followeth thee, full well may say,
He goeth right : and while he holds that way
He neuer needes to feare that he shall stray.

*Sara comming out of the same*
*house sayth.*
In thinking and bethinking me what store
[35.] Of benefits I haue had erst heretofore,
Of thee my God which euer hast prouided
To keepe my mind and bodie undefiled,

And

[18]

And furthermore according to thy word
(Which I tooke then as spoken but in boord)
[40.] Hast blist my aged time aboue all other,
By giuing me the happy name of mother.
I am so rauisht in my thought and mind,
That (as I would full fayne) no meane I find
The least of all the benefits to commend,
[45.] Which thou my God doest daily still me send.
Yit sith alone with thee Lord here I am,
I will thee thanke at least wise as I can.
But is not yun my husband whom I see ?
I thought he had bin further of from me.

*Abraham.*

[50.] Sara Sara, thy mind I well allow,
Nought hast thou sayd but I the same auow.
Come on, and let us both giue thankes togither
For Gods great mercy since our comming hither
The frute thereof as both of us hath found :
[55.] Let prayse & thankes from both of us resownd.

*Sara.*

Contented Sir, how might I better doe,
Than you to please in all you set me too ?
And euen therefore hath God ordeyned me.
Agein, wherein can time spent better be,
[60.] Than in the setting forth of Gods dew praise,
Whose maiestie doth shew it selfe alwayes,
Aboue and eke beneath, before our eyes?

Bii

[19]

*Abraham*
Of truth no better can a man deuise,
Than of the Lord to sing the excellence,
[65.]  For none can pay him other recompence
For all his giftes which daily he doth send,
Than in the same, his goodnes to commend

*The Song of Abraham and Sara.*
Come on then, let us now begin to sing
            with hartes in one accord,
[70.]  The prayses of the souerein heauenly king
            our onely God and Lord.
His onely hand doth giue us whatsoeuer
We haue, or shall hereafter haue for euer

It is alonly he that doth mainteine
[75.]            the heauen that is so hie,  -
So large in compasse and in space so mayne :
            and eke the starrie skie,
The course whereof he stablisht hath so sure,
That ay withouten fayle it doth endure

[80 ]  The skorching heate of sommer he doth make,
            the haruest and the spring :
And winters cold that maketh folke to quake,
            in season he doth bring.
Both wethers, faire, and fowle, both sea & land,
[85.]  Both night and day be ruled by his hand.

Alas good Lord ! and what are we that thou

                                    didst

didst choose and enterteyne
Alonly us of all the world, and now
doth safely us mainteine
[90.] So long a time from all the wicked rowtes
In towne & country where we come throughouts.

Thou of thy goodnes drewest us away
from places that are giuen
To serue false gods : and at this present day
[95.] hast wandringly us driuen,
To trauell still among a thowsand daungers,
In nacions unto whom we be but straungers.

The land of Egypt in our chiefest neede
thou madst to haue a care,
[100.] Thy seruants bodies to mainteine and feede
with fine and wholsom fare,
And in the ende compelledst Pharao,
Full sore against his will, to let us goe.

Foure mightie Kinges that were already gon
[105.] away with victorie,
I ouertooke and put to flight anon
before they could me spie.
And so I saw the feeldes all stained red
With blud of those which through my sword lay dead.

[110.] From God receiued well this benefite :
for he doth mind us still,
As his deere freendes in whom he doth delight,

Biii

[21]

and we be sure he will,
Performe us all thinges in dew time and place,
[115.] As he hath promist of his owne free grace.

To us and unto our posteritie
     this land belongs of right,
To hold in honor and felicitie
     as God it hath behight,
[120.] And we beleue it surely shall be so,
For from his promise God will neuer goe.

Now tremble you ye wicked wights therefore,
     which sowed are so thicke
Throughout the world, & worship now such store
[125.]      of gods of stone and sticke,
which you your selues with wicked hands do carue,
To call upon and vainly for to serue

And thou O Lord whom we doe know to be
     the true and liuing God,
[130.] Come from thy place, that we may one day see
     the vengeance of thy rodde
Upon thy foes, that they may come to nowght
With all their gods deuizd through wicked thowght.

*Abraham*
Go to my Sara, that great God of ours
[135.] Hath blist us, to thintent that we all howres
Should for his giftes which he alone doth giue,

                           Him

Him serue and prayse as long as we doe liue.
Now let us hence and chiefly take good heede,
We hazard not our sonne to much in deede,
[140.] By suffering him to haunt the company
Of wicked folke, with whom you see we be.
A new made vessell holdeth long the sent
Of that that first of all is in it pent.
A child by nature nere so well dispozed,
[145.] By bringing up is quite and cleane transpozed.

*Sara.*

Sir, I doe hope my dewtie for to doe,
Therefore the thing that we must looke unto,
Is that Gods will may be fulfild in him.
Right sure I am we shall him weeld so trim,
[150.] And that the Lord will blisse him so : as all
Shall in the ende to his high honor fall.

*Satan in the habit of a Monke.*

I goe, I come, I trauell night and day,
I beate my braynes, that by no kind of way
My labour be in any wise misspent.
[155.] Reigne God aloft aboue the firmament,
The earth at least to me doth wholly draw,
And that mislikes not God nor yet his lawe
As God by his in heauen is honored :
So I on earth by myne am worshipped.
[160.] God dwells in heauen, and I on earth likewize :

Biiii

[23]

God maketh peace, and I doe warres deuize.
God reignes aboue, and I doe reigne belowe :
God causeth loue, and I doe hatred sowe.
God made the starrie skies and earthy clodds :
[165.] I made much more . for I did make the godds.
God serued is by Angells full of light ·
And doe not my faire Angells glister bright ?
I trow there is not one of all my swine,
Whose grooyn I make not godlike for to shine
[170.] These lechours, drunkards, gluttons ouerfedd,
Whose noses shine faire tipt with brazell redd,
Which weare fine precious stones uppon their skinnes,
Are my upholders & my Cherubins.
God neuer made a thing so perfect yit, -
[175.] That could the makers full perfection hit.
But I haue made, (whereof I glory may)
A thowsand worser than my selfe farre way.
For I beleue and know it in my thought,
therz but one God, & that my self am nowght
[180.] But yit I know there are whose foolish mind
I haue so turned quite against the kind,
That some (which now is common long agone)
Had leuer serue a thowsand gods than one.
And others haue conceiued in their brayne,
[185.] That for to thinke there is a God is vayne
Thus since the time that man on mowld was made,
With happy lucke I followed haue this trade

               And

And follow wil (come losse or come there gain)
So long as I this habit may mainteine,
[190.] I say this habit wherewithall as now
The world is unacquainted : but I vow
The day shall come it shall be knowne so rife,
Of euery wight, both child, yea man, and wife,
That nother towne nor village shall scape free
[195.] From seeing it to their great miserie.
O cowle, o cowle, such mischef thou shalt wurk,
And such abuse shall underneath thee lurke
At high noone daies : O Cowle, o Cowle I say,
Such mischief to the world thou shalt conuey,
[200.] That if it were not for the spitefulnesse,
Wherewith my hart is frawghted in excesse:
Euen I my selfe the wretched world shall rew,
To see the things that shall through thee insew.
For I, than who, of all none worse can be,
[205.] Am made yit worse by putting on of thee.
These thinges shall in their time without all faile
Be brought to passe.  As now I will assaile
One Abraham, who onely with his race
Withstands me, and defies me to my face.
[210.] In deede I haue him often times assailed :
But euer of my purpose I haue failed.
I neuer saw olde fellow hold such tack.
But I will lay such loade upon his backe,
That (as. I hope) ere long I shall him make

[25]

[215.] A sonne of myne    I know that he doth take
    The true Creator for his onely hold
    To trust unto : and that doth make him bold
    In deede he hath alliance with the trew
    Creator, who hath promist him a new
[220] Right wondrous thinges, according whereunto
    He hath already done, and still will doe.
    But what for that ?   If stedfastnes him faile
    To hold out still : what shall his hope auaile ?
    I trow I will so many blowes him giue,
[225.] That from his hold at length I shall him driue
    His elder sonne I feare not    and the other
    Shal hardly scape these hands of mine : the mother
    Is but a woman . as for all the meynie
    That serue him, they be simple sowles as enie
[230.] Can lightly be . there is a ragged rowt
    Of sillie shepherds, nother skild nor stowt
    Ynough against my wily sleights to stand.
    But hence I will and worke so out of hand,
    To haue them, that unlesse I misse my marke,
[235.] Anon I will deceiue their greatest Clarke

*Abraham comming out of his house*
*agein sayth*

What euer thing I doe or say,
I weery am thereof streit way,
How meete so euer that it bee,

[26]

Soe wicked nature reignes in me.
[240.] But most of all it me mislikes,
And to the hart with sorrow strikes,
That seeing God is neuer tyrde
In helping me, yea undezyrde :
I also likewise doe not streyne
[245.] My selfe, unweerie to remayne,
In dew and trew acknowledgment,
Of his great mercie to me sent,
As well with mouth as with my hart.

*The Angell.*

Abraham, Abraham.

*Abraham.*

Lord here I am.

*Angell.*

[250.] Goe take thyne onely deerebeloued sonne,
Euen Isaac, and bring him to the place
which hight the myrrh of God : which being done,
Slea him in sacrifice before my face :
And burne him whole upon a hill which I
[255.] Will shew thee there, goe hye thee by and by.

*Abraham.*

What ! burne him ! burne him ! wel I wil do so.
But yit my God, the thing thou putst me to
Seemes very straunge and irksom for to be ·
Lord, I beseech thee, wilt thou pardon me ?

[27]

[260.] Alas, I pray thee giue me strength and power,
To doe that thou commaundest me this howre.
I well perceiue and plainly now doe find,
That thou art angrie with me in thy mind.
Alas my Lord I haue offended thee.
[265]. O God by whom both heauen & earth made be,
With whom intendest thou to be at warre ?
And wilt thou cast thy seruaunt downe so farre ?
Alas my sonne, alas, what shall I doe ?
This matter askes aduised looking too

*A companie of Shepherdes comming out of*
*Abrahams house*
*The one halfe of them*

[270.] Hie time it is Sirs as I trow
We hie us packing on a row
To our companions where they be.

*The other halfe.*
Euen so thinkes me.
For if we all togither were
[275.] We should the lesser neede to feare.

*Isaac*
How Sirs, I pray you tary.  Will
You leaue me so behind you still ?

*Shepherds.*
Good child abide you there,

[28]

Or else our maister your father
[280.] And our mistresse your mother may,
Be angrie for your going away :
The time will come by Gods good grace,
That you shall grow and proue a pace :
And then ye shall perceiue the charge,
[285.] Of keeping flocks in feelds at large,
What daungers come from hill and dale,
By rauening beasts that lye in stale,
Among the couerts of the woode,
To kill our cattell for their foodd.

*Isaac.*

[290.] And doe ye thinke I would,
Goe with you though I could,
Before I knew my fathers mind ?

*Shepherds.*

In deede a child of honest kind,
And well brought up, ought euermore
[295.] His fathers and his mothers lore
In all his doings to obey.

*Isaac.*

I will not fayle it (if I may)
To die therefore : but will ye stay
A while untill I ronne and know
[300.] My fathers will ? *Shep.* Yea, therefore goe.

[29]

*The Song of the Shepherds*

O happy is the wight
That grounds him selfe aright
On God, and maketh him his shield :
And lets the worldly wize,
[305.]   Which looke aboue the skies,
Goe wander where they list in field.

No rich, ne poore estate,
Can puffe or yit abate,
The godly and the faithfull hart :
[310.]   The faithfull goeth free
Although he martred be
A thowsand times with woe and smart.

The mighty God him leeds,
In chiefest of his needes,
[315.]   And hath of him a speciall care,
To make him to abide,
Euen at the poynt to slide,
When worst of all he seemes to fare.

Whereof a proofe we see
[320.]   Our maister well may be :
For why, the more him men assayle
And urge on euery side ·
Lesse feare in him is spyde,
And lesse his courage doth him fayle.

[325.]   He left his natiue soyle,

                    Hard

[30]

Hard famin did him foyle,
Which draue him into Egypt land,
And there a king of might,
Tooke Sara from his sight,
[330.]    Uniustly euen by force of hand.

But streit on sute to God,
The king through Gods sharp rod,
Did yeeld to him his wife streit way,
And Abraham neuer stayd,
[335.]    But as the king him prayd,
Departed thence without delay.

And during this his flight,
He grew to so good plight,
That Loth to part away was faine :
[340.]    Bycause, as stoode the case,
To litle was the place,
To keepe the flockes of both them twayne.

There fell a sodeyn iarre
Betweene nine Kings through warre,
[345.]    Wherein fiue kings were put to flight,
And Loth him selfe, with all
His goods both great and small,
Away was caried cleane and quite.

Our faithfull Maister streit,
[350.]    On newes of this conceit,
Made fresh pursute immediatly :

And hauing but as then
Three hundred eighteene men,
Did make the enmies all to fly.

[355].    And of the reskewd pray
The tenth to the Preest did pay.,
And hauing done ech man his right,
Returned home anon,
With  commendacion,
[360.]    For putting so his foes to flight.

But nother sonne he had,
Nor daughter him to glad.
Which thing when Sara did perceiue,
She put her maid in bed,
[365.]    To serue her husbands sted,
Bycause her selfe could not conceiue.

So Agar bare a sonne
A thirteene yeares outronne,
Whose name is called Ismael.
[370.]    And to this present day,
Our maisters goods are ay
Increaced passing wondrous well.

Then for the couenants sake
Which God him selfe did make,
[375.]    Betwene him and our maister deere,
Our maister and we all,
As well the great as small,
At once all circumcized were.

                                        Isaac

*Isaac.*

My fellowes : God hath shewed himselfe to us,
[380.] So good, so louing and so gracious,
That I can neuer any thing yit craue
Ne small ne great, but that I much more haue,
Than I desire. I would haue gone with you
(As you doe know) to see full fayne : but now
[385.] Behold my father commeth here at hand.

*Abraham and Sara.*

But it behoueth us to understand,
That if God will us any thing to doe,
We must streyt wayes obedient be thereto,
And nother striue nor speake against his will.

*Sara.*

[390.] In deede Sir so I thinke and purpose still.
But yit I pray you thinke not straunge, that I
Doe take this matter somewhat heauily.

*Abraham.*

A good hart (wife) doth shew it self at neede.

*Sara.*

Thats trew : & therfore lets be sure in deede,
[395.] It is Gods will and mind we should doe so.
We haue but this child onely and no mo
Who yit is weake : in him stands all the trust
Of all our hope, with him it falls to dust.

C

[33]

*Abraham*
Nay rather in God.

*Sara*
But giue me leaue to say

*Abraham*
[400]    Can euer God his word once sayd unsay ?
No no, and therefore be you out of dowt,
That God wil keepe & prosper him throughout.

*Sara*
Yea, but will God haue us to hazard him ?

*Abraham.*
No hazarding it is where God doth gard him.

*Sara.*
[405.]    My hart misgiueth some mishappe

*Abraham.*
I nother dread nor dowt of any hap.

*Sara*
There is in hand some secret enterpryze.

*Abraham.*
What ere it be, it doth from God aryze.

*Sara.*
At least, if what it were you wist.

*Abraham*
[410.]    I shall ere long, if God so list.

*Sara*

                        So

[34]

So long away the child will neare abide.

*Abraham.*

For that our God will well ynough prouide.

*Sara.*

Yea but the wayes now full of daungers are.

*Abraham.*

Who dyes in following God needs neuer care.

*Sara.*

[415.]    If he should dye, then farewel our good dayes.

*Abraham.*

God doth foresett mens dying times alwayes.

*Sara.*

It were much better here to sacrifyze.

*Abraham.*

What euer you thinke, God thinks otherwise.

*Sara.*

Well then Sir, sith it must be so

[420.] The grace of God with both you goe.

Adiew my sonne.

*Isaac.*

Good mother eke adieu.

*Sara.*

My sonne obey thy father still,

'And God thee saue : that if it be his will

Thou mayst in health returne right soone agein.

Cii

[35]

[425.] My child I can not me refreyne
But that I needes must kisse the now.

*Isaac.*
Good mother, if it should not trouble you,
I would desire you one thing ere I went.

[WOOD-CUT]

*Sara.*
Say on my sonne : for I am well content
[430.] To graunt thee thy request.

*Isaac.*
I humbly doe you pray
To put this greef away.
These teares of yours refreyne,
I shall returne ageine
[435.] (I hope) in better plyght,

ſhan

My child I can not me refreyne
But that I needes must kiſſe the now.
Iſaac.
Good mother, if it ſhould not trouble you,
I would deſire you one thing ere I went,

Sara.
Say on my ſonne: for I am well content
To graunt thee thy requeſt.
Iſaac.
I humbly doe you pray
To put this greef away.
Theſe teares of yours refreyne,
I ſhall returne ageine
(I hope) in better plyght.

Than

Than now I am in syght :
And therefore stay this greef and wo.

*Abraham.*
My fellowes : we haue now to goe
Good six daies iorney ere we rest :
[440.] See that your cariages be prest
And all the things that we shall neede.

*The Compauie.*
Sir, as for that let us take heede.
Doe you no more but onely shew your will.

*Abraham.*
On then : and God be with you still.
[445.] The mightie God who of his goodnesse ay,
From time to time euen to this present day,
So kind and gracious unto us hath be,
Be helpfull still both unto you and mee.
Deale wisely howsoeuer that you fare :
[450.] I hope this iorney which we going are
Shall be performed happily.

*Sara.*
Alas alas full litle wote I
When I shall see you all ageine.
The Lord now with you all remayne.

*Isaac.*
[455.] Good mother God you guyde.

C iii

[37]

*Abraham*

Farewell.

*The Companie.*

God guide, and keepe you through his grace.

*Abraham*

Gowe on Sirs, let us hence apace.

*Satan.*

But is not this ynough to make me mad,
That whereas I make euery man to gad,
[460.] And all the world to follow after me,
If they my finger doe but hild up see,
And therwithall set all thinges on a rore :
Yit for all that I neuer could the more
This false olde fellow bring unto my lure,
[465.] For any thing that yit I can procure ?
Behold he is departed from this place
Gods will full bent tobey in euery cace,
Although the matter neuer be so straunge.
But yit it may be that his mind will chaunge,
[470.] Or that he shall him sacrifyze in deede,
And so he shall if I may help him speede.
For if he doe, then Isaac shall be dead,
Whereby my hart shall be deliuered
Of that same feare least God in him fulfill,
[475.] The threate whereby he promist me to spill.
And if he chaunge his mind, then may I say
The

[38]

The gold is wonne. For may I once so play
My part, as for to make him disobey
Almighty Gods commaundment, or repyne :
[480.] Then were he banisht from the grace diuine.
That is the marke whereat I alwayes shoote,
Now hye thee Cowle, set forth the better foote :
Lets ronne apace, and by some cunning drift
Foyle him in feeld, or put him to his shift.

### A PAUUZE.

*Abraham.*

[485.]    My children : this is now the third day
That we haue traueld making little stay.
Here must you tarry : as for me, I will
With Isaac, goe yit further onward still,
Unto a place from hence yet distant more
[490.] Which God almighty shewed me before,
Where I must pray and offer sacrifyze
As he requires. Wherefore in any wyze
Abide you here, and stirre not hence. But thou
Sonne Isaac shalt goe with me as now :
[495.] For God requires in this behalfe thy presence.

*The Shepherds*
Sir, sith you forbid us we will not hence.

*Abraham.*
This bundle unto him betake,
And I the fire and knife will take.

Ciiii

[39]

We shal (God willing) come agein right soone
[500.] But in the meane while, wot ye what to doone ?
Pray ye to God both for your selues and us.
Alas, alas, was neuer wyght, ywus.

*Shepherds.*
We will not fayle

*Abraham.*
That had such neede as I.
Well Sirs, I say no more but God be wy.

*Shepherds*
And with you too.

*Halfe the Shepherds.*
It greatly mazeth me.

*Halfe the Shepherds.*
And me likewyze.

*Halfe the Shepherds.*
And me too, for too see
Him so dismayd which hath so stowtly borne
All haps that haue befalne him heretooforne.

*Halfe the Shepherds.*
To say he is afrayd of warre
[510.] Debate, or strife, or any iarre
It were no reason : for we knowe,
Abimelech the king did showe
Such honor to our maisterward,
That he not onely had regard

To

[40]

[515.] To visit him, but eke did knit
A leage with him which lasteth yit.
And as for howshold matters, what
Can he desire which he hath nat ?

*Halfe the Shepherds.*
He liues in outward peace and rest :
[520.] But age perchaunce doth woork unrest.

*Halfe the Shepherds.*
Of zunnes he hath but onely one
But in the world mo such are none.
His cattell thryue in such great store,
As God doth seeme to giue him more,
[525.] Than he him selfe can wish or craue.

*Halfe the Shepherds.*
Nothing ye can so perfect haue,
But alwaies sumwhat is amisse.
I pray to God him so to blisse,
As soone to cure this his disease.

*Halfe the Shepherds.*
[530.] Amen, say I, if it him please.

*Halfe the Shepherds.*
Sure ʌ suppoze how ere the cace doth stand
He hath this time some weightie thing in hand.

*The song of the Shepherds.*
As howge as is the world we see
With all the things that in it be,

[535.]    Yet nothing is so strong and sure,
          That can for euer here endure.
          Almighty God which all mainteynes,
          Can nothing spie that ay remaynes,
          Except him selfe : all else ech one
[540.]    Indure short time, and soone are gone.
          The sunne with bright and burning beames
          Goes casting forth his cheerefull gleames,
          As long as day in skie doth last.
          Then darksom night doth ouer cast,
[545 ]    All kind of thinges both fowle and fayre,
          With coleblacke winges aloft in ayre.
          And of the moone what shall we say,
          Which neuer keepeth at a stay ?
          Sometimes with hornes she doth appeere :
[550.]    Sometime halfe fast : now thicke, now cleere ·
          Anon with rownd and fulsom face
          The night she fro the skie doth chace.
          The twincling starres aboue on hye
          Ronne rolling rownd about the skye,
[555.]    One while with wether fayre and cleere,
          Another while with lowring cheere.
          Two dayes togither match, and ye
          Them like in all poynts shall not see
          The one doth passe more swift away,
[560.]    The other longer while doth stay :
          The one, as though it did us spyght,
                              Bereeues

Bereeues us of the cheerfull lyght :
The other with his color bryght
Doth ioy our hart and dim our sight.
[565.] One burnes the world with heate from skyes,
With frost and cold another dyes.
With purple, greene, blew, white, and red
The earth earwhile is ouerspred.
Anon a blast of nipping cold
[570.] Maks freshest thinges looke seare and old.
The riuers with their waters moyst
Aboue their bankes are often hoyst,
And passe their bownds with rage so farre,
That they the plowmans hope doe marre.*j*
[575.] And afterward they fall within
Their chanells, ronning lank and thin.
And therefore whoso doth him grownd,
On awght that in the world is fownd,
Beneath or in the starrie skyes,
[580.] I say I count him nothing wyze ?
What then of him is to be sayd,
Whose hope on man is wholly stayd ?
Ech liuing creature subiect is
To endlesse inconueniencis :
[585.] And yit among them all, the sunne,
In all his course which he doth runne,
Beholdeth not a feebler wyght,
Than man is in his cheefest plyght.

[43]

For he that is most wyze and stowt,
[590.]    Is so beseeged rownd abowt,
And so assayld with vices strong,
That often he is throwen along.
What a foole is he, whose hart
Thinks to be free from wo and smart,
[595.]    So long as he doth liue on mowld ?
But if that any creature wowld
Be sure taccumplish that desire :
He must goe set his hart more higher.
Whereof our maister rightly may
[600.]    A good example bee that way.

*Halfe the Shepherds*
The best I thinke that can be now espyde,
Is for too draw us one asyde,
That ech of us may by him selfe alone
Pray God to send our maister which is gone,
[605.]    A safe returne with gladnesse.    gowe

*Halfe the Shepherds.*
I will not be behind I trowe.

*A pause.*

*Isaac*
My father.

*Abraham.*
Alas a poore father am I.

*Isaac.*

                        Sir

[44]

Sir here is woode, with fire, and knyfe redy:
But as for sheepe or lambe I see none here.
For you to offer.

*Abraham.*

O my sonne most deere,
God will prouide. Abide thou heere I say,
While I to God a litle whyle doo pray.

*Isaac.*

Good father go : but yit I pray you showe
Me whereupon this greef of yours doth growe,
Which doth (I see) so greatly you appall.

*Abraham.*

At my returne, my sonne, thou shalt know all,
But in the meane tyme pray thy selfe heere too.

Sir here is woode, with fire, and knyfe redy :
But as for sheepe or lambe I see none here
[610.]    For you to offer.

*Abraham.*
O my sonne most deere,
God will prouide.  Abide thou heere I say,
While I to God a litle whyle doo pray.

[WOOD-CUT]

*Isaac.*
Good father go : but yit I pray you showe
Me whereupon this greef of yours doth growe,
[615.]    Which doth (I see) so greatly you appall.

*Abraham.*
At my returne, my sonne, thou shalt know all.
But in the meane tyme pray thy selfe heeretoo.

[45]

*Isaac*

It is good reason that I should so doe.
And therewithall I will ech thing addresse.
[620.] That first this wood may be in redinesse.
This billet first shall gin the order heere :
Then this, then that shall cloze togither neere.
Thus all these thinges are redie now and prest :
My father shall prouide for all the rest.
[625.] And now O God I will aside retyre,
To pray to thee, as reason doth requyre

*Sara*

The more we liue, the more we see, alas,
What life it is that in this world we passe.
Was neuer woman borne upon the mowld,
[630.] That for hir husband or hir yssue could
Hirselfe with me in happinesse compare.
But yit I haue indurde such greefe and care
These last three dayes since they went hence, that well
I am not able for my life to tell,
[635] Which of the twayne hath greater to me beene,
The former ioy, or present peyne I meene
Which I haue felt these last 3 dayes, since they
Haue bin away : for nother night nor day
Haue I tane rest, bycause my mind doth ronne
[640.] On nothing but my husband and my sonne
And of a truth I was to blame as tho,
In that I suffered them away to goe,
             And

[46]

And went not with them.   Of the six dayes three,
Alas but three my God, yit passed bee,
[645.] And yit three mo my patience still must proue.
Alas my God which seest me from aboue,
Both outwardly and inwardly alway,
Vowtsafe to shorten these three yeeres I say,
For were they much more shorter than they be,
[650.] They be not dayes, but moneths & yeeres to me
My God, thy promis putts me out of dowt :
But if thou long delay the falling out,
I feare I shall haue neede of greater strength,
To beare the peyne in holding out at length.
[655.] Wherefore my God, now graunt thou unto me
I may with ioy right soone my husband see,
And eke mine Isaac in mine armes embrace
Returnd in helth and saftie to this place.

*Abraham.*

O God my God, thou seest my open hart,
[660.] And of my thowghts thou seest ech secret part,
So that my cace I neede not to declare.
Thou seest, alas thou seest my wofull care.
Thou onely canst me rid of my diseaze,
By graunting me (if that it might thee pleaze)
[665.] One onely thing the which I dare not craue.

*Satan.*

An other song then this yit must we haue.

[47]

*Abraham.*

What ? what ?  and is it possible that Gods
Behest and deede should euer be at oddes ?
Can he deceiue ?  euen to this present day
[670.] He hath kept towche in all that he did say.
And can he now unsay his word ?  no, no.
But yit it would ensew he should doe so,
If he my sonne should take away as now.
What say I ?  O my God, my God, sith thow
[675.] Doost bid me, I will doe it.  Is it right
That I so sinfull and so wretched wight,
Should fall to scanning of the iudgements
Of thy most perfect pure commaundements.

*Satan*

My cace goes ill.  O Cowle we must yit find
[680.] Some other way tassault this hagards mind.

*Abraham.*

It maybe that I haue imagined
Amisse : the more it is examined,
The more the cace seemes straunge.  It was perchaunce
Some dreame or wicked feend that at a glaunce
[685.[ Did put this matter in my head for why,
So cruell offrings please not God perdye.
He cursed Cayne for killing of his brother :
. And shall I kill myne Isaac and none other ?

*Satan*

No

[48]

No no. Neuer doe soe.

*Abraham.*

[690.] Alas alas what ment I so to sayne ?
Forgiue me, Lord, and pluck me backe agein
From this leawd race wherein my sin gan go :
O Lord my God deliuer me from this wo.
This hand of mine shall certeinly him smight.
[695.] For sith it is thy will, it is good right
It should de doone. Wherfore I will obey.

*Satan.*

But I will keepe you from it if I may.

*Abraham.*

So doing I should make my God untrew,
For he hath told me that there should insew,
[700.] So great a people out of this my sonne,
As ouer all the earth should spred and ronne,
And therefore if that Isaac once were kild,
I see not how this couenant could be hild.
Alas Lord, hast thou made him then for nowght ?
[705.] Alas Lord, is it vaine that thou so oft
Hast promist me such things in Isaake,
As thou wooldst neuer doo for others sake ?
Alas and can the things repealed be,
Which thou so oft hast promist unto me ?
[710.] Alas and shall my hope haue such an end ?
Whereto should then mans hope & trusting tend?

D

[49]

The summe of all I minded to haue sayd,
Is that to thee I hartily haue prayd,
To giue me yssue : hoping that when thow
[715 ] Hadst graunted it, I should haue liued.now
In ioy and pleasure . but I see full well,
The contrary to my desire befell.
For of my sonns, which were no mo but twayn,
To put away the one my selfe was fayne :
[720 ] And of the other (O hard extremitee)
Both father I, and tormenter must be,
Yea tormenter, yea tormenter, alas.
But are not thou the selfe same God, which was
Contented for too heere me patiently,
[725.] When I did pray to thee so instantly,
Euen in the midds of all thy wrath and yre,
When Sodom thou didst mind to burne with fire ?
Now then my God and king, wilt thou say nay,
When for my selfe I unto thee doe pray ?
[730.] Whom I begate him must I now deface.
O God, at leastwise graunt me yit this grace.

*Satan*

Grace ? in my book that word I neuer found

*Abraham*

Some other man my sonne to death may wownd
Alas my Lord, and must this hand of myne
[735.] To such a stroke against all kind declyne ?
How will it towch his wofull mother neere,

when

[50]

When of his violent death she needes shal heere ?
If I alledge thy will for my defence,
Who will beleue that thou wilt so dispence ?
[740.] And if men doe not credit it : what fame
Will fly abrode to my perpetuall shame ?
I shall be shund of all men more and lesse,
As paterne of extremest cruelnesse.
And as for thee, who will unto thee pray,
[745.] Or on thy word and promise euer stay ?
Alas, may these hore heares of myne abide
The sorrow that is likely to betide ?
Haue I alredy past so many daungers,
Haue I so traueld countries that are straungers,
[750.] In heate and cold, in thirst and hunger still,
Continewally obedient to thy will :
Haue I so long time liued lingringly,
Now in the end to dye unhappily ?
O hart of mine, clyue, clyue, asunder clyue :
[755.] And linger heere no longer time aliue.
The speedier death, the lesser is the greef.

Satan.

Now is he downe, if God send no releef.

Abraham.

What sayd I ? what intend I ?  O my God
Which didst create and make me of a clod,
[760.] Thou art my Lord, and I thy seruant trew.
Out of my natiue countrie thou me drew.

D ii

[51]

How oftentimes hast thou assured me,
That unto mine this land should lotted be ?
And when thou gaue me Isaac, didst not thow
[765.] Most faithfully and constantly auow,
That out of him such offspring should be bred,
As should this land throughout all ouerspred ?
Then if thou wilt needs take him now away,
What should I thereunto ageinst thee say ?
[770.] He is thine owne, I had him of thy gift.
Take him therfore.  Thou knowest best how to shift.
I know thou wilt to life him rayze againe,
Rather than that thy promis should be vaine,
Howbeit Lord, thou knowest I am a man,
[775.] No good at all or doo or thinke I can.
But yit thy power which ay is inuincible,
Doth to beleef make all things possible.
Hence flesh, hence fond affections euerychone :
Ye humane passions let me now alone.
[780.] Nothing to me is good or reasonable,
Which to Gods will is not agreeable

*Satan.*

' Well, well, then Isaac shall dye · and wee
What will insew thereof shall after see
O false old hag, thou makste me soft to grone.

*Abraham.*

[785.]     See where my sonne walks up & downe alone.
O silie child ! O wretched men, death oft
                                    Within

[52]

Within our bosoms lodgeth him full soft,
When furthest of we take him for too be.
And therfore right great need alwaies haue we
[790.] To leade such life, as if we fayne would die.
But wotest thou my sonne (alas) what I
Intend to say ?

*Isaac.*

What pleaseth you good father.

*Abraham.*

Alas, that word doth kill my hart the rather.
Yit must I better corage to me take.
[795.] Isaac my sonne : alas my hart doth quake.

*Isaac.*

Father, me thinks that feare hath you dismayd.

*Abraham.*

O my deere child : it is as thou hast sayd.
Alas my God.

*Isaac.*

Sir if it may you pleaze,
Be bold to tell me what doth you diseaze.

*Abraham.*

[800.]        Ah my deere child, wist thou what thing it were
Mercie good Lord, thy mercie graunt us here.
My sonne my sonne, beholdest thou this lyne.
This wood, this fire, and eke this knife of myne ?
This geere my Isac serueth all for thee.

[53]

*Satan*

[805.] Of God and nature enmie though I bee :
Yit is this thing so hard a cace to see,
That euen almost it is a greef to mee.

*Abraham*

Alas my sonne

*Isaac*

Alas my father deere,
Uppon my knees I humbly pray you heere,
[810.] My youthfull yeeres to pitie, if you may.

*Abraham*

O of mine age the only staffe and stay,
My derling, O my derling, faine would I
That I for thee a thowsand times might dye :
But God will haue it otherwise as now.

*Isaac.*

[815.]    Alas my father, mercie I kry you.
Alas alas I want both tung and hand,
Ageinst you in mine owne defence to stand.
But see, but see my teares for natures sake,
None other fence I can or will now make
[820.] Ageinst you.  I am Isaac, none other
But Isaac, your only by my mother.
I am your sonne that through your self hath life
And will you let it be bereft with knife ?
Howbeit, if you do't to'bey the Lord,

[54]

[825.] Then on my knees I humbly doe accord,
To suffer all that euer God and yow,
Shall think expedient for too doo as now.
But yit what deeds, what deeds of mine deserue
This death O God.  my God my life preserue.

*Abraham.*

[830.] Alas my sonne, God hath commaunded me
To make an offring unto him of thee,
To my great greef, to my great greef and pine,
And endlesse wo.

*Isaac.*

Alas poore mother mine.
How many deathes shall my death giue to thee ?
[835.] But tell me yit, my killer who shall be ?

*Abraham.*

Who ? my deere son ! my God my God graunt grace,
That I may dy now present in this place.

*Isaac.*

O father mine.

*Abraham.*

Alas, no whit that name
Agrees to me.  yit should we be to blame
[840.] If we obeyd not God. *Isaac.* Sir I am redy.

*Satan.*

Who would haue thought he would haue bin so stedie ?
D iiii

[55]

*Isaac*

Now then my father, well I see in deede
That I must dye    Lord help me at my neede.   ·
My God, my God, now strengthen thou my mind
[845.] And at thy hand such fauor let me find,
That of my selfe I may the upper hand
Obteyne, ageinst this sodein death to stand.
Now bind me, kill me, burne me, I am prest
To suffer all, sith God so thinks it best.

*Abraham*

[850.]    Ah what a thing, a what a sight is heere !
Mercie good God, now for thy mercie deere.

*Isaac.*

Thou Lord hast made me and created me,
Thou Lord upon the earth hast lodged me,
Thou hast me giuen the grace to knowledge thee :
[855.] Yit haue I not so well obeyed thee              .:
My Lord and God as dewtie doth require :
Which me to pardon lowd I thee desire
And whereas I to you my Lord and father
Haue not alwaies such honor yeelded rather,
[860.] As your great kindnesse did deserue to haue :
Therfore forgiuenesse humbly I doe craue.
My mother : she is now a great way hence,
Wherfore my God vowtsafe hir thy defence,
And so preserue hir through thy speciall grace,
                                        As.

[56]

[865.] As she no whit be trubbled at my cace.

*Here Isaac is bound.*

Alas, I go to deepe and darksom night :
Farewell as now for ay all worldly light.
But sure I am I shall at Gods hand find
Farre better things than these I leaue behind.
[870.] Good father, I am redy at your will.

*Satan.*

Was neuer child that spake with better skil.
I am ashamde, and therfore take my flight.

*Abraham.*

Alas my sonne, before thou leaue this light
And that my hand doe giue thunkindly blowe,
[875.] Upon thy mouth let me a kisse bestowe.
Isac my sonne, let this same arme of mine
Which must thee kil, imbrace this neck of thine.

*.Isaac.*

With right good will and hartie thankes.

*Abraham.*

Ye skyes the great gods woork ay glistring
in our eyes
[880.] Which well haue seene how God (who still is trew)
Did me with frute by Isaac here indew :
And thou O land fiue times to me behight,
Beare witnesse that my fingers doo not smight
This child of mine for hatred or for vengance,

[57]

[885.] But only for to yeeld my dew obeysance,
 To that great God which hath created me,
 And all the thinges that liue or moue or be :
 Who saues the good that put in him their trust,
 And stroyes the bad that serue their wicked lust.
[890 ] Beare witnesse that I faithfull Abraham,
 Through gods great goodnes stil so stedfast am
 As notwithstanding all that humane wit
 Can say or think, to make me now to flit :
 In one beleef I euer doo remaine,
[895 ] That not one word of God doth happen vaine.
 But now my hand, high time it is that thow
 Doo gather strength to execute thy vow
  *Heere the knife falles out of his hand*
 That by thy killing of mine only sonne,
 Thy deadly stroke may through my hart eke ronne

     *Isaac*
 What doe I heere ?
Alas my father deere !

     *Abraham*
 A, a, a, a.
     *Isaac*
 I am at your will.
Am I now well ? your pleasure then fulfill.

    *Abraham*
 Did euer man so piteous cace yit find ?

        Was

Was euer any frendship yit so kind?
And was there euer yit so pyteous case,
I dye my sonne, I dye before thy face,

*Isaac.*

Away with all this feare of yours I pray,
Will you from God yit longer time me stay?

*Abraham.*

*Heere he intendeth to stryke him.*

Alas who euer yit so stowt a mind
Within so weake a bodie erst did find?
Alas my sonne I pray thee me forgiue
Thy death. It kills me that thou may not liue,

*The Angell.*

Abraham, Abraham.

Was euer any frendship yit so kind ?
[905.] And was there euer yit so piteous cace.
I dye my sonne, I dye before thy face.

*Isaac.*
Away with all this feare of yours I pray.
Will you from God yit longer time me stay ?

*Abraham.*
*Heere he intendeth to stryke him.*
Alas who euer yit so stowt a mind
910.] Within so weake a bodie erst did find ?
Alas my sonne I prey thee me forgiue
Thy death.   It kills me that thou may not liue.

[WOOD-CUT]

*The Angell.*
Abraham, Abraham.

[59]

*Abraham.*

My God heere I am.

*Angell.*

Into the sheath put up thy knife,
[915.] And see thou doe not take his life,
Nor hurt the child in any wyse.
For now I see before mine eyes,
What loue thou bearest to the Lord,
And honor unto him auord,
[920.] In that thou doost so willingly
Thy sonne thus offer euen to dye.

*Abraham.*

O God.

*Isaac.*

O God.

*Abraham.*

O Lord a man may see.

*Heere he takes the sheepe.*

How good it is obedient for to bee
To thee : the cace is fitly furnished.
[925.] I will go take him tyed by the head.

*Angell.*

O Abraham.

*Abraham.*

Lord heere I am.

*Angell.*

[60]

Thus sayth the Lord, I promis thee
By my eternall maiestie,
And by my Godhead : sith that thow
[930.] Hast shewed thy self so willing now,
Me to obey, as to forbeare
Thine only Isaks life : I sweare,
That mawgre Satan to his face,
I will thee blisse and all thy race.
[935.] Considrest thou the lightsom skye,
And on the shore the grauell drye ?
I will increace thyne offspring more,
Than starres in heauen, or sand on shore.
Their enmies they shall ouercome,
[940.] And of thy bodie one shall come,
By whom my blissing shall spred foorth
On all the nations of the earth.
By him the treasures of my loue
And mightie power, shall from aboue
[945.] Be sheaded downe on all mankind,
Bycause thou hast obeyd my mind.

## THE CONCLVSION.

EE *here the mightie power of earnest faith,*
*And what reward the trew obedience payth*
*VVherfore ye Lords & Ladies I you pray,*
*VVhen you from hence shall go agein away,*

[61]

## The Conclusion

[5.]    *Let not this trew and noble storie part*
*Out of the mind and tables of your hart.*
*It is no lye, it is no peynted tale,*
*It is no feyned iest nor fable stale.*
*It is a deede, a deede right trew, of one*
[10.]   *That was Gods faithfull seruant long agone.*
*VVherefore ye maisters and ye mistresses,*
*Ye Lords and Ladies all both more and lesse,*
*Ye rich and poore, ye sorie and ye sad,*
*And you also whose harts with mirth are glad,*
[15.]   *Behold, and looke upon your selues ech one,*
*In this so fayre example heere foregone.*
*Such are trew glasses, shewing to our sight,*
*The fayre, the fowle, the crooked, and the right.*
*For whoso doth unfeynedly indeuer*
[20.]   *(As Abraham) to keepe Gods sayings euer,*
*And (notwithstanding all the reasons which*
*His mind alledgeth backward him to twich)*
*Doth still referre him selfe and all his deedes*
*To God : with much more happy yssue speeds,*
[25.]   *Than he can wish : for come there stormes or winds,*
*Come greef, come death, come cares of sundry kinds,*
*Let earthquake come, let heauen & skyes downe fall;*
*Let dark confuzion ouercouer all :*
*The faithfull hart so stedfastly is grownded,*
[30.]   *As it abideth euer unconfownded.*
*Contrariwise the man that trusteth too*

*His owne selfwit, therafter for to doe,*
*And standeth in his owne conceyt shall find,*
[35.] *The more he goes, the more he comes behind.*
*And euery litle puffe and sodein blast*
*From his right course shal quite & cleane him cast*
*Agein, his owne selfwilled nature will*
*Him ouerthrowe and all his dooings spill.*
[40.] *Now thou great God which makest us to knowe*
*The great abuses which doo plainly showe*
*The wretched world to be peruerted quite,*
*Make all of us to take such warning by'te,*
*As ech of us may fare the better by*
[45.] *The liuely faith set foorth before our eye*
*In Abraham that holy personage,*
*VVhose dooings haue bin playd upon this stage.*
*Lo maisters heere the happie recompence*
*VVhich God doth giue you for your gentle silence.*

FINIS.
ALL PRAYSE AND THANKS BEE GIUEN
TO GOD. AMEN.

NOTES

# NOTES.

---

*To the Readers.*

"It is now a two yeares," etc. Beza's conversion to Protestantism took place in 1548. A few months after the publication of his *Juvenilia* he suffered a severe illness, and on recovering he decided to give up all his brilliant prospects in France in order to go to Geneva, where he might enjoy religious freedom, and where he was to become one of the most famous of the leaders of French Protestantism.

"there came a desire vppon me," etc. It was while the first bitterness of exile and of loneliness was strong upon him that he felt the analogy between his fate and that of Abraham who had also suffered much,

> *Depuis le temps que tu m'as retiré*
> *Hors du pays où tu n'est adoré,*

but who was also conscious of the many blessings which God had showered upon him. The actual prompting to composition may be ascribed to this feeling, to Beza's desire to write a didactic play which should be acted by his students at Lausanne, and to his natural literary instinct, rather than to the more conventional reasons which are here alleged—and, indeed, Beza confesses this in part in the next sentence.

"it greueth me right sore," etc. Beza here refers to his *Juvenilia*, published in 1548, a volume of verses almost all of which were written before he was twenty years of age, and which had circulated for some years in manuscript among his friends. They consisted of imitations of Catullus, Ovid and Virgil, and although Beza condemned them in unmeasured terms in his later life they are not really very objectionable. At the time of their publication no one, not even Beza himself, felt that the poems were open to criticism, as is shown by the fact that the young author dedicated the volume to Melchior Wolmar, the eminent scholar in whose school at Orleans both Beza and Calvin had been students. Before accepting the professorship of Greek in the Academy of Lausanne a few months after his conversion (1549) Beza publicly made confession of his sin in having written the *Juvenilia*, and called the attention of the ecclesiastical council to the book. Indeed it was only on the earnest solicitation of Calvin that he accepted the office, so conscious was he of the degree to which his youthful Muse had compromised his standing as a leader in the Reformed Church.

Beza's misgivings were well grounded, for this volume provided his enemies with their strongest argument in their attempt to malign his character and his work. During his lifetime the most bitter of these attacks was made by Hieronymus Bolsec in his *Historia de vita, moribus, doctrina et rebus gestis Theod. Beza*, etc., which was published in 1582 together with extracts from the *Juvenilia* [Brit. Mus., 1193.h.30.(10)]. In 1577 Bolsec had published at Lyons a similar attack on Calvin. This volume was republished at Lyons as late as 1875, 'avec une introduction, des extraits de la vie de Th. de Bèze, par le même, & des notes d'appui,' by M. Louis-François Chastel, Magistrat. That the evil men have done lives after them is illustrated by the following extract from the Introduction. . . . . . "le libertinage à double fin, les débauches même séniles de de Bèze, l'opinion que l'on doit avoir de ses écrits poétiques ou religieux, de ses sermons, de ses perfidies, de ses persécutions contre ses contradicteurs, de ses provocations à des révoltes dont il se tenait par prudence personnellement éloigné, nous avouons que nous avons trouvé ces détails trop dégoûtants ou trop peu intéressants pour les mettre sous les yeux de nos lecteurs. De Bèze est d'ailleurs un personnage trop secondaire pour qu'on s'en occupe longtemps." (*Brit. Mus.* 4867.f.4.p.XVI.)

A copy of the *Juvenilia* is preserved in the Bodleian Library, the sub-title of which reads *Poemata amatoria ab ipso adolescente edita et ab ipso post damnata. 1548.*

"the translating of the Psalmes." Marot had begun the work in 1533 when he published a French translation of the sixth psalm. Twelve others from his pen appeared in 1539, a collection of thirty in 1541, and finally a complete collection of fifty in 1543. His death in the following year cut short his work, and Beza's continuation of the task—"que i'ay maintenant en main"—bore fruit in 1551, about a year after the publication of *Le Sacrifice d'Abraham*. This edition contained thirty-four of the psalms. In 1552 he republished these, together with forty-nine of those contained in Marot's collection. The remaining sixty-seven did not appear until 1562, in which year at least twenty-five editions were published of the complete translation of the Psalter—a record far surpassing that of any other book of the time. *Les Pseavmes de David, mis en rime Françoise, par Clement Marot et Theodore de Bèze* has maintained its position as the generally accepted French Psalter even to the present day. To the edition of 1552 Beza prefaced an epistle 'À l'eglise de nostre Seigneur,' in which he urges 'good wits' to give themselves to similar holy tasks—in language bearing close resemblance to that which he had used in the preface we are considering, *e.g.*:

> " Sus donc esprits de celeste origine,
> Monstrez ici vostre fureur Diuine :
> Et cette grace autant peu imitable
> Au peuple bas, qu'aux plus grands admirable,
> Soient desormais vos plumes addonnées
> A louer Dieu, qui les vous a données," etc.

(*Les Pseavmes de David*, Paris, 1642.)

The first English version of the French psalter was that published by Arthur Golding in 1571, together with Calvin's *Commentaries on the Psalms*. A second edition appeared in 1576. Another English translation, the work of Anthony Gilby, was published in 1581, and two more editions of this second version followed in 1590. In the Bodleian Library there are copies of all three editions of Gilby's translation.

"And woulde God that the great number of good witts which I know in Fraunce," etc. It is hardly possible that the succeeding lines were not inspired by Beza's opposition to some of the theories promulgated in Joachim du Bellay's *Defense et Illustration de la Langue Françoise*. This famous book had appeared about eighteen months before Beza wrote the preface to *Le Sacrifice d'Abraham*, and had occasioned a storm of criticism. That Beza, the young poet and accomplished classical scholar, should be in touch with contemporary literary theories would seem certain on *a priori* grounds. The *Quintil Horatian,* a celebrated pamphlet attacking Du Bellay's work, had appeared in this very year, 1550, from the pen of another of Wolmar's old students—Barthélemy Aneau, who was at this time professor of rhetoric and principal of the college at Lyons. Beza's preface distinctly suggests to us the author's interest in the discussion of these vital questions, and his intellectual sympathy with the "bons esprits que ie cognoy en France," in spite of his own religious preoccupation. In the *Defense et Illustration* the author is rather contemptuous of much that French literature has as yet produced, "comme rondeaux, ballades, virelais, chants royaux, chansons et autres telles espiceries, qui corrompent le goust de nostre langue et ne servent sinon à porter tesmoignage de notre ignorance" (p. 30). Nevertheless he has unbounded faith in the possibilities of the language. . . . "j'ay toujours estimé nostre poésie françoise estre capable de quelque plus haut et meilleur stile que celuy dont nous sommes si longuement contentez" (p 26), and in an address to the 'lecteur studieux de la langue françoise,' he declares : "[je] ne te puis mieux persuader d'y escrire, qu'en te montrant le moyen de *l'enrichir* et illustrer, qui est l'imitation des Grecs et Romains" (p. 28). The whole work is an amplification of this statement. In writing the strictures contained in this address to the reader Beza seems to have had in mind especially the fourth chapter of the second book of the *Defense et Illustration,* the title of which is *Quels Genres de Poèmes doit élire le Poète François.* To the 'poète futur' Du Bellay addresses, among others, the following counsels : "Jette-toy à ces *plaisans epigrammes,* non point comme font aujourd'huy un tas de faiseurs de comtes nouveaux . mais à l'imitation d'un Martial ou de quelqu'autre bien approuvé, *si la lascivité ne te plaist,* mesle le profitable avecques le doux. *Distile* avecques un stile coulant et non scabreux, ces pitoyables elegies, à l'exemple d'un Ovide, d'un Tibule et d'un Properce, y entremeslant quelquefois de ces fables anciennes. . Si tu ne voulois, à l'exemple des anciens, en vers heroiques . . sous le nom de *satyre* taxer modestement les vices de ton temps Tu as pour cecy Horace, qui selon Quintilian, tient le premier lieu entre les satyriques.   Sonne-moy ces beaux *sonnets* non moins docte que plaisante invention italienne . . . . Pour le sonnet doncques tu as *Petrarque* et quelques modernes Italiens " (p. 30).  In the sixth chapter of the second book—*D'Inventer des Mots*, etc., the author declares . . . . "je veux bien avertir celuy qui entre-prendra un grand oeuvre, *qu'il ne craigne point d'inventer, adopter et composer à l'imitation des Grecs, quelques mots françois* comme Ciceron se vante d'avoir fait en sa langue" (p.33).  In these extracts I have italicized the words and phrases to which, it would seem, Beza refers directly.

In working over the material of a mystery play into an approximation to the form of a Greek drama, however, Beza follows the injunctions of Du Bellay : "Quant aux comedies et tragedies, si les roys et les republiques les vouloient restituer en leur ancienne dignité, qu'ont usurpée les farces et moralités je seroy bien d'opinion que tu t'y employasses, et si tu le veux faire pour l'ornement de ta langue, tu sçais où tu en dois trouver les archetypes" (p. 31).  (J. Du Bellay, *Oeuvres Complètes*, ed. Léon Séché, Paris, 1903, Tome i.)

It may be added that Arthur Golding, too, did also "desyre too enryche [his] native language with thinges not hertoofore published in the same." (V. prose dedication to Leicester of the first four books of the *Metamorphoses* (1564); v. also his stanzas prefixed to Baret's *Alvearie* which are quoted in the introduction.)

"thinges which beare the readers on hande," etc, *i.e.* deceive by false pretences.  Cf.
"How you were borne in hand, how cross'd, the instruments,
  Who wrought with them," etc.

*Macbeth*, III, i, 80-81.

"two-edged epigrams," etc.  A reference to the *Juvenilia*. The volume contained "vier Sylven, zwölf Elegien, viele Epitaphien und dann nehmen die Epigramme fast die letzte Hälfte des Buches ein." (Baum, *Theodor Beza*, vol i, p. 69.) For an analysis of the contents of the *Juvenilia* see pages 69-81. Baum reprints several of the pieces (pp. 93-102).  His judgment of the volume is summed up in the following sentence :

[71]

"Wer Sinn für Poesie hat wird Beza und Wolmarn danken dasz sie uns diese mannichfaltigen, in üppiger Natürlichkeit ausgeschossenen Jugenderzeugnisse nicht vorenthalten haben" (p. 80).

"I thought best to name it a tragedie." This statement illustrates the vagueness of the term "comedy" and "tragedy" throughout the Middle Ages. They did not even refer specifically to the drama, and the distinction between them had to do more frequently with considerations of style or the character of the ending than with the predominance of the more serious or lighter matter. In dedicating the *Paradiso* to Can Grande della Scala, Dante gives his reasons for calling his great epic a comedy : "Ed è la Commedia un certo genere di poetica narrazione, diverso da ogni altro. Quanto alla materia, differisce dalla tragedia, perchè questa in principio è ammirabile e quieta, nel fino od esito sozza ed orribile. . . . Laddove la Commedia incomincia con alcun che di avverso, ma termina felicemente. . . . Parimente la Tragedia e la Commedia tengono differente modo nel parlare : l'una, alto e sublime; l'altra, dimesso e umile . . . ." (*La Divina Commedia* ed. Camerini, Milano, 1893, p. 20.) Chaucer's definition of tragedy is, "Tragedye is to seyn a dite of a prosperite for a tyme that endeth in wrecchidnesse." (*Boece*, Bk. II, Prosa ii, Glose.) A distinction similar to that of Dante is given in the *Catholicon* of Johannes Januensis (1286) : "differunt tragoedia et comoedia, quia comedia privatorum hominum continet facta, tragoedia regum et magnatum. Item comoedia humili stilo describitur tragoedia alto. Item comoedia a tristibus incipit sed cum laetio desinit, tragoedia e contrario." (Quoted by Chambers in *The Mediæval Stage*, II, 209.) See also Cloetta, *Beiträge zur Litteraturgeschichte des Mittelalters*, I, s. 140-4.

In the prologue to the *Amphitryon* of Plautus there is a discussion as to whether the play is to be a comedy or a tragedy and it is assumed that the question is to be decided by the worldly dignity of the *dramatis personæ* : since a servant is to be introduced besides the kings and gods who are the chief characters the author decides to call the play a tragi-comedy. Another point of resemblance between this prologue and Beza's may be mentioned here : in both great profit is promised to the audience if they will but preserve silence during the presentation of the play.

"I passed so little," etc., *i.e.* I cared so little. Cf. "I will not greatly care, or passe, whether they beleeue, or no. Haud in magno ponam discrimine."

Baret's Alvearie s.v.

"I pass not for his threats."

Tamburlaine, Part I, i.

"I pass not for thy anger."

Edward II, I, iv.

"I report me to Aristophanes," etc. Beza probably refers to *The Frogs* ll. 907 +. For the reflexive use of the verb 'report,' see the *Century Dictionary*, s.v. 6 +. Cf. also,

"As for the common sort of Ballads which now are used in the world I report me to every good man's conscience, what wicked fruits they bring." *The Gude and Godlie Ballates*, 1573, ed. Laing, Preface.

"As touching the ortographie," etc. Beza here refers to the devotees of spelling reform in France, the chief of whom were Jacques Peletier and Louys Maigret. In the *Defense et Illustration* Du Bellay has only a passing and non-commital reference to the subject—"si l'orthographe françoise n'eust point été depravée par les praticiens." In his preface to the second edition of *L'Olive* (1550) he says : "C'est encor' la raison pourquoy j'ay si peu curieusement regardé à l'orthographe, la voyant aujourd'huy aussi diverse qu'il y a de sorte d'escrivains. J'approuve et loue grandement les raisons de ceux qui l'ont voulu reformer; mais voyant que telle nouveauté desplaist autant aux doctes comme aux indoctes, j'aime beaucoup mieux louer leur intention que la suyvre." (*Oeuvres* Tome I, p. 96). Du Bellay's well-known friendship for Peletier would naturally dispose him to look kindly on the new theories. Ronsard had announced in the "Avertissement" to his *Odes*, which were published in the same year (1550), his determination to follow to a great extent the principles laid down by Maigret. As this work was the first of those written in confessed conformity to the doctrines of the Pléiade, the

[73]

author's attitude to the new theories regarding spelling reform would have the effect of identifying the Pléiade with the movement.   It is quite possible, if not probable, that Beza wrote the criticisms we are considering when he was fresh from a perusal of Du Bellay's or Ronsard's preface   The similarity of Beza's language to that of Du Bellay quoted in the extract given above is at least worthy of attention.

The question of spelling reform was one of general concern in the sixteenth century   An interesting reference to the anomalies which Englishmen felt existed in the preservation of an orthography which no longer corresponded to the pronunciation of the language is found in Baret's *Alvearie* (1580) under the letter E :  "Then must both we and many other nations, geld out many idle dumme E, ees, especially in the latter end of our wordes, (As glasse, rodde, etc ) which signifie nothing . . . This one rule therefore being well weighed, and the similitude diligently marked, will suffice to mend a great deale of our corrupt writing, and reduce it againe to true Orthographie .  .  For surely, we may still wonder & find fault with our Orthographie (or rather Cacographie in deed .)  but it is impossible (in mine opinion) for any private man to amend it, untill the learned Universities haue determined upon the truth thereof, & after the Prince also with the noble Councell, ratified and confirmed the same, to be publikely taught and used in the Realme."

Camden in his *Remains concerning Britain* refers to contemporary orthography and the efforts that have been made to improve it, but "that Tyrant Custome," he admits, makes any reform difficult (pp 36 +)

"they should first learn to pronounce "  Beza was much interested in the question of pronunciation.  In 1584 he published at Geneva *De Francicae linguae recta pronunciatione tractatus*, now one of the rarest of his works (a copy is in the Bodleian), but accessible in a reprint (Paris, 1868, 12mo )   In 1580 and 1587 he published short treatises on the pronunciation of Latin and Greek.  A copy of the latter is preserved in the Bodleian in a small octavo volume the title of which is *De vera pronuntiatione Gr  et Latinae linguae, commentarii doctiss. virorum. Quorum primus qui est De pronuntiatione Graecae linguae Theod. Bezam autorem habet.*

*The Argument.*
" . . . . take thyne onely sonne out of hande," *i.e.* immediately.
Cf.
 . . . . "also [he] told me he intended to print it out of hand."
Preface to Baret's *Alvearie.*

and

"But gather we our forces out of hand<br>And set upon our boasting enemy."
*Henry VI, Part I*, IV., ii, 102.

*The Prologue.*

Line 4. "such preace," *i.e.* crowd. A common enough Elizabethan usage frequently met in Golding. Cf.
" . . .. Within the courts is preace
Of common people."
(Golding's translation of Ovid's *Metamorphoses*, Bk. XII, l. 56. Reprinted by the De La More Press, London, 1904, W.H.D.Rouse ed.)

Line 9. "alonly." The form is also used in lines 17 of the Prologue and 74 and 88 of the regular text of the play, as well as in others of Golding's works. Cf., *e.g.* the *Metamorphoses*, Bk. XI, 286; Bk. XII, 96. Nares derives it from "alone," V. *Glossary*, s. v., but the New English Dictionary says it is a combination of "all" and "only," and that it was therefore originally an emphatic form of "only." *Jamieson's Scottish Dictionary* gives this derivation also. It is certainly used in this sense whenever it occurs in the present play. The corresponding adjective form is also used : "There lives the phœnix one alone bird ever." Marlowe, *Ovid's Elegies*, Book II, Elegia VI. The Scottish form is " allanerlie." Cf. "We trow in God allanerlie." *The Gude and Godlie Ballates* (1573) ed. Laing, p. 9. Cf. also
"Except thow weschin be,<br>With Christis blude allanerlie,<br>Thow art condampnit man." *Ibid*, p. 148.
The form became obsolete in the seventeenth century.

[75]

Line 10. "VVhat weene you," etc. "Ween, to fancy, to hope (erroneously)." Schmidt, *Shakespeare-Lexicon*, s.v.
Cf. "They that be in Hell ween there is no other Heaven "
Camden's *Proverbs* in *Remains*, p. 334.

Line 11. "VVe nother can nor will away with that," *i e.* endure that Cf "Away with, as when wee can not away with one, or with such fashions as he useth." Baret, *op. cit.* s v.
"She could never away with me."
*Henry IV, Part II*, III, 11, 213.

Line 21. "to be in place," *1 e.* present Cf.
"And yet here's one in place I cannot pardon."
*Measure for Measure*, V, 504.

Line 23. "For Lausan is not here." For similar juggling as to the scene of the play compare the Prologue to the *Truculentus* of Plautus

Line 27. "As now this is the land of Palestine." The redundant "as" before expressions of time is common in many Elizabethan writers. V. Abbott, *A Shakespearian Grammar*, 114. For 'the land of Palestine' Beza wrote 'le pays des Philistins.' Cf "The people shall hear, and be afraid; sorrow shall take hold on the inhabitants of Palestina "
*Exodus*, chap. XV, 14.
Cf. also
"A thousand foreskins fell, the flower of Palestine,
In Ramath-lechi, famous to this day."
*Samson Agonistes*, 1,144

Line 52 "grave and wondrous geere " The use of 'geere' in the indefinite sense of "business" or "matter" was very common. Cf. "I am sore afraid how this matter will fall out, or what will be the end of this geare."
Baret's *op cit.* s.v. "fall."
"And that these covenantes may never be broken, but stand or hold forever; or for the better assuring, or making sure, and confirming of this geare." *Ibid* s.v. "hold " (543).

Line 53. "And that we will his ears to him restore," etc. A similar witticism occurs in the prologue to the *Casina* of Plautus where the attention of the audience is requested if their ears are disengaged.

[76]

*Abraham's Sacrifice.*

Line 19. "fee"—"Goods, possessions, wealth." V. *New Eng. Dict.* s.v. 2.

Line 35. Here, and in line 44, "benefits" is a dissyllabic word, but in line 6 it is trisyllabic as also in line 110.

Line 39. "Spoken but in boord," *i.e.* jest. Cf.

Sumtyme with pleasaunt boords
And wanton toyes he dalyingly dooth cast foorth amorous
woords." *Metamorphoses*, Bk. X, 279.

Cf. also the Scotch "baur." "Soth bourde is no bourde" is a very old saying (it is in Heywood's *Proverbs*, ed. Sharman, p. 150), which has persisted until modern times in Scotland. Cf. "A sooth boord is no boord." *Quentin Durward*, Abbotsford edition, p. 256.

"The sooth bourd is nae bourd." *Redgauntlet*, The Scott Society, p. 293.

See an interesting note in Jamieson's *Scottish Dictionary* s.v. on "The Bourd of Brechen." Chambers refers to a Dutch "Boerd," or farce about 1400. V. *The Mediaeval Stage*, Vol. II, p. 150.

Line 50. In this speech Abraham uses the familiar 'thou' in addressing Sara ; elsewhere he always uses 'you'—probably because of the greater solemnity of the succeeding scenes. Sara, the reverential wife, who remembers that "therefore hath God ordeyned me" always uses 'you' in addressing Abraham. In speaking to his parents Isaac uses 'you' except in his apostrophe to his absent mother.

"Alas poore mother mine.
How many deathes shall my death giue to thee?
(ll.833-4.)

where the passionate exaltation of the speech explains the usage.

Line 50. "thy mind I well allow." "to Alowe : to make good or allowable : to declare to be true."

Approbo . . . . *appouuer* [sic] *du tout, trouuer bon.*

No man better esteemed or alowed of his countrie men.

To alowe. approbare & laudare. Cic.
(Baret *op. cit.* s. v.)

"to praise, commend, approve of." *New Eng. Dict.* s.v.

Cf
"O heavens,
If you do love old men; if your sweet sway
Allow obedience"                                         *Lear*, II, iv, 192-4.
and "He understanding not hir thought, did well her woordes
allow"                                         *Metamorphoses*, X, 410

Line 76. "in space so mayne" "Mayne" or "main"
means "vast in extent" Cf. "The large mayne poole of water
neere at hand."                                         *Metamorphoses*, XI, 411.

Line 91 "throughouts." The form would seem to be an
arbitrary one coined for the sake of the rhyme

Line 122. "Now tremble you, ye wicked wights." An
example of the regular change from "you" to "ye" in direct,
and especially in impassioned, address. Cf line 3 of the Conclusion. Cf. also

"Therein, ye gods, you make the weak most strong."

*Julius Cæsar* I, iii, 91

Line 142. "A new-made vessell," etc. The proverb is
quoted in Hazlitt's *English Proverbs*, p. 375, in the form, "The
cask savours of the first fill" Hazlitt adds "See a note by
Weber in Dyce's *Beaumont and Fletcher*, IV 462 The following apposite passage from Horace is quoted *ibidem* :

"Quô semel est imbuta recens servabit odorem
Testa diu."

Line 157. "That mislikes not God." Cf. also line 240.
"to Displease, to mislike." Baret's *Alvearie* s.v. "displease"
This somewhat rare impersonal use of the verb became obsolete
in the seventeenth century. Cf. "All they would do was to
allow Mr Bruce to come out if he heard anything that misliked
him." Bruce, *Sermons* (1631) 69, ed 1843 · (Quoted in
Wright's *English Dialect Dictionary*, s v ) Shakespeare uses
"likes" very frequently impersonally, e g "This likes me well,"
*Hamlet* V, ii, 249, but "mislikes" only in a personal sense, *e.g.*
"Mislike me not for my complexion," *Merchant of Venice* II,
i, 1. This personal use of "mislike" is very common in
Elizabethan authors.

Line 165 "I did make the godds." The belief that the
heathen deities were originally the angels who had rebelled
with Satan was general in the Middle Ages, and prevailed until

comparatively modern times. Hooker tells us that "These wicked spirits [*i.e.* the fallen angels] the heathens honoured instead of gods, both generally under the name of *dii inferi*, 'gods infernal'; and particularly some in oracles, some in idols, some as household gods, some as nymphs." *The Laws of Ecclesiastical Polity*, Bk. I, chap. iv, 3. Milton also accepts the theory:

> "Then were they [*i.e.* the fallen angels] known to men by
>     various names,
> And various idols through the Heathen World."
>
> *Paradise Lost*, Bk. I, ll, 374-5.

Line 171. "brazell redd." "Brazell' is a variant of 'brazil'—"of unknown origin ; perh. a corruption of an Oriental name of the dye-wood originally so called. On the discovery of an allied species, also yielding a dye, in South America, the territory where it grew was called *terra de brasil*, 'red-dye-wood land,' afterwards abbreviated to Brasil, 'Brazil.' Brazil-wood was thus not named from the country, but the converse was the case. Formerly pronounced in English *bra.zil* as shown by rimes and spellings." *New Eng. Dict.* s. v. The present case is an instance of the word's being accented on the first syllable.

Lines 174-5. Cf. also lines 526-7—

> "Nothing ye can so perfect have,
>     But alwaies sumwhat is amisse."

Similar ideas very frequently find expression in Elizabethan literature. Perhaps the most famous example is that which occurs in Marlowe's *Tamburlaine* V, ii, beginning "If all the pens that ever poets held," etc.

Line 181. "the kind," *i.e.* nature, as usually in Middle English.

Line 186. "on mowld." Cf. also ll. 595 and 629. A Middle English word meaning earth. Cf.:

> "Certes thanne schulde I be fryke
>     And a mery man on molde."
>
> *The Castell of Perseverance*, ll, 153-4, ed. Pollard.

Cf. also "She did not live above the molde," etc.

> *Metamorphoses*, I, 725.

and "*Homo*, for that he was made of mold."

Camden, op. cit., p 11.

Line 192. "rife." "Currently; commonly; frequently "

V Cent. Dict, s v 3

Line 202. "Euen I my selfe the wretched world shall rew "
V also lines 305-8. Cf. Milton's Satan

"yet no purposed foe
To you, whom I could pity thus forlorn,
Though I unpitied "

Paradise Lost, Bk. IV, ll. 373-5

and again,

"And, should I at your harmless innocence
Melt, as I do, yet public reason just—
Honour and empire with revenge enlarged
By conquering this new World—compels me now
To do what else, though damned, I should abhor."

Ibid. IV, ll 388-393

Line 212 "hold such tack " "To hold tack—to keep one
at bay." *Nares*, s v., where the following passage is quoted :

"They hew his armour peece-meale from his backe,
Yet still the valiant prince maintaines the fray,
Though but halfe-harnest, yet he holds them tacke "

Heywood's Troia Britanica, 1609.

Line 230                    "there is a ragged rowt
Of sillie shepherds, nother skild nor stowt."
This inevitably suggests "the rakehellye route of our ragged
rymers" mentioned by E.K. in his Epistle to Mayster Gabriell
Harvey prefaced to the *Shepheards Calendar* (Globe edition,
p. 442).

Line 235. "their greatest Clarke." Cf.:
"The greatest Clerkes be not the wisest men "
*The Proverbs of John Heywood*, ed. Sharman, p. 115.
The same proverb is quoted by Camden, *op. cit*, p. 332

Line 251 "Isaac" is here used as a trisyllabic word. Cf.
also ll. 494, 706, 782, 820, 821. More frequently it is dissyllabic as in ll. 657, 688, etc.

Line 252. "which hight the myrrh of God " In Genesis
the place is referred to as 'the land of Moriah,' and the hill

has been doubtfully identified by tradition with that on which Solomon's Temple was built in Jerusalem. The A. B. and C. versions of *Le Viel Testament* read simply " dessus les montaignes," and "une montaigne, Dessus la quelle," etc., in the command of God to the angel and the angel's command to Abraham respectively. The E. and F. versions both read "au mont de Vision" and "la terre de Vision" in the corresponding passages, following the Vulgate version,—"Vade in terram visionis." (The York, Towneley and Brome plays also mention the land of Vision.) The Vulgate interpretation is based on the Hebrew forms *Mar'è* (Vision) > *mārè* > vulgarly *maure*, and *Yah* < *Yahwè* (Jehovah) = Maureyah. Beza has preferred to derive the form from Hebrew *mōr* < *murr* > μυρρο and *Yah* < *Yahwè* = Moryah = Moriah. Beza's opinion of the Vulgate is well known, and his contempt was evidenced by the fact that he himself translated the New Testament into Latin. For half a century before his death he enjoyed a very high reputation both as a Hebrew and a classical scholar. The esteem in which he was held among contemporary English theologians is shown by a glance at such a work as Fulke's *Defence of the English Translations of the Bible* (Parker Society, *passim*).

Line 271. "We hie us packing on a row." "*To go packing*, to go away about one's business. *Var. dial.*" (*Halliwell.*) Cf.

"Make speede to flee : be packing and awaie. Maturate fugam. Virg." (*Baret*, s.v. "packe") Cf. also

"When we would be rid of one, we use to say, 'Be going, trudge, pack, be faring, hence away, shift.'"

Camden, *op. cit.*, p. 49.

"on a row," *i.e.* one after the other,—often used jocosely.
Cf. "In jolly ruffe he passed streyght from him
Too *Coryt*, and Enagrus, and too Dryant on a rowe."

*Metamorphoses*, XII, 319.

" Where Prophets, 'Postles, and just folk,
With Martyrs on a row do walk,—
The Angels sweetly caroling."

*The Gude and Godlie Ballates*, (L. IX).

Lines 276-7. The Elizabethan confusion between the use of "you "and "ye " is illustrated in Isaac's speeches addressed to the shepherds : Cf.

"Will ye leave me . . . . ?" (ll. 276-7). "And doe ye thinke . . . . ?" (l. 290.) "But will ye stay . . . . ?" (l.298). "As you doe know . . . . ?" (l. 384).

The confusion cannot be explained by any considerations regarding accented and light words, or ordinary and impassioned speech, although conformably to Elizabethan usage, "ye" is restricted to interrogations. In the accusative "you" is always used. The shepherds in addressing Abraham and Isaac always use "you" except in line 284:

"And then ye shall perceiue the charge."
Here "ye" is used probably to avoid repeating "you" from the preceding line, and because it is more euphonious for the unaccented syllable. Abraham addresses the shepherds as "you" except in ll. 500-501, where the use of "ye" may be attributed to the sudden exaltation of the style.

Line 283. "and proue a pace," *i.e.* thrive. The word which also means "to be with young" is generally applied to cattle, and is therefore especially appropriate in the speech of the shepherds.

Line 287. "that lye in stale." Nares says, "To lie in stale meant to lie in wait, or ambush, for any purpose," and quotes :

"This find I true, for as I lay in stale,
To fight with the Duke Richard's eldest son,
I was destroy'd, not far from Dintingdale."

*Mirr. Mag.* p. 366.
Cf. "The unjust judge for bribes becomes a stale."

Marlowe's *Ovid's Elegies*, Book I, Elegia X.
where "stale" means "bait" or "decoy."

Line 293. "of honest kind," *i.e.* nature.

Line 305. "which looke aboue the skies." Cf., the obsolete expression "to look aloft" which means "to aspire," "be ambitious." V. *New Eng. Dict.*, s.v. "look," 28.

"Look not too high, lest a chip fall into thine eye."
Camden's *Proverbs*, in *Remains*, p. 327.

Line 338. "so good plight." Cf. also line 435, "in better plight." The use of 'plight' in the sense of 'state' or 'condition' was general in Middle English, and was common in Shakespeare's day. Cf. "I think myself in better plight for a leader than you are." *Merry Wives of Windsor*, II, ii, 172. Cf. also

"(Achilles) lives still in healthfull plyght."
*Metamorphoses*, XII, 654.

Line 350. "this conceit." Probably used here in the sense of "trick": V. *New Eng. Dict.*, s.v. 8 b, where the following illustrative quotations are given: "A pretie conceyt that happened in this gathering" (*Grafton Chron.* II, 719), and "Practise some pleasant conceit vpon thy poore patient" (Lyly, *Euphues*, ed. Arb., 67).

Lines 367-9. The translation is very awkward, but a reference to the original makes the meaning quite clear.

Line 415. In the original a printer's error makes this line read as follows: "If he should dyeth, ē farewel our good dayes.'

Line 440. "See that your cariages be prest." Cf. ll. 623 and 848. 'Prest' means 'ready'—a common Elizabethan usage. Cf. "So prest are we." *Tamburlaine*, Part II, Act I, Sc. i., and, "Who warn me of such danger prest at hand."
*Dido, Queen of Carthage*, Act III, Sc. ii.

Line 447. The tendency to drop final -en has been strengthened in this case by the necessity for a rhyme.

Line 459. "to gad";—"To go wandering in desire or thought; to leave the path. Now *rare*." (*New Eng. Dict.*, s.v. 2). "to Gadde, and iet up and downe, &c. Volitare, & vagari in foro. Cicer. Hac illac itare & circumcursare." *Baret* s.v. Cf.

"And millions both of trothes and lyes ronne gadding every where." *Metamorphoses*, XII, 58.

Line 462. "on a rore." "Rore (2) Trouble, stir, noise. Hence perhaps, the name of *Roaring-boys*." *Halliwell*. Cf.

"The zhore
And zea is staynd with blood, and all the ven is on a rore."
*Metamorphoses*, XI, 431.

[83]

NOTES

Line 482. "set forth the better foote." Still a common proverbial expression. Cf.

"Nay, but make haste; the better foot before."
*King John*, IV, ii, 170.

"And with the better foote before the fleeing Nymph to chace." *Metamorphoses*, I, 648.

Line 483. "some cunning drift." *i.e.* scheme or plot. Cf.

"I will so plead
That you shall say my cunning drift excels."
*Two Gentlemen of Verona*, IV, ii, 83.

and

"That drifte by the Queene not vnwiselye deuised."
Sir T. More, *Richard III* (Works, p. 40, col. i.). (Quoted in Notes to *Hamlet*, Clark and Wright, eds., II, ii, 11).

"The Gods, defenders of the innocent
Will neuer prosper your intended drifts."
*Tamburlaine*, Part I, I, ii.

Line 502. "ywus." This form of the adverb is used elsewhere by Golding for the sake of the rhyme. Cf.

"but (he) sayde unto him thus.
No marvell though thou be so proude and full of wordes ywus."
*Metamorphoses*, I, 949.

In the present case Abraham's sentence is broken into two parts by the speech of the shepherds.

Line 504. "God be wy." One of the many contracted forms of 'God be with you (or ye).' Among the variants given in the *New English Dictionary* there is none exactly like that of our text, the nearest approach to it being 'God b'wy' and 'God be wy you.'

Line 511. "It were no reason." Cf. "It is good reason." (l. 618) and "it is good right" (l. 695). V. *New Eng. Dict.* s.v., 14.a., where the following example is given : "It is good reason to sowe timely in wette groundes." (B. Googe *Heresbach's Husb.* 1. (1586) 25 b.) Cf. also

"It is no reason that he, etc."

"Whom you (as meete and reason was) resisted.
*Quibus* tu (ut par erat) restitisti." *Baret, s.v.*

Line 513. "maisterward." "-Ward or -Wards. As a termination, implying *towards* was often arbitrarily added to any other word, as to *us-ward*, to *God-ward*, etc., in the authorized version of the Bible." Nares, *Glossary*, s.v.

Golding in his translation of the *Metamorphoses* uses "Godward" (XII, 171), and "seaward" (VII, 1054). V. a note by Rolfe in his edition of *Coriolanus* on "to bedward" (I, vi, 32).

Line 521. "zuunes." The dialectic form is used as appropriate to the shepherds. Cf. the speech of the herdsman, Anætor the Phocayan, in Golding's translation of the *Metamorphoses* (XI,ll.409-435), where initial "s" is always written "z." (A quotation from this speech is given in the note to line 462, above.) Edgar in addressing Oswald also changes s's to z's (V. *Lear* IV, vi, 211+).

Line 533. "howge." Golding uses this form interchangeably with "huge."

Line 550. "Halfe-fast," *i.e.* half-faced, or partially hidden by the clouds. Cf.

"whose hopeful colours
Advance our half-faced sun, striving to shine."
*Henry VI, Part II*, IV, i, 98.

Line 551. "fulsom." V. *New Eng. Dict.* s.v.i, where the following quotation is given : "For alwey God gaf hyr to her presence So fulsom lyght of heuenly influence." Lydgate, *Lyfe our Ladye* (Caxton) A.v. The word was also used in its modern signification. Cf.

"Fat love, and too much fulsome me annoys,,
Even as sweet meat a glutted stomach cloys."
Marlowe, *Ovid's Elegies*, Bk. II, Elegia XIX.

Line 588. "his cheefest plyght." For 'plight' see note on line 338. 'Chief' is here used in the obsolete sense of 'pre-eminent in excellence.' V. *New Eng. Dict.*, s.v. 5 and 8. In line 98 "chiefest" means simply "greatest."

Line 592. "throwen along." Cf. "as he lay along under an oak." *As You Like It*, II, i, 30.
and                                "when he lies along
After your way, his tale pronounc'd shall bury
His reasons with his body." *Coriolanus*, V, vi, 57-59.

Line 602. Both the metre and sense would be improved by reading

"Is for too drawen us ech one asyde."

Golding uses the old forms of the infinitive elsewhere in the play, *e.g.* "to doone" (l.500) and "to sayne" (l.690); in the *Metamorphoses* I have found "to beene" and "to gone"—always, however, for the sake of the rhyme. At any rate the line is evidently imperfect.

Line 619. "I will ech thing addresse." "Address. To prepare for anything; to get ready. (Fr.) A very common use of the word in our old dramatists." *Halliwell*, s.v.

Line 652. "the falling out," *i.e.* fulfillment. V. *New Eng. Dict.* s.v. "fall," 93, g., where the meaning of 'fall out' is given as 'come to pass.' V. also quotation from Baret's *Alvearie* in the note on line 52.

Line 670. "He hath kept towche." "To keep touch. To be faithful, to be exact to an appointment." Nares, *Glossary*, s.v. "keep."

Line 680. "this hagards mind." Cf. " O false old hag" (l.784). "Haggard. A wild and intractable person (at first, a female); one not to be captured. Obs." *New Eng. Dict.* s.v. 1.+b. fig.

Line 684. "at a glaunce." This would seem to be a reference to the evil eye.

Line 692. "this leawd race," *i.e.* wicked course. V. *New Eng. Dict.* for the numerous meanings of this word. Baret has " Lewd, ungratious naughtie. Improbus," as one meaning, and this is the sense in which it is used in the present instance.

Line 723. "are not thou." Cf. also line 761.—"thou me drew," and line 764—"thou gave me." The regular form of the verb in the second person singular is avoided in the first and third cases for the sake of euphony, in the second case for the sake of the rhyme. V. Abbott, *A Shakespearian Grammar*, 340.

Line 730. "deface." "To deface . . . . to kill." *Baret*, s.v.

Line 739. "dispence," *i.e.* govern. V. *New Eng. Dict.*, s.v. 2.b., where the following quotation is given : "a 1633 Austin *Medit.* 106. Lest hee should not dispense and governe well."

The word is used in a different sense in line 24 of the Prologue.

Line 784. "O false old hag." Golding has used the term as applied to a man in his translation of the *Metamorphoses*, and also in his translation of De Mornay's *Worke Concerning the Trewnesse of Christian Religion*. Both are quoted in the *New Eng. Dict.*, s.v. 3.c.

Line 793. "rather." Cf. also line 859. The word is used in the old sense of "more quickly."

Line 804. "geere." "Any special set of things forming essential parts or appurtenances, or utilized for or connected with some special act." *Century Dictionary*, s.v. 3.

Line 854. "to knowledge thee." "Knowledge" is an old variant of acknowledge, though it sometimes meant "to know." Cf. "But wel Ich wot he wepte faste watur with his eighen,
    And knouhlechede his gult to Crist."

> *Piers Plowman*, A—Text, Passus V, ll.255-6.

Line 879. It is perhaps unnecessary to point out that the first two words complete the preceding metrical line.

Line 880. Abraham's turning in his isolation to the skies and land, which alone seem stable at this juncture, suggests Lear's apostrophe to the heavens under somewhat similar circumstances, or that of Constance in King John.

Line 919. "auord." Apparently a form of "afford." I have met the word only once elsewhere—in Golding's *Metamorphoses*, I, 124.
"The ground untilde, all kinde of fruits did plenteously auorde"
For the omission of the second person singular ending v. note on line 723.

Line 931. "to forbeare." "To give up, part with or from, lose. Obs." *New Eng. Dict.*, s.v. 4.b. The following example is given :"c. 1430 *Syr Gener* (Roxb.) 146. Sith I haue this hert lorn, And my goode men forborn." A closely related meaning is illustrated in Golding's use of the word in *Metamorphoses*, I, 114.
"The worlde was suche, that souldiers helpe might easily be forborne."

Line 935. "the lightsom skye." Cf. "darksom night" (1.866.) "Lightsome. (2) Light; full of light. 'Lightsome glass-window,' Davies, ed. 1672, p. 52." *Halliwell*. The word is a favorite with Golding. The "lightsome skye" is referred to twice in the first book of the *Metamorphoses* (ll. 22 and 77), and I have noticed "the lyghtsum Lucifer" (*Ibid. XI*, 662), and the "lyghtsum Titan" (*Ibid. XI*, 293).

*Conclusion.*

Line 7. "it is no peynted tale." "Peynted" here means "artificial, counterfeit, unreal," as frequently in Shakespeare. V. Schmidt's *Shakespeare-Lexicon* s.v. "Paint" (4). Perhaps there is also an implied reference to the "painted cloth" pictures and emblems which are usually referred to disparagingly because of their cheapness as compared to tapestry.

Line 17. "trew glasses." Cf. such book titles as *The Mirrour for Magistrates, A Looking Glasse for London and England*, etc. V. an interesting note on the frequent use of such terms in English and French literature, in Ward's *History of English Dramatic Literature* I, p. 402. (London, 1899. 3 vols.)

# APPENDIX

## ABRAHAM SACRIFIANT

(REPRINTED FROM THE EDITION OF J. G. FICK, GENEVA, 1874)

# ABRAHAM
## SACRIFIANT,

Tragedie Françoise

PAR THEODORE DE BESZE.

GEN. XV, ROM. IIII.
Abraham a creu à Dieu, & il luy a esté
reputé à iustice.

## THEODORE DE BESZE
### aux Lecteurs, Salut en nostre Seigneur.

IL y a enuiron deux ans, que Dieu m'a fait la grace d'abandonner le pays
auquel il est persecuté, pour le seruir selon sa saincte volonté: durant lequel
temps, pource qu'en mes afflictions, diuerses fantasies se sont presentées à mon
esprit, i'ay eu mon recours à la parolle du Seigneur, en laquelle i'ay trouué
deux choses qui m'ont merueilleusement consolé. L'vne est vne infinité de
promesses, sorties de la bouche de celuy qui est la verité mesmes, & la parolle
duquel est tousiours accompaignée de l'effect : l'autre est vne multitude
d'exemples, desquels le moindre est suffisant non seulement pour enhardir,
mais aussi pour rendre inuincibles les plus foibles & descouragés du monde.
Ce que nous voyons estre auenu, si nous considerons par quels moyens la verité
de Dieu a esté maintenue iusqu'icy. Mais entre tous ceux qui nous sont mis
en auant pour exemple au vieil Testament, ie trouue trois personnages,
ausquels il me semble que le Seigneur a voulu representer ses plus grandes
merueilles, assauoir Abraham, Moyse & Dauid: en la vie desquels si on se miroit
auiourdhuy, on se cognoistroit mieux qu'on ne fait. Lisant donc ces histoires
sainctes auec vn merueilleux plaisir & singulier profit, il m'est pris vn desir de
m'exercer à escrire en vers tels argumens, non seulement pour les mieux con-
siderer & retenir, mais aussi pour louer Dieu en toutes sortes à moy poffibles.
Car ie confesse que de mon naturel i'ay tousiours pris plaisir à la poesie, & ne
m'en puis encores repentir : mais bien ay-ie regret d'auoir employé ce peu de
grace que Dieu m'a donné en cest endroit, en choses desquelles la seule souuen-
ance me fait maintenant rougir. Ie me suis doncques addonné à telles
matieres plus sainctes, esperant de continuer cy apres : mesmement en la
translation des Pseaumes, que i'ay maintenant en main. Que pleust à Dieu
que tant de bons esprits que ie cognoy en France, en lieu de s'amuser à ces
malheureuses inuentions ou imitations de fantasies vaines & deshonnestes
(si on en veut iuger à la verité) regardassent plustost à magnifier la bonté de ce
grand Dieu, duquel ils ont receu tant de graces, qu'à flatter leurs idoles, c'est
à dire, leurs seigneurs ou leurs dames, qu'ils entretiennent en leurs vices par
leurs fictions & flatteries. A la verité il leur seroit mieux seant de chanter
vn cantique à Dieu, que de petrarquiser vn Sonnet, & faire l'amoureux transi,
digne d'auoir vn chapperon à sonnettes : ou de contrefaire ces fureurs poeti-
ques à l'antique, pour distiller la gloire de ce monde & immortaliser cestuy-cy

ou ceste-la    choses qui font confesser au lecteur, que les autheurs d'icelles
n'ont pas seulement monté en leur mont Parnasse, mais sont paruenus iusqu'au cercle de la Lune    Les autres (du nombre desquels i'ay esté à mon
tresgrand regret) aiguisent vn Epigramme trenchant a deux costez, ou piquant
par le bout    les autres s'amusent à tout renuerser, plustost qu'à tourner·
autres cuidans enrichir nostre langue, l'accoustrent à la Grecque & à la
Romaine    Mais quoy ? dira quelcun, i'attendoye vne Tragedie, & tu nous
donnes vne Satyre    Ie confesse que pensant à telles phrenesies, ie me suis
moy-mesmes transporté    toutesfois ie n'entens auoir mesdict des bons esprits,
mais bien voudroy-ie leur auoir descouuert si au clair l'iniure qu'ils font à
Dieu, & le tort qu'ils font à euxmesmes, qu'il leur print enuie de me surmonter
en la  description de tels argumens, dont ie leur enuoye l'essay  comme ie say
qu'il leur sera bien aisé, fi le moindre d'eux s'y veut employer.    Or pour venir
à l' argument que ie traite, il tient de la Tragedie & de la Comedie & pour
cela ay-ie separé le prologue, & diuisé le tout en pauses, à la façon des actes
des Comedies, sans toutesfois m'y assuiettir    Et pource qu'il tient plus de
l'vn que de l'autre, i'ay mieux aimé l'appeller Tragedie    Quant à la maniere
de proceder, i'ay changé quelques petites circonstances de l'histoire, pour
m'approprier au theatre    Au reste i'ay poursuiuy le principal au plus pres
du texte que i'ay peu, suyuant les coniectures qui m'ont semblé les plus
conuenables à la matiere & aux personnes    Et combien que les affections
soyent des plus grandes, toutesfois ie n'ay voulu vser de termes ne de manieres
de parler trop eslongnées du commun    encores que ie sache telle auoir esté la
façon des Grecs & des Latins, principalement en leurs Chorus (ainsi qu'ils les
nomment).    Mais tant s'en faut qu'en cela ie les veuille imiter, que tout au
contraire ie ne trouue rien plus mal-seant que ces translations tant forcées, &
mots tirés de si loing qu'ils ne peuuent iamais arriuer à poinct    tesmoin
Aristophane, qui tant de fois & à bon droit en a repris les Poetes de son temps.
Mesmes i'ay fait vn cantique hors de Chorus, & n'ay vsé de strophes, anti-
strophes, epirremes, parecbases, ny autres tels mots, qui ne seruent que
d'espouanter les simples gens    puis que l'vsage de telles choses est aboly, &
n'est de soy tant recommendable qu'on se doyue tourmenter à le mettre sus
Quant à l'orthographie, i'ay voulu que l'imprimeur suiuist la commune, quelques maigres fantasies qu'on ait mis en auant depuis trois ou quatre ans ença,
& conseilleroye volontiers aux plus opiniastres de ceux qui l'ont  changé
(s'ils estoyent gens qui demandassent conseil à autres qu'à eux mesmes) puis
qu'ils la veulent ranger selon la prononciation, c'est à dire, puis qu'ils veulent
faire qu'il y ait quasi autant de manieres d'escrire, qu'il y a non seulement de
contrées, mais aussi de personnes en France  ils apprennent à prononcer
deuant que vouloir apprendre à escrire    car (pour parler & escrire à leur
façon) celuy n'est pas digne de bailler les reigles d'escrire nostre langue, qui
ne la peut parler.    Ce que ie ne dy pour vouloir calomnier tous ceux qui ont
mis en auant leurs difficultés en ceste matiere, laquelle ie confesse auoir bon
besoin d'estre reformée: mais pour ceux qui proposent leurs resueries comme
certaines reigles que tout le monde doit ensuiure    Au surplus, quant au profit
qui se peut tirer de ceste singuliere histoire, outre ce qui en est traité en infinis
passages de l'Escriture, i'en laisseray faire à celuy qui parlera en l'Epilogue.
vous priant, quiconques vous soyez, receuoir ce mien petit labeur, d'aussi bon
cœur qu'il vous est presenté    De Lausanne, ce premier d'Octobre.    M. D L.

## ARGVMENT DV

### XXII CHAPITRE

de Genese.

ET apres ces choses, Dieu tenta Abraham, & luy dit, Abraham. Et il respondit, Me voicy. Puis luy dit, Pren maintenant ton fils vnique, lequel tu aimes : Ifaac, dy-ie, & t'en va au pays de Moria & l'offre là en holocauste sur vne des montagnes laquelle te diray. Abraham donc se leuant de matin, embasta son asne, & print deux seruiteurs auec luy, & Isaac son fils : & ayant coupé le bois pour l'holocauste, se leua, & s'en alla au lieu que Dieu luy auoit dit. Au troisieme iour Abraham leuant ses yeux, vit le lieu de loing, & dit à ses seruiteurs, Arrestez-vous icy auec l'asne : moy & l'enfant cheminerons iusques là : & quand aurons adoré, nous retournerons à vous. Et Abraham print le bois de l'holocauste, & le mit sur Isaac son fils. Et luy print le feu en sa main & vn glaiue, & s'en allerent eux deux ensemble. Adonc Isaac dit à Abraham son pere, Mon pere. Abraham respondit, Me voicy mon fils. Et il dit, Voicy le feu & le bois, mais où est l'agneau pour l'holocauste ? Et Abraham respondit, Mon fils, Dieu se pouruoira d'agneau pour l'holocauste. Et cheminoyent tous deux ensemble. Et estans venuz au lieu que Dieu luy auoit dit, il edifia illec vn autel, & ordonna le bois : si lia Isaac son fils, & le mit sur l'autel par dessus le bois: & auançant sa main, empoigna le glaiue pour decoler son fils. Lors luy cria du ciel l'Ange du Seigneur, disant, Abraham, Abraham : lequel respondit, Me voicy. Et il luy dit, Tu ne mettras point la main sur l'enfant, & ne luy feras aucune chose. Car maintenant i'ay cognu que tu crains Dieu, veu que tu n'as espargné ton fils, ton vnique, pour l'amour de moy. Et Abraam leua ses yeux, & regarda : & voicy derriere luy vn mouton retenu en vn buisson par ses cornes. Adonc Abraham s'en va & print le mouton, & l'offrit en holocauste en lieu de son fils. Et Abraham appella le nom de ce lieu-la, Le Seigneur verra, dont on dit auiourdhuy de la montagne, Le Seigneur sera veu. Et l'Ange du Seigneur appella Abraham du ciel pour la seconde fois, disant : I'ay iuré par moy-mesme, dit le Seigneur: Pourtant que tu as fait ceste chose, & que tu n'as point espargné ton fils, ton vnique, ie te beniray, & multiplieray ta semence comme les estoilles du ciel & comme le sablon qui est sur le riuage de la mer : & ta semence possedera la porte de tes ennemis. Et toutes nations de la terre seront benites en ta semence, pource que tu as obey à ma voix.

# PERSONNAGES.

PROLOGVE.

ABRAHAM.

SARA.

ISAAC.

LA TROUPE des bergers de la maison d'Abraham d uisée en deux parties.

L'ANGE.

SATAN.

## PROLOGVE.

IEU vous gard' tous, autant gros que
    menuz,
Petits & grans, bien soyez-vous venus.
Long temps y a, au moins comme il
    me semble,
Qu'icy n'y eut autant de peuple ensemble:
[5] Que pleust à Dieu que toutes les sepmaines,
Nous peussions voir les eglises si pleines.
    Or ça messieurs, & vous dames honnestes,
Ie vous supply' d'entendre mes requestes:
Ie vous requier vous taire seulement.
[10] Comment ? dira quelcune, voirement
Ie ne saurois, ny ne voudrois auec.
Or si faut-il pourtant clorre le bec,
Ou vous & moy auons peine perdue :
Moy de parler, & vous d'estre venue.
[15] Ie vous requier tant seulement silence :
Ie vous supply' d'ouyr en patience.
    Petits & grans ie vous diray merueilles.
Tant seulement prestez-moy vos aureilles.
Or doncques peuple, escoute vn bien grand cas :
[20] Tu penses estre au lieu où tu n'es pas.
Plus n'est icy Lausanne, elle est bien loing :
Mais toutesfois quand il sera besoing,
Chacun pourra, voire dedans vne heure,
Sans nul danger retrouuer sa demeure.
[25] Maintenant donc icy est le pays
Des Philistins. Estes-vous esbahis ?
Ie dy bien plus, voyez-vous bien ce lieu ?
C'est la maison d'vn seruiteur de Dieu,
Dict Abraham, celuy mesme dequel
[30] Par viue foy le nom est immortel.
    En cest endroit vous le verrez tenté,
Et iusqu'au vif attaint & tourmenté.
Vous le verrez par foy iustifié :
Son fils Isaac quasi sacrifié.
[35] Bref, vous verrez estranges passions,

La chair, le monde, & ses affections
Non seulement au vif representées,
Mais qui plus est, par la foy surmontées.
    Et qu'ainsi soit, maint loyal personnage
[40] En donnera bien tost bon tesmoignage :
Bien tost verrez Abraham & Sara,
Et tost apres Isaac sortira.
Ne sont-ils point tesmoins tresueritables ?
    Qui veut donc voir choses tant admirables,
[45] Nous le prions seulement d'escouter,
Et ce qu'il a d'aureilles nous prester :
Estant tout seur qu'il entendra merueilles :
Et puis apres luy rendrons ses aureilles.

    *ABRAHAM* parle, sortant de sa maison

Depuis que i'ay mon pays delaissé,
Et de courir çà & là n'ay cessé :
Helas, mon Dieu, est-il encore vn homme
Qui ait porté de trauaux telle somme ?
[5] Depuis le temps que tu m'as retiré
Hors du pays où tu n'es adoré :
Helas, mon Dieu, est-il encore vn homme
Qui ait receu de biens si grande somme ?
Voila comment par les calamitez,
[10] Tu fais cognoistre aux hommes tes bontez :
Et tout ainsi que tu fis tout de rien,
Ainsi fais-tu sortir du mal le bien :
Ne pouuant l'homme à l'heure d'vn grand heur
Assez au clair cognoistre ta grandeur.
[15] Las, i'ay vescu septante & cinq années,
Suyuant le cours de tes predestinées,
Qui ont voulu que prinse ma naissance
D'vne maison riche par suffisance.
Mais quel bien peut l'homme de bien auoir,
[20] S'il est contrainct, contrainct (dy-ie) de voir,
En lieu de toy, qui terre & cieux as faicts,
Craindre & seruir mille dieux contrefaicts ?
Or donc sortir tu me fis de ces lieux,
[96]

Laisser mes biens, mes parens & leurs dieux,
[25] Incontinent que i'eu ouy ta voix.
Mesmes tu sais que point ie ne sauois
En quel endroit tu me voulois conduire :
Mais qui te suit, mon Dieu, il peut bien dire
Qu'il va tout droit :  & tenant ceste voye,
[30] Craindre ne doit que iamais se fouruoye.

*Sara sortant d'vne mesme maison.*

Apres auoir pensé & repensé
Combien i'ay eu de biens le temps passé,
De toy, mon Dieu, qui tousiours as voulu
Garder mon cœur & mon corps impollu :
[35] Puis m'as donné, ensuyuant ta promesse,
Cest heureux nom de mere en ma vieillesse:
En mon esprit suis tellement rauie,
Que ie ne puis, comme i'ay bonne enuie,
A toy, mon Dieu, faire recognoissance
[40] Du moindre bien dont i'aye iouyssance.
Si veux-ie au moins, puis qu'à l'escart ie suis,
Te mercier, Seigneur, comme ie puis.
Mais n'est-ce pas mon seigneur que ie voy ?
Si le pensoy'-ie estre plus loing de moy.

*Abraham*

[45] Sara, Sara, ce bon vouloir ie loue :
Et n'as rien dit, que tresbien ie n'aduoue.
Approche-toy, & tous deux en ce lieu
Recognoissons les grans bienfaits de Dieu.
Commune en est à deux la iouyssance,
[50] Commune en soit à deux la cognoissance.

*Sara*

Ha monseigneur, que sauroy'-ie mieux faire,
Que d'essayer tousiours à vous complaire ?
Pour cela suis-ie en ce monde ordonnée.
Et puis comment sauroit-on sa iournée
[55] Mieux employer, qu'à chanter l'excellence
De ce grand Dieu, dont la magnificence
Et haut & bas se presente à nos yeux ?

*Abraham*

L homme pour vray ne sauroit faire mieux,
Que de chanter du Seigneur l'exce lence :
[60] Car il ne peut, pour toute recompense
Des biens qu'il a par luy iournellement,
Rien luy payer qu'honneur tant seulement.

*Cantique* d'Abraham & de Sara

Or sus donc commençons
Et le los annonçons
[65] Du grand Dieu souuerain.
Tout ce qu'eusmes iamais,
Et aurons desormais,
Ne vient que de sa main.
C'est luy qui des hauts cieux
[70] Le grand tour spacieux
Entretient de là haut,
Dont le cours asseuré
Est si bien mesuré,
Que iamais ne defaut.
[75] Il fait l'esté bruslant :
Et fait l'hyuer tremblant :
Terre & mer il conduit,
La pluye & le beau temps :
L'automne & le prin-temps,
[80] Et le iour & la nuict
Las, Seigneur, qu'estions-nous,
Que nous as entre tous
Choisiz & retenus ?
Et contre les meschans,
[85] Par villes & par champs,
Si long temps maintenus ?
Tiré nous as des lieux
Tous remplis de faux dieux,
Vsant de tes bontez :
[90] Et de mille dangers
Parmy les estrangers
Tousiours nous as iettez.
En nostre grand besoin

Egypte a eu le soin
[95] De nous entretenir :
Puis contrainct a esté
Pharaon despité
De nous laisser venir.
  Quatre Rois furieux,
100] Desia victorieux,
Auons mis à l'enuers.
Du sang de ces meschans
Nous auons veu les champs
Tous rouges & couuers.
[105]  De Dieu ce bien nous vient :
Car de nous luy souuient,
Comme de ses amis.
Luy donc nous donnera,
Lors que temps en sera,
[110] Tout ce qu'il a promis.
  A nous & nos enfans
En honneur triomphans
Ceste terre appartient :
Dieu nous l'a dit ainsi,
[115] Et le croyons aussi :
Car sa promesse il tient.
  Tremblez doncques, peruers,
Qui par tout l'vniuers
Estes si dru semez :
[120] Et qui vous estes faits
Mille dieux contrefaits
Qu'en vain vous reclamez.
  Et toy Seigneur vray Dieu,
Sors vn iour de ton lieu,
[125] Que nous soyons vengez
De tous tes ennemis :
Et qu'à neant soyent mis
Les dieux qu'ils ont forgez.

*Abraham.*

Or sus, Sara, le grand Dieu nous benie :
[130] A celle fin que durant ceste vie,

[99]

Pour tant de biens que luy seul nous ottroye,
A le seruir chacun de nous s'employe.
Retirons-nous, & sur tout prenons garde
A nostre fils, que trop ne se hazarde,
[135]  Par frequenter tant de malheureux hommes,
Parmy lesquels vous voyez que nous sommes.
Vn vaisseau neuf tient l'odeur longuement
Dont abbreuué il est premierement.
Quoy qu'vn enfant soit de bonne nature,
[140]  Il est perdu sans bonne nourriture.

*Sara*

Monsieur, i'espere en faire mon deuoir :
Et pour autant qe'en luy nous deuons voir
De nostre Dieu le vouloir accomply,
Seure ie suis qu'il prendra si bon ply,
[145]  Et le Seigneur si bien le benira,
Qu'à son honneur le tout se conduira.

*Satan* en habit de moyne.

Ie vay, ie vien, iour & nuict ie trauaille,
Et m'est aduis, en quelque part que i'aille,
Que ie ne pers ma peine aucunement.
[150]  Regne le Dieu en son haut firmament :
Mais pour le moins la terre est toute à moy,
Et n'en deplaise à Dieu ny à sa Loy.
Dieu est aux cieux par les siens honnoré :
Des miens ie suis en la terre adoré.
[155]  Dieu est au ciel : & bien, ie suis en terre.
Dieu fait la paix : & moy, ie fay la guerre.
Dieu regne en haut   & bien, ie regne en bas.
Dieu fait la paix : & ie fay les debas.
Dieu a crée & la terre & les cieux :
[160]  I'ay bien plus fait, car i'ay crée les dieux.
Dieu est seruy de ses Anges luisans :
Ne sont aussi mes anges reluisans ?
Il n'y a pas iusques à mes pourceaux,
A qui ie n'aye enchassé les museaux.
[165]  Tous ces paillars, ces gourmans, ces yurongnes
Qu'on voit reluire auec leurs rouges trongnes,

Portans sapphirs, & rubis des plus fins,
Sont mes supposts, sont mes vrais Cherubins.
Dieu ne fit onc chose tant soit parfaite
[170] Qui soit egale à celuy qui l'a faicte :
Mais moy i'ay fait, dont vanter ie me puis,
Beaucoup de gens pires que ie ne suis.
Car quant à moy, ie croy & say tresbien
Qu'il est vn Dieu, & que ie ne vaux rien :
[175] Mais i'en say bien à qui totalement
I'ay renuersé le faux entendement :
Si que les vns (qui est vn cas commun)
Aiment trop mieux seruir mille dieux qu'vn :
Les autres ont fantasie certaine,
[180] Que de ce Dieu l'opinion est vaine.
Voila comment depuis l'homme premier,
Heureusement i'ay suiuy ce mestier :
Et poursuiuray, quoy qu'en doyue aduenir,
Tant que pourray cest habit maintenir.
[185] Habit encore en ce monde incogneu :
Mais qui sera vn iour si bien cognu,
Qu'il n'y aura ne ville ne village
Qui ne le voye à son tresgrand dommage.
O froc, ô froc, tant de maux tu feras,
[190] Et tant d'abus en plein iour couuriras !
Ce froc, ce froc vn iour cognu sera,
Et tant de maux au monde apportera,
Que si n'estoit l'enuie dont i'abonde,
I'aurois pitié moymesme de ce monde.
[195] Car moy qui suis de tous meschans le pire,
En le portant, moymesme ie m'empire.
  Or se feront ces choses en leurs temps :
Mais maintenant assaillir ie pretens
Vn Abraham, lequel seul sur la terre
[200] Auec les siens m'ose faire la guerre.
De faict, ie l'ay maintesfois affailly,
Mais i'ay tousiours à mon vouloir failly :
Et ne vis onc vieillard mieux resistant.
Mais il aura des assaux tant & tant,

[205] Qu'en brief sera, au moins comme i'espere,
Du rang de ceux desquels ie suis le pere.
Vray est qu'il a au vray Dieu sa fiance,
Vray est qu'il a du vray Dieu l'alliance,
Vray est que Dieu luy a promis merueilles
[210] Et desia fait des choses nompareilles :
Mais quoy ? s'il n'a ferme perseuerance,
Que luy pourra seruir son esperance ?
Ie feray tant de tours & çà & là,
Que ie rompray l'asseurance qu'il a.
[215] De deux enfans qu'il a, l'vn ie ne crains .
L'autre à grand peine eschappera mes mains.
La mere est femme : & quant aux seruiteurs,
Sont simples gens, sont bien poures pasteurs,
Bien peu rusez encontre mes cautelles.
[220] Or ie m'en vay employer peines telles
A les auoir, que ie suis bien trompé,
Si le plus fin n'est bien tost attrappé.

*Abraham* resortant de la maison.

Quoy que ie die ou que ie face,
Rien n'y a dont ie ne me lasse,
[225] Tant me soit l'affaire agreable :
Telle est ma nature damnable.
Mais sur tout ie me mescontente
De moymesme,& fort me tormente,
Veu que Dieu iamais ne se fasche
[230] De m'aider : pourquoy ie me tasche
A ne me fascher point aussi
De recognoistre sa mercy,
Autant de bouche que de cœur.

*L'Ange.*

Abraham, Abraham.

*Abraham.*

Seigneur,

[235] Me voicy.

*L'Ange.*

Ton fils bien-aimé,
Ton fils vnique Isaac nommé,

[102]

Par toy soit mené iusqu'au lieu
Surnommé la Myrrhe de Dieu :
Là deuant moy tu l'offriras,

[240] Et tout entier le brusleras,
Au mont que ie te monstreray.

*Abraham.*

Brusler ! brusler ! ie le feray.
Mais, mon Dieu, si ceste nouuelle
Me semble fascheuse & nouuelle,

[245] Seigneur, me pardonneras-tu ?
Helas, donne-moy la vertu
D'accomplir ce commandement.
Ha bien cognoy'-ie ouuertement,
Qu'enuers moy tu es courroucé

[250] Las, Seigneur, ie t'ay offensé,
O Dieu qui as fait ciel & terre,
A qui veux-tu faire la guerre ?
Me veux-tu donc mettre si bas ?
Helas, mon fils, helas, helas !

[255] Par quel bout doy-ie commencer ?
La chose vaut bien l' penser.

*Troupe* des bergers sortans de la maison d'Abraham.

*Demie troupe.*

Amis, il est temps, ce me semble,
Que nous retournions tous ensemble
Vers nos compagnons.

*Demie troupe.*

Ie le veux.

[260] Car si nous sommes auec eux,
Ils en seront plus asseurez.

*Isaac.*

Hola, ie vous pri', demeurez.
Comment ?  me laissez-vous ainsi ?

*Troupe.*

Isaac, demeurez icy :

[265] Autrement monsieur vostre pere,
Ou bien madame vostre mere

En pourroyent estre mal contens.
Il viendra quel<sup> </sup>e iour le temps
Que vous serez grand. si Dieu plaist:
[270] Et lors vous cognoistrez que c'est
De garder aux champs les troupeaux,
En danger par monts & par vaux,
De tant de bestes dangereuses,,
Sortans des forests ombrageuses.

*Isaac.*

[275] Pensez-vous aussi que voulusse
Departir deuant pue ie seusse
Si mon pere ainsi le voudroit ?

*Troupe*

Aussi faut-il en tout endroict,
Qu'vn fils ưonneste & bien appris,
[280] Quelque cas qu'il ait entrepris,
A pere & à mere obeisse.

*Isaac.*

Ie n'y faudray point que ie puisse,
Et fust-ce iusques au mourir.
Mais tandis que ie vay courir
[285] Iusqu'à mon pere, pour cognoistre
Quelle sa volonté peut estre,
Voulez-vous pas m'attendre icy ?

*Troupe.*

Allez, nous le ferons ainsi.

*Cantique* de la Troupe

O l'homme heureux au monde
[290] Qui dessus Dieu se fonde,
Et en fait son rampart :
Laissant tous ce<sup> </sup> hautains,
Et' tant sages mondains
S'esgarer à l'escart.

[295] Poureté ne richesse
N'empesche ny ne blesse
D'vn fidele le cœur.
Quoy qu'il soit tormenté
Et mille fois tenté,

[104]

[300]      Le fidele est vainqueur.
        Ce grand Dieu qui le meine,
        Au plus fort de sa peine,
        En prend vn si grand soing,
        Qu'il le vient redresser
[305]      Estant prest de glisser,
        En son plus grand besoing.
        Cela peut-on cognoistre
        D'Abraham nostre maistre :
        Car tant plus on l'assaut
[310]      Et deçà & delà,
        Tant moins de peur il a,
        Et moins le cœur luy faut.
        Il a laissé sa terre,
        Faim luy a fait la guerre :
[315]      En Egypte est venu.
        Sara il voit soudain
        Rauie de la main
        D'vn grand Roy incognu.
        A Dieu fait sa demande,
[320]      Soudain le Roy le mande,
        Et sa femme luy rend :
        Le prie de vuider.
        Abraham sans tarder,
        Autre voye entreprend.
[325]      Mais durant ceste fuitte,
        Son bien si bien profite,
        Que pour s'entretenir,
        De Loth il se depart :
        Pource qu'en mesme part
[330]      Deux ne pouuoyent tenir.
        Vne guerre soudaine
        Entre neuf Rois se meine.
        Parmy ces grans combats,
        Loth perd auec les siens
[335]      Sa franchise & ses biens :
        Cinq Rois sont mis à bas.
        Nostre maistre fidelle

Oyant ceste nouuelle
Viuement les poursuit,
[340] Les atteint & desfait,
N'ayant d'hommes de faict
Que trois cens dix & huit.

Leur arrache leur proye,
La disme au Prestre paye,
[345] A chacun fait raison.
Puis de tous hautement
Loué tresiustement,
Retourne en sa maison
Or parmy sa famille
[350] N'auoit-il fils ne fille.
Sara qui cela voit,
Ne pouuant conceuoir,
Luy fait mesmes auoir
Agar qui la seruoit.

[355] D'Agar donc nostre maistre
Ismael se vit naistre.
Treize ans ainsi passa,
Voyant deuant ses yeux
Aller de bien en mieux
[360] Les biens qu'il amassa.
Lors pour signifiance
De la saincte alliance
Du Seigneur & de nous,
Autant petits que grans
[365] Iusqu'aux petits enfans
Circoncis fusmes tous.

*Isaac*

Mes amis, Dieu se monstre à nous.
Si bon, si gracieux, si doux,
Que iamais ie ne luy demande
[370] Chose tant soit petite ou grande,
Que ie ne me voye accordé
Trop plus que ie n'ay demandé.
I'auois, comme sauez, vouloir

De vous suyure, afin d'aller voir :

[375]    Mais voicy mon pere qui vient.

       *Abraham* sortant auec Sara.

Mais tant y a qu'il appartient,
Quand Dieu nous enioint vne chose,
Que nous ayons la bouche close,
Sans estriuer aucunement

[380]    Contre son sainct commandement :
S'il commande, il faut obeir.

         *Sara*

Ie vous pri' ne vous esbahir
Si le cas bien fascheux ie trouue.

        *Abraham.*

Au besoin le bon cœur s'esprouue.

        *Sara.*

[385]    Il est vray : mais en premier lieu,
Sachez donc le vouloir de Dieu.
Nous auons cest enfant seulet.
Qui est encore tout foiblet :
Auquel gist toute l'asseurance

[390]    De nostre si grande esperance.

        *Abraham.*

Mais en Dieu.

        *Sara.*

       Mais laissez-moy dire.

        *Abraham.*

Dieu se peut-il iamais desdire ?
Partant asseurée soyez
Que Dieu le garde :  & me croyez.

        *Sara.*

[395]    Mais Dieu veut-il qu'on le hazarde ?

        *Abraham.*

Hazardé n'est point que Dieu garde.

        *Sara.*

Ie me doutte de quelque cas.

        *Abraham.*

Quant à moy ie n'en doutte pas.

*Sara*

C'est quelque entreprise secrette.

*Abraham.*

[400]  Mais telle qu'elle est, Dieu l'a faicte.

*Sara*

Au moins si vous sauiez où c'est.

*Abraham*

Bien tost le sauray, si Dieu plaist.

*Sara*

Il n'ira iamais iusques là.

*Abraham*

Dieu pouruoira à tout cela.

*Sara*

[405]  Mais les chemins sont dangereux.

*Abraham*

Qui meurt suyuant Dieu, est heureux.

*Sara*

S'il meurt, nous voila demeurez.

*Abraham*

Les morts de Dieu sont asseurez.

*Sara*

Mieux vaut sacrifier icy

*Abraham*

[410]  Mais Dieu ne le veut pas ainsi.

*Sara*

Or sus, puis que faire le faut,
Ie prie au grand Seigneur d'enhaut,
Monseigneur, que sa saincte grace
Tousiours compagnie vous face.
[415]  Adieu mon fils.

*Isaac*

Adieu ma mere.

*Sara.*

Suyuez bien tousiours vostre pere,
Mon amy, & seruez bien Dieu,
Afin que bien tost en ce lieu
Puissiez en santé reuenir.

[420] Voila, ie ne me puis tenir,
Isaac, que ie ne vous baise.

*Isaac.*

Ma mere, qu'il ne vous desplaise,
Ie vous veux faire vne requeste.

*Sara.*

Dites, mon amy, ie suis preste
[425] A l'accorder.

*Isaac.*

Ie vous supplye
D'oster ceste melancholie.
Mais, s'il vous plaist, ne plourez point,
Ie reuiendray en meilleur poinct :
Ie vous pri' de ne vous fascher.

*Abraham.*

[430] Enfans, il vous faudra marcher
Pour le moins six bonnes iournées :
Voila vos charges ordonnées,
Et tout ce qui fait de besoin.

*Troupe.*

Sire, laissez-nous en le soin,
[435] Tant seulement commandez-nous.

*Abraham.*

Or sus, Dieu soit auecques vous :
Ce grand Dieu qui par sa bonté
Iusques icy nous a esté
Tant propice & tant secourable,
[440] Soit à vous & moy fauorable.
Quoy qu'il y ait, monstrez-vous sage :
I'espere que nostre voyage
Heureusement se parfera.

*Sara.*

Las, ie ne say quand ce sera
[445] Que reuoir ie vous pourray tous.
Le Seigneur soit auecques vous.

*Isaac.*

Adieu ma mere.

[109]

*Abraham.*
Adieu.

*Troupe.*
Adieu.

*Abraham.*
Or sus, departons de ce lieu.

*Satan.*
Mais n'est-ce pas pour enrager ?
[450] Moy qui fais vn chacun ranger,
Qui say tirer le monde à moy,
Ne faisant signe que du doy :
Moy qui renuerse & trouble tout,
Ne puis pourtant venir à bout
[455] De ce faux vieillard obstiné.
Quelque assaut qu'on luy ait donné,
Le voila party de ce lieu,
Et tout prest d'obeir à Dieu,
Quoy que le cas soit fort estrange.
[460] Mais au fort, soit que son cœur change,
Ou qu'il sacrifie en effect,
Ce que ie pretens sera faict.
S'il sacrifie, Isaac mourra,
Et mon cœur deliuré sera
[465] De la frayeur qu'en sa personne
La promesse de Dieu me donne.
S'il change de cœur, ie puis dire
Que i'ay tout ce que ie desire :
Et voila le poinct où ie tasche.
[470] Car si vne fois il se fasche
D'obeir au Dieu tout-puissant,
Le voila desobeissant,
Banny de Dieu & de sa grace.
Voila le poinct que ie pourchasse.
[475] Sus donc, mon froc, courons apres
Pour le combatre de plus pres.

PAVSE.

[110]

*Abraham.*

Enfans, voicy arriué le tiers iour,
Que nous marchons sans auoir fait seiour
Que bien petit : reposer il vous faut :
[480] Car quant à moy, ie veux monter plus haut,
Auec Isaac, iusqu'en vn certain lieu,
Qui m'a esté enseigné de mon Dieu.
Là ie feray sacrifice & priere,
Comme il requiert : demourez donc derriere,
[485] Et vous gardez de marcher plus auant.
Mais vous, mon fils Isaac, passez deuant,
Car le Seigneur requiert vostre presence.

*Troupe.*

Puis que telle est, Sire, vostre defense,
Nous demourrons.

*Abraham.*

Baillez-luy ce fardeau,
[490] Et ie prendray le feu & le cousteau.
Bien tost serons de retour, si Dieu plaist.
Mais cependant sauez-vous bien que c'est ?
Priez bien Dieu, & pour nous & pour vous.
Helas i'en ay

*Troupe.*

Ainfi le ferons-nous.

*Abraham.*

[495] Autant besoin qu'eut onc poure personne.
Adieu vous dy.

*Troupe.*

Adieu.

*Demie Troupe.*

Mais ie m'estonne
Tresgrandement.

*Demie Troupe.*

Et moy aussi.

*Demie Troupe.*

Et moy.
Comment ? de voir en tel esmoy

[111]

[500]
Cil qui si bien a resisté
A tant de maux qu'il a porté !

*Demie Troupe*
De dire qu'il craigne la guerre,
Estant en ceste estrange terre,
Il n'y auroit point de raison :
Car nous sauons qu'vne saison
[505] Abimelech, qui est seigneur
Du pays, luy fit cest honneur
De le visiter, & prier
Qu'à luy se daignast allier,
De sorte qu'en solennité
[510] L'accord de paix fut arresté.
Au surplus, quant à son mesnage,
Que peut-il auoir dauantage ?

*Demie Troupe*
Il vit en paix & en repos.
Il est vieil, mais il est dispos.

*Demie Troupe.*
[515] Il n'a qu'vn fils, mais Dieu sait quel :
Au monde il n'en est point de tel.
Son bestail tellement foisonne,
Qu'il semble à voir que Dieu luy donne
Encore plus qu'il ne souhaitte.

*Demie Troupe*
[520] Il n'y a chose tant parfaicte,
Qu'il n'y ait tousiours à redire.
Ie prie à Dieu qu'il le retire
Bien tost de la peine où il est.

*Demie Troupe*
Ainsi le face, s'il luy plaist.

*Demie Troupe.*
[525] Quoy qu'il y ait, ie presuppose
Que ce soit quelque grande chose.

*Cantique* de la Troupe
Quoy que soit cest vniuers
Tant spacieux & diuers,

[112]

Il n'y a rien tant soit ferme,
[530]    Rien n'y a qui n'ait son terme.
    Dieu tout puissant qui tout garde,
Rien icy bas ne regarde,
Qui tousiours dure de mesme,
S'il ne regarde soy-mesme.
[535]    Le grand soleil reluisant,
Va son flambeau conduisant
Autant comme le iour dure :
Puis reuient la nuict obscure,
Couurant de ses noires ailes
[540]    Choses & laides & belles.
    Que dirons-nous de la lune,
Qui iamais ne fut tout vne ?
Ores apparoist cornue,
Puis demie, puis bossue,
[545]    Puis esclaire toute ronde
Les tenebres de ce monde.
    Les grans astres flamboyans,
Cà & là vont tournoyans,
Peignans leur diuers visage
[550]    Et de beau temps & d'orage.
    Si deux iours on met ensemble,
L'vn à l'autre ne ressemble :
L'vn passe legerement,
L'autre dure longuement.
[555]    L'vn est sur nous enuieux
De la lumiere des cieux.
L'vn auec sa couleur bleue
Nous veut esblouir la veue :
L'vn veut le monde brusler,
[560]    L'autre essaye à le geler.
    Ores la terre fleurie
Estend sa tapisserie :
Ores d'vn vent la froidure
Change en blancheur sa verdure.
[565]    L'onde en son humide corps
S'enfle par dessus les bords,

Pillant par tout à outrance
Du laboureur l'esperance :
Puis en sa riue premiere
570] Sera bien tost prisonniere.

Parquoy celuy qui se fonde
En rien qui soit en ce monde,
Soit en haut ou soit en bas,
Ie dy que sage n'est pas.
[575] Qu'est-ce donques de celuy
Qui des hommes fait appuy ?

Parmy tous les animaux
Suiets à dix mille maux,
Le soleil qui fait son tour,
[580] Du monde tout à l'entour,
Ne vit onc, pour dire en somme,
Chose si foible que l'homme.
Car tous les plus vertueux
Par les flots impetueux
[585] Sont tellement combatus,
Qu'on en voit maints abatus.

O combien est fol qui cuide
De fascherie estre vuide
Tant qu'icy bas il sera !
[590] Mais cil qui desirera
D'estre affeuré, il luy faut
Son cœur appuyer plus haut :
Dont il aura bon exemple,
Si nostre maistre il contemple.

*Demie Troupe.*
[595] Or le mieux que nous puissions faire,
Ie croy que c'est de se retraire
En quelque coin plus à l'escart :
Afin que chacun de sa part,
Prie le Seigneur qu'il luy plaise
[600] Le ramener mieux à son aise.
Allons.
*Demie Troupe.*
Ie vay tant que ie puis.

PAVSE.

*Isaac.*

Mon pere.

*Abraham.*

Helas, las, quel pere ie suis !

*Isaac.*

Voila du bois, du feu, & vn cousteau,
Mais ie ne voy ne mouton ny agneau,
[605] Que vous puissiez sacrifier icy.

*Abraham.*

Isaac mon fils, Dieu en aura soucy :
Attendez-moy, mon amy, en ce lieu,
Car il me faut vn petit prier Dieu.

*Isaac.*

Et bien, mon pere, allez : mais ie vous prie,
[610] Me direz-vous quelle est la fascherie,
Dont ie vous voy tourmenté iusqu'au bout ?

*Abraham.*

A mon retour, mon fils, vous saurez tout :
Mais cependant prier vous faut aussi.

*Isaac.*

C'est bien raison : ie le feray ainsi,
[615] Et quant & quant le cas appresteray.
En premier lieu ce bois i'entasseray:
Premierement ce baston sera là,
Puis cestuy-cy, puis apres cestuy-la.
Voila le cas : mon pere aura le soin,
[620] Quant au surplus qui nous fait de besoin.
Prier m'en vay, ô Dieu, ta saincte face :
C'est bien raison, ô Dieu, que ie le face.

*Sara.*

Plus on vit, plus on voit, helas,
Que c'est que de viure cy bas !
[625] Soit en mari, soit en lignée,
Il n'y eut oncques femme née
Autant heureuse que ie suis.
Mais i'ay tant enduré d'ennuis
Ces trois derniers iours seulement,

[115]

[630] Que ie ne say pas bonnement
 Lequel est le plus grand des deux :
 Ou le bien que i'ay receu d'eux,
 Ou le mal que i'ay enduré
 En trois iours qu'ils ont demeuré.

[635] Ne nuict ne iour ie ne repose,
 Et si ne pense à autre chose
 Qu'à mon seigneur & à mon fils.
 A vray dire, assez mal ie fis
 De les laisser aller ainsi,

[640] Ou de n'y estre allée aussi.
 De six iours sont passez les trois :
 Que trois, mon Dieu ! & toutesfois
 Trois autres attendre il me faut.
 Helas, mon Dieu, qui vois d'enhaut

[645] Et le dehors & le dedans,
 Vueilles accourcir ces trois ans :
 Car à moy ils ne sont point iours,
 Fussent-ils trente fois plus cours.
 Mon Dieu, tes promesses m'asseurent :

[650] Mais si plus long temps ils demeurent,
 I'ay besoin de force nouuelle,
 Pour souffrir vne peine telle.
 Mon Dieu, permets qu'en toute ioye
 Bien tost mon seigneur ie reuoye,

[655] Et mon Isaac que m'as donné,
 I'accolle en santé retourné.

*Abraham.*

O Dieu, ô Dieu, tu vois mon cœur ouuert,
Ce que ie pense, ô Dieu, t'est descouuert :
Qu'est-il besoin que mon mal ie te die ?

[660] Tu vois, helas, tu vois, ma maladie.
Tu peux tout seul gairison m'enuoyer,
S'il te plaisoit seulement m'ottroyer
Vn tout seul poinct que demander ie n'ose.

*Satan.*

Si faut-il bien chanter quelque autre chose.

[116]

*Abraham.*

[665] Comment ? comment ? se pourroit-il bien faire,
Que Dieu dist l'vn, & puis fist du contraire ?
Est-il trompeur ? si est-ce qu'il a mis
En vray effect ce qu'il m'auoit promis.
Pourroit-il bien maintenant se desdire ?
[670] Si faut-il bein ainsi conclurre & dire,
S'il veut rauoir le fils qu'il m'a donné.
Que dy-ie ? ô Dieu, puis que l'as ordonné,
Il le feray : las, est-il raisonnable
Que moy qui suis pecheur tant miserable,
[675] Vienne à iuger les secrets iugemens
De tes parfaits & tressaincts mandemens ?

*Satan.*

Mon cas va mal : mon froc, trouuer nous faut
Autre moyen de luy donner assaut.

*Abraham.*

Mais il peut estre aussi que i'imagine
[680] Ce qui n'est point : car tant plus i'examine
Ce cas icy, plus ie le trouue estrange.
C'est quelque songe, ou bien quelque faux ange
Qui m'a planté cecy en la ceruelle :
Dieu ne veut point d'offrande si cruelle.
[685] Maudit-il pas Cain n'ayant occis
Qu'Abel son frere ? & i'occiray mon fils !

*Satan.*

Iamais, iamais.

*Abraham.*

Ha, qu'ay-ie cuidé dire ?
Pardonne moy, mon Dieu, & me retire
Du mauuais pas où mon peché me meine.
[690] Deliure moy, Seigneur, de ceste peine.
Tuer le veux moy-mesme de ma main.
Puis qu'il te plaist, ô Dieu, il est certain
Que c'est raison : parquoy ie le feray.

*Satan.*

Mais si ie puis, ie t'en engarderay.

*Abraham*

[695]    Mais le faisant, ie feroy' Dieu menteur :
Car il m'a dit qu'il me feroit cest heur
Que de mon fils Isaac il sortiroit
Vn peuple grand qui la terre empliroit.
Isaac tué, l'alliance est desfaicte.
[700]    Las est-ce en vain, Seigneur, que tu l'as faicte ?
Las est-ce en vain, Seigneur, que tant de fois
Tu m'as promis qu'en Isaac me ferois
Ce que iamais à autre ne promis ?
Las pourroit-il à neant estre mis
[705]    Ce dont tu m'as tant de fois asseuré ?
Las est-ce en vain qu'en toy i'ay esperé ?
O vaine attente, ô vain espoir de l'homme,
C'est tout cela que ie puis dire en somme,
I'ay prié Dieu qu'il me donnast lignée,
[710]    Pensant, helas, s'elle m'estoit donnée,
Que i'en aurois vn merueilleux plaisir :
Et ie n'en ay que mal & desplaisir.
De deux enfans, l'vn i'ay chassé moy mesme:
De l'autre il faut, ô douleur tresextreme !
[715]    Que ie sois dit le pere & le bourreau !
Bourreau, helas ! helas, ouy, bourreau !
Mais n'es-tu pas celuy Dieu proprement,
Qui m'escoutas ainsi patiemment,
Voire, Seigneur, au plus fort de ton ire,
[720]    Quand tu partis pour Sodome destruire ?
Maintenant donc veux-tu, mon Dieu, mon Roy,
Me repousser quand ie prie pour moy ?
Engendré l'ay, & faut que le defface.
O Dieu, ô Dieu, au moins fay-moy la grace

*Satan*

[725]    Grace ! ce mot n'est point en mon papier.

*Abraham*

Qu'vn autre soit de mon fils le meurtrier
Helas, Seigneur, faut-il que ceste main
Vienne à donner ce coup tant inhumain ?
Las que feray-ie à la mere dolente,

[118]

[730] Si elle entend ceste mort violente ?
Si ie t'allegue, helas, qui me croira ?
S'on ne le croit, las, quel bruit en courra ?
Seray-ie pas d'vn chacun reietté
Comme vn patron d'extreme cruauté ?

[735] Et toy, Seigneur, qui te voudra prier ?
Qui se voudra iamais en toy fier ?
Las pourra bien ceste blanche vieillesse
Porter le fais d'vne telle tristesse ?
Ay-ie passé parmy tant de dangers,

[740] Tant trauersé de pays estrangers,
Souffert la faim, la soif, le chaud, le froid.
Et deuant toy tousiours cheminé droict :
Ay-ie vescu, vescu si longuement,
Pour me mourir fi malheureusement ?

[745] Fendez mon cœur, fendez, fendez, fendez,
Et pour mourir plus long temps n'attendez :
Plustost on meurt, tant moins la mort est greue.

*Satan.*

Le voila bas, si Dieu ne le releue.

*Abraham.*

Que dy-ie ? où suis-ie ? ô Dieu mon createur,

[750] Ne suis-ie pas ton loyal seruiteur ?
Ne m'as-tu pas de mon pays tiré ?
Ne m'as-tu pas tant de fois asseuré,
Que ceste terre aux miens estoit donnée ?
Ne m'as-tu pas donné ceste lignée,

[755] En m'asseurant que d'Isaac sortiroit
Vn peuple tien qui la terre empliroit ?
Si donc tu veux mon Isaac emprunter,
Que me faut-il contre toy disputer ?
Il est à toy : mais de toy ie l'ay pris.

[760] Et pourautant quand tu l'auras repris,
Resusciter plustost tu le feras,
Que ne m'aduinst ce que promis tu m'as.
Mais, ô Seigneur, tu sais qu'homme ie suis,
Executer rien de bon ie ne puis,

[765] Non pas penser : mais ta force inuincible

Fait qu'au croyant il n'est rien impossible.
Arriere chair, arriere affections,
Retirez-vous, humaines passions,
Rien ne m'est bon, rien ne m'est raisonnable,
[770]    Que ce qui est au Seigneur agreable

*Satan.*

Et bien, & bien, Isaac donc mourra,
Et nous verrons apres que ce sera.
O faux vieillard, tant me donnes de peine !

*Abraham*

Voila mon fils Isaac qui se pourmeine.
[775]    O poure enfant, ô nous poures humains,
Cachans fouuent la mort dedans nos seins,
Alors que plus en pensons estre loing !
Et pourautant il est tresgrand besoing
De viure ainsi que mourir on desire
[780]    Or ça mon fils : helas que veux-ie dire !

*Isaac*

Plaist-il mon pere ?

*Abraham*

Helas ce mot me tue.
Mais si faut-il pourtant que m'esuertue.
Isaac mon fils : helas, le cœur me tremble.

*Isaac*

Vous auez peur, mon pere, ce me semble.

*Abraham.*

[785]    Ha mon amy, ie tremble voirement.
Helas, mon Dieu !

*Isaac.*

Dites-moy hardiment
Que vous auez, mon pere, s'il vous plaist.

*Abraham*

Ha mon amy, si vous sauiez que c'est.
Misericorde, ô Dieu, misericorde !
[790]    Mon fils, mon fils, voyez-vous ceste corde,
Ce bois, ce feu, & ce cousteau icy ?
Isaac, Isaac, c'est pour vous tout cecy.

*Satan.*

Ennemy suis de Dieu & de nature,
Mais pour certain ceste chose est si dure,
[795]    Qu'en regardant ceste vnique amitié,
Bien peu s'en faut que n'en aye pitié.

*Abraham.*

Helas Isaac !

*Isaac.*

Helas pere tresdoux,
Ie vous supply, mon pere, à deux genoux
Auoir au moins pitié de ma ieunesse.

*Abraham.*

[800]    O seul appuy de ma foible vieillesse !
Las mon amy, mon amy ie voudrois
Mourir pour vous cent millions de fois :
Mais le Seigneur ne le veut pas ainsi.

*Isaac.*

Mon pere, helas, ie vous crie mercy.
[805]    Helas, helas, ie n'ay ne bras ne langue
Pour me defendre, ou faire ma harangue !
Mais, mais voyez, ô mon pere, mes larmes,
Auoir ne puis ny ne veux autres armes
Encontre vous : ie suis Isaac, mon pere :
[810]    Ie suis Isaac, le seul fils de ma mere :
Ie suis Isaac, qui tien de vous la vie :
Souffrirez-vous qu'elle me soit rauie ?
Et toutesfois si vous faites cela
Pour obeir au Seigneur, me  voila,
[815]    Me voila prest, mon pere, & à genoux,
Pour souffrir tout, & de Dieu & de vous.
Mais qu'ay-ie fait, qu'ay-ie fait pour mourir ?
He Dieu, he Dieu, veuille me secourir.

*Abraham.*

Helas mon fils Isaac, Dieu te commande
[820]    Qu'en cest endroit tu luy serues d'offrande,
Laissant à moy, à moy ton poure pere,
Las quel ennuy !

*Isaac.*

Helas ma poure mere,
Combien de morts ma mort vous donnera !
Mais dites-moy aumoins qui m'occira ?

*Abraham.*

[825]     Qui t'occira, mon fils ?  mon Dieu, mon Dieu,
Ottrope-moy de mourir en ce lieu !

*Isaac.*

Mon pere.

*Abraham.*

Helas, ce mot ne m'appartient.
Helas Isaac, si est-ce qu'il conuient
Seruir à Dieu.

*Isaac.*

Mon pere, me voila.

*Satan.*

[830]     Mais ie vous pri', qui eust pensé cela ?

*Isaac.*

Or donc mon pere, il faut, comme ie voy,
Il faut mourir. Las mon Dieu, aide-moy !
Mon Dieu, mon Dieu, renforce-moy le cœur !
Rend-moy, mon Dieu, sur moymesme vainqueur.

[835]     Liez, frappez, bruslez, ie suis tout prest
D'endurer tout, mon Dieu, puis qu'il te plaist.

*Abraham.*

A, a, a, a, & qu'est-ce, & qu'est ceci ?
Misericorde, ô Dieu, par ta mercy.

*Isaac.*

Seigneur, tu m'as & creé & forgé.
[840]     Tu m'as, Seigneur, sur la terre logé,
Tu m'as donné ta saincte cognoissance,
Mais ie ne t'ay porté obeissance
Telle, Seigneur, que porter ie deuois :
Ce que te prie, helas, à haute voix,
[845]     Me pardonner. Et à vous, mon seigneur,
Si ie n'ay fait tousiours autant d'honneur
Que meritoit vostre douceur tant grande,
Treshumblement pardon vous en demande.

Quant à ma mere, helas, elle est absente.
[850] Veuille, mon Dieu, par ta faueur presente
La preseruer & garder tellement,
Qu'elle ne soit troublée aucunement.

     *Icy est bandé Isaac.*

Las ie m'en vay en vne nuict profonde,
Adieu vous dy la clarté de ce monde.
[855] Mais ie suis seur que de Dieu la promesse
Me donnera trop mieux que ie ne laisse.
Ie suis tout prest, mon pere, me voila.

     *Satan.*

Iamais, iamais enfant mieux ne parla.
Ie suis confus, & faut que ie m'enfuye.

     *Abraham.*

[860] Las mon amy, auant la departie,
Et que ma main ce coup inhumain face,
Permis me soit de te baiser en face.
Isaac mon fils, le bras qui t'occira
Encore vn coup au moins t'accolera.

     *Isaac.*

[865] Las, grand mercy.

     *Abraham.*

O ciel, qui es l'ouurage
De ce grand Dieu, & qui m'es tesmoignage
Tressuffisant de la grande lignée
Que le vray Dieu par Isaac m'a donnée :
Et toy la terre à moy cinq fois promise,
[870] Soyez tesmoins que ma main n'est point mise
Sus cest enfant par haine ou par vengeance,
Mais pour porter entiere obeissance
A ce grand Dieu, facteur de l'vniuers,
Sauueur des bons & Iuge des peruers.
[875] Soyez tesmonis qu'Abraham le fidele,
Par la bonté de Dieu, a la foy telle,
Que nonobstant toute raison humaine,
Iamais de Dieu la parolle n'est vaine.
Or est-il temps, ma main, que t'esuertues,

[880] Et qu'en frappant mon seul fils, tu me tues.
*Icy le cousteau luy tombe des mains.*

*Isaac.*

Qu'est-ce que i'oy, mon pere ? helas mon pere !

*Abraham.*

A, a, a, a.

*Isaac.*

Las ie vous obtempere.
Suis-ie pas bien ?

*Abraham.*

Fut-il iamais pitié,
Fut-il iamais vne telle amitié ?
[885] Fut-il iamais pitié ? a, a, ie meurs,
Ie meurs, mon fils.

*Isaac.*

Ostez toutes ces peurs,
Ie vous supply', m'empescherez-vous doncques
D'aller à Dieu ?

*Abraham.*

Helas, las qui vit onques
En petit corps vn esprit autant fort ?
[890] Helas, mon fils, pardonne-moy ta mort.
*Icy le cuide frapper.*

*L'Ange.*

Abraham, Abraham.

*Abraham.*

Mon Dieu.

*L'Ange.*

Remets ton cousteau en son lieu :
Garde bien de ta main estendre
Dessus l'enfant, ne d'entreprendre
[895] De l'outrager aucunement.
Or peux-ie voir tout clairement
Quel amour tu as au Seigneur,
Puis que luy portes cest honneur
De vouloir, pour le contenter,
[900] Ton fils à la mort presenter.

*Abraham.*

O Dieu !

*Isaac.*

O Dieu !

*Abraham.*

Seigneur, voila que c'est
De t'obeir.  Voicy mon cas tout prest :
Prendre le veux.

Icy prend le mouton.

*L'Ange.*

Abraham.

*Abraham.*

Me voicy,
Seigneur, Seigneur.

*L'Ange.*

Le Seigneur dit ainsi :
[905]   Ie te promets par ma grand' maiesté,
Par la vertu de ma diuinité,
Puis que tu as voulu faire cela,
Puis que tu m'as obey iusques là,
De n'espargner de ton seul fils la vie :
[910]   Maugré Satan & toute son enuie,
Benir te veux auec toute ta race.
Vois-tu du ciel la reluisante face ?
Vois-tu les grains de l'arene au riuage ?
Croistre feray tellement ton lignage,
[915]   Qu'il n'y a point tant d'estoiles aux cieux,
Tant de sablon par les bords spacieux
De l'Ocean qui la terre enuironne,
Qu'il descendra d'enfans de ta personne.
Ils domteront quiconques les haira,
[920]   Et par celuy qui de toy sortira,
Sur toutes gens & toutes nations
Ie desploiray mes benedictions
Et grans thresors de diuine puissance,
Puis que tu m'as porté obeissance.

[125]

### EPILOGVE.

OR voyez-vous de foy la grand' puissance,
  Et le loyer de vraye obeissance.
Parquoy, messieurs, & mes dames aussi,
Ie vous supply', quand sortirez d'icy,
[5]  Que de vos cœurs ne sorte la memoire
  De ceste digne & veritable histoire.

  Ce ne sont point des farces mensongeres,
Ce ne sont point quelques fables legere s :
Mais c'est vn faict, vn faict tresueritable,
[10]  D'vn serf de Dieu, de Dieu tresredoutable.
Parquoy seigneurs, dames, maistres, maistresses,
Poures, puissans, ioyeux, pleins de destresses,
Grans & petits, en ce tant bel exemple
Chacun de vous se mire & se contemple.
[15]  Tels sont pour vray les miroirs où l'on voit
Le beau, le laid, le boussu, & le droit.
Car qui de Dieu tasche accomplir sans feinte,
Comme Abraham, la parole tressaincte,
Qui nonobstant toutes raisons contraires,
[20]  Remet en Dieu & soy & ses affaires,
Il en aura pour certain vne issue
Meilleure encor' qu'il ne l'aura conceue.
Vienent les vents, vienent tempestes fortes,
Vienent tormens, & morts de toutes sortes,
[25]  Tournent les cieux, toute la terre tremble,
Tout l'vniuers renuerse tout ensemble,
Le cœur fidele est fondé tellement,
Que renuerser ne peut aucunement :
Mais au rebours, tout homme qui s'arreste
[30]  Au iugement & conseil de sa teste :
L'homme qui croit tout ce qu'il imagine,
Il est certain que tant plus il chemine,
Du vray chemin tant plus est escarté,
Vn petit vent l'a soudain emporté :
[35]  Et qui plus est, sa nature peruerse
En peu de temps soymesme se renuerse.
  Or toy grand Dieu, qui nous as fait cognoistre

Les grans abus esquels nous voyons estre
Le poure monde, helas, tant peruerty,
Fay qu'vn chacun de nous soit aduerty
En son endroit, de tourner en vsage
La viue foy de ce sainct personnage.
  Voila, messieurs, l'heureuse recompense
Que Dieu vous doint pour vostre bon silence.

CPSIA information can be obtained at www.ICGtesting.com
Printed in the USA
LVOW051408160412

277797LV00014B/34/P